Collected Poems

C. K. STEAD

Collected Poems 1951–2006

AUCKLAND UNIVERSITY PRESS

First published 2008

Auckland University Press
University of Auckland
Private Bag 92019
Auckland 1142
New Zealand
www.auckland.ac.nz/aup

© C. K. Stead, 2008

ISBN 978 1 86940 418 5

National Library of New Zealand Cataloguing-in-Publication Data
Stead, C. K. (Christian Karlson), 1932-
Poems.
Collected poems : 1951-2006 / C.K. Stead.
Includes index.
ISBN 978-1-86940-418-5
I. Title.
NZ821.2—dc 22

Cover design: Sarah Maxey
Cover photograph: Marti Friedlander, 2006
Printed by South Wind Productions, Singapore

Contents

FOREWORD

This collected volume follows the order of my published books of poems from
the earliest to the latest, except in a few cases where there have been overlaps and
repetitions. I have tried, on the whole, to represent my own history as it occurred,
and not make it look better, or myself wiser, more mature, more adroit, than I was
at the time. I recognise the truth in Paul Valéry's 'a poem is never finished, merely
abandoned'; but revision after many years often produces, not a better poem of the
same kind, but a poem (better or worse) of another kind.

Nothing is simple, however, and there are exceptions to the rough rule I made for
myself, especially in the early work where some poems have been revised and a few
deleted. These changes have been indicated in the notes at the back of the book.

In particular, in assembling the 'Early Uncollected' section, I did allow myself any
number of revisions. These were poems which, for one reason or another, had not
made it into my first book, *Whether the Will is Free* (1964); and in retrieving them
here, mostly from periodicals, a few from manuscripts, I felt I had the distance, and the
authority, to dress them better and tidy their hair. This does not conceal their (i.e. my)
weaknesses; but it does overcome some matters of presentation.

One thing that interested me especially in looking back over so many decades
was the recognition that I have been concerned (it might not be too much to say
obsessed) with poetic form throughout; but that the forms I used to begin with were
much more conventional, obvious and external than they later became. I am an ear
person, and poetry, word by word, line by line, and equally in its larger structures, is,
as I experience and conceive it, more closely related to music than to anything else.
Language is what distinguishes us on our planet, and poetry pushes that everyday
currency out into new territories of sense – sensory and semantic. I think of writing a
poem as putting oneself in the moment *at* the moment – an action more comprehensive,
intuitive and mysterious than mere thinking, governed partly by history (the poet
works in a tradition), but equally by individual temperament and voice, and by a
feeling for what is harmonious, fresh, surprising, and even, occasionally, wise.

Some of the notes and acknowledgements at the back of the book are taken
from the original published collections; many more have been added. A particular
acknowledgement is due to Creative New Zealand for the Michael King Fellowship,
the work on this collected volume being the most important of the projects I
undertook to do while holding that generous award. And finally, there is the huge
acknowledgement to Kay, which the poems themselves make in so many different
ways, overt and oblique, from *Whether the Will is Free* all the way through to *The
Black River*.

C.K.S.

Whether the Will is Free: Poems 1954–62

1964

'Kay'

Whatever answers to a name
Loses itself in answering.
Whatever does not answer dies.

Here is a world I cannot give
To name yet would not lose from words.
Here is the word I cannot crack.

One

And could he now . . .

And could he now go back? – to the milky mornings
Waking to Daisy's bell, a dance of dogs,
And the nipping early air in a yard all mud;
Summer mirrored on the dam, the cut scrub burning,
The gorse bright yellow until the time for logs –
Then damp days heavy with the axe's thud.

Rabbit or hawk in trap on moon full nights
By water glistening, and under hanging trees
The creeping quiet where loony Stanley crooned;
Go back to the long kitchen, candle for light,
Moreporks at brass bed time, and the mason bees
Stuffing the ears of the house with their waxy drone.

Leather and horse smell, smell of privy and pine,
And the muddy matron sow with her snouts of squeals
Escaping, jolting through scrub that climbed the hill.
But not the ash-white roads nor clacking lines
That led the boy, counting on flying wheels,
Can find him these, where time is quick to kill.

Trapped Rabbit

When the rabbit rattled the drag of a grasping trap,
Ran a few steps, laid back the flaps
Of ears against quivering fur, then seemed to play,
Lifting a twitching face that grinned and prayed;
When it tripped and ran to the tune of the wind-singing fence,
Stepping light-footed in exquisite, nervous dance
On the knife-edge knowledge of death; then heard our steps,
Its graceful frenzy bound in the weight of the trap
Collapsing clenched against steel and the waiting earth;
O when the hands made hard by the cycle of birth
And pain, closed on the warm-furred neck, and the bone
Clicked crisp in crystal air, the small stone
Of the head drooping towards earth as though
To burrow in shame from the blue
Of a sky that could only smile: then I felt
Neither guilt nor superfluous pity, but smelt
Clay at my heels, manuka breath
In clean air, denying this shapeless death.

Elements

i Iron Gully

Sky is hard in which the hawk hangs fire,
Rocks unflinching under imperious sun;
Water avoids this place, and leaf, and man
Pitched softer than its shrilling silences.

Praise here the forge and metal of the will,
Tenacious thorn, hawk dropping to kill,
Stone unmerged in stone, where all things know
It is the rain that softens us to love.

ii The Garden

From remembered rain beating a small dense garden
Nothing divides me. Not distance, nor the years that harden

Mind's clay and the mould of the face, can alter those small
Worm-wristed lilac-branches beside an ivied wall.

Heavy, flat down the rain comes, and is taken
Still by the mothering grass ignorant of time.
The leaves of the lemon tree wax, each separately shaken,
And enclosing stone stands firm, too tall to climb.

Dissolution

Street lights are marbling designs on the rain-glazed eye,
Shadows sprawling beyond wet hedges
Where charcoal trees sketch rough-and-ready edges
On the smudged grey backdrop of a winter-waking sky.

Sight blurred by rain, nerves on the soothing spools
Of its spinning sound; voices trapped beneath eaves;
Grass sighing underfoot and aging leaves
Soaking their wrinkles out in reflective pools.

This is the season's collapse, the dead-pan sky
Weeping of age to listless, listening trees,
Houses winking through blinds with the light that sees
Peace in the closing of summer's assertive eye.

So cooling sense dissolves across the brain
Spinning this winter mesh of drifting rain.

Night Watch in the Tararuas

Moon bathes the land in death, throws shadows down
From thorn and manuka over the stunted ground;
A gravel stream rasps smooth the butts of stone,
Moulds pebbles, waters sheep ragged as the land.
Rabbits thump their warnings through earth hard
As the carved gleam of Holdsworth against the sky
Whose upright, white-capped miles catch the moon's eye.

Placed now alone I shape for you the word –
Mind's genesis that would create you here
And make this place an Eden where the blurred
Shades of my lives resolve to one, and where
Art is the vision our conjunction yields.
So duty holds me, but commanding love,
Itself a discipline, is free to move.

And watching the ghosts of sheep in scrubby fields
Prisoned by walls of stone war-prisoners built
I know myself more bound by what love yields
Than by the laws that thought as often flouts
As hand obeys; so seem a slave to commands
I least respect, while yet all thought walks free
Into your greater serfdom, binding me.

For even here where beauty's large demands
Are met in thorn, unsentimental stone –
The cracking earthen bowl of a course-grained land –
Man's common fall impels the gentler vision.
Disease at the rugged root of Adam's tree
Restores green sensual time whose fertile dream
Makes clear the valley's hard, contrasting theme.

Here I recall night's fall to crumpled day,
Soft folds of morning under your sleeping face,
Mouth curved on memory, the opening eye
Holding a dream too full for the timid grace
Of innocence, yet waking to the toils of thought –
Blind disarray in slatted lines of light
Groping for truths that fade in day's dull sight.

No death more urgent than that waking, yet
In rock and thorn, night-settled dust, a land
Watered by one uncertain stream that's fed
From the white, religious mountain, I understand
The choice we make binding ourselves to love;
And know that though death breeds in love's strange bones
Its fading flesh lives warmer than the stone.

While down the fleeces of our sky . . .

Our glassed-in shell is busy trapping sun.
My work is done: matting covers the boards,
Books and our pottery dishes upright in
Their standing frames of smooth-grained furniture.
Cushions have captured cocks of strutting red –
A low divan suggests you fall among them:
Composite image of bright concupiscence.

Beyond the wax of pumpkins, peppers drying,
Summer fruit and pohutukawa leaves,
A ship sails out, islands sprawl in the sun.
Close in our white blades knife a harmless breeze,
Children brawl, the Gulf winks and beckons,
While down the fleeces of our sky blue signals ride
From far dark worlds where it is always raining.

Letter to R. R. Dyer

Wave lifts; late-angled sunlight frames
Far out its white collapse whose sound
Rolls shoreward in its own good time.
That big surf breaking – noisy, blind
Sculptor mad with the work in hand –
Out of his own, is on my mind.

So the wind inflates the truth.
Old Duncan in the flat next door
Sees his dead son in each brown youth.
So, I suppose, I hoped the sea
Might beat and on my thoughts confer
Its eloquent tenacity.

The world rolls on the brink of fire,
Children play games, we play our own.
Full of ourselves, we both aspire
To write – most often write a lie.
I share this beach-oblivion;
You find tall truths in short supply.

A storm is brewing, but all day
Children on the brazen sand
Have gulled sharp cries along the bay.
Picnics, bodies barely made,
Lovers spanning time on hand,
Ebbed and flowed between the shade.

The houses here were pioneers' –
Those gentle-tough who never knew
A writer's cramp. The buttered years
Feed leisure uselessly unless
We make their language fit this view,
This beach that is our new address.

Is there a truth concealed in granite
Bitten by a mad-dog surf?
It won't be told by chance or habit –
Our borrowed styles are antique swords.
One sea is difficult enough,
But snow confounds our Christmas cards.

And now a head Del Sarto drew
Out of his time and place, distracts.
Irrelevant? It's in my view!
I set that sure and casual eye
In judgement on us, Rob, who lack
The means to speak so candidly.

But you have chosen Greece, alone,
While I, a husband grateful where
Your blessings on us both have shone,
Watch from this shell the breeding storm
And trust that love outlasts our fears
When ocean's ominous winds are born.

Three Imperatives in White

i

Walk, girl, the dead sand
Barefoot. Your body bends
To skirt the wind,
And the leaf of your hand
Blows from your flying hair.

ii

Climb moon, the grave sky,
Sail easy there
Darkly shading
Your full face, riding
A path splashed down on the sea.

iii

White trunks, resist
(Enamelled hip to wrist
By mist and moon)
The threatening gun
In the hard heart of the storm.

Carpe Diem

Since Juliet's on ice, and Joan
Staked her chips on a high throne

Sing a waste of dreams that are
Caressing, moist, familiar:

A thousand maidens offering
Their heads to have a poet sing;

Hard-drinking beaches laced with sun,
The torn wave where torn ships run

To wine and white-washed bungalows.
This summer sing what winter knows –

Love keeps a cuckoo in his clock
And death's the hammer makes the stroke.

Two

Letter to Frank Sargeson
from Armidale, N.S.W.

If I shut my eyes here to the violent death
Alight in every tree as never at home,
It's quite an easy matter to catch my breath
Blowing old phantoms under a chilly moon,
And just step out again along the sand.
Here there's no water dashing at the land.

In such impossible moods I take the road
Up past the bakery (that world rebuilds,
Each sense takes up an old, accustomed load –
Green, garlic, Bach, new bread, a stroking sea)
And walk in on you telling Janet lies,
Cooking perhaps, writing – scenes multiply,

I cannot get them straight but all the same
Feel for the moment I'm again at home.
Escapes like these don't last of course, the shame
Is that they come at all, and leave behind
A fight in which I try to hold the scene,
But lose it to (say) someone round or lean

Coming to hand her latest essay in.
Soon there'll be snow here, and the English trees –

Sheltering as yet that least original sin
Practised by students – will be out of work,
Rooted upways in a watery dirt of sky.
(Season's disasters need a poet's eye.)

The windy gallows of these trees are right
For hanging thoughts of death on, but their mould
Dies a red that rages at the sight –
Burns on the roadside with a martyr's faith:
Maybe my numbering the leaves is wrong
Finding more cause in this than spring, for song.

Over the rasp of grass a breezy knife
Sharpens the morning, is by midday hot.
Nostalgia's tossed off with the bedclothes, life
Moves in the usual dust of compromise.
All roads lead to (or allow) return.
No Nero I, watching this autumn burn.

À la recherche du temps perdu

i *L'acte gratuit*

He walks where they have spent
Warm nights, branches over-bent

And street lights drumming. Now
Rain falls on him, leaves flow

Choking the drains, and over
Rain-blackened rocks like a lover

Ivy sprawls. Green to brown
To puddled slush, and down

The streaked air slide the lights of cars.
This street, this house, were hers –

She, the once beloved
Who chose the worst to prove

The choice was hers. Not loss
But a death, like the bones of trees

Above this thudding rain.
They may not keep even their pain.

ii Le cauchemar

In wind they walk above the town, the grey
Clouds low-racing, and in a high house
Shutters banging beyond a ruined gate;
All overgrown there under birch and elm
Yellowing, looking out on the valley town.

Here they turn, finding a stony path
Climbing through scrub. Sun slips away
Discreetly. He hears a distant night-bird drop
Malicious notes, round stones in a deep well.
A tree-frog buzzes like a broken wire.

Where is she now? He tries to call the name
He can't recall, while every moment adds
More scraping insect legs, more wattled throats
Blown up unseen into a glottal threat.
He fears the shadows, fights them, wakes alone.

Four Minute Miler

None better knows what hunts us all
Around fixed circuits, in determined lanes,
The needle bearing down on those who fall,
The strong ones making gains.

Frustration too – the goal that moves
While we approach, as when a rail track sends
Its shafts ahead to meet like perfect loves
(Point never reached that lends

Grace to our dreams). So he will squeeze
The fractured seconds down till limbs protest;
Still the mechanic arm flicks on, with ease
Out-pacing his best.

As well scholar, priest, king,
Eye fixed beyond, glory mounting behind,
Ambitious man hunts with him the dear thing
He shall not find.

Letter to Eve in London

Your letter on my desk. I imagine now
Around the famed Monopoly board of London
You walking, a fierce untidy girl, bearing
Your body like a postcard, more or less on sale.

How do I choose between them – the city and you?
That big name, survivor of centuries and bombs,
And the poor flesh that God knows what smart gun
Will shock to life with a hot, careless bullet.

Both are perhaps fictions, but art is a power
In the city I see you jostle and stalwartly tramp;
Arches are frozen, the fountain stands at ease;
The streets, the river, balance their shares of light.

Forgive my uncertain praise, but you are the heart
(How ill we choose the region of metaphor)
From which I shy toward imperious stone –
Yet grateful for the apple you brought me once.

Four Harmonics of Regret

i Party
Assured of my own sobriety, the first lurch
Is Revelation. The safest knee gives way,
And multi-coloured, -voiced, the peopled room
Flicks open like a fan, and shut again.

Gingerly, through the jittering screen of jazz
I pick-path to the bathroom and sit down.
How blue the tiles, blue that weary retching
Beyond a curtain which I dare not draw.

ii Tall Girl
The tall girl with brown arms is walking
Between the elms in bluest evening,
Her breasts full of a melancholy sway,
Her face browner with the sun half-gone.

The tall girl is walking towards the hills.
She crosses a thin creek and rushy grass,
She crosses the line of my eyes that follow her
And fades among the great breasts of the hills.

iii Campfire
We light dry eucalypt under a knife of moon
And pare our hearts offering slices round.

Sue's is a watermelon of generous tears,
Jane's a delicious little foreign cheese,
Pip's a pound of butter unpleasantly melting,
And mine, o heart! – such a plain loaf of bread.

iv Red
Red, the martyr's colour, flames
Cloud-splashed at day's back door or flakes

(An autumn) from the iron hull.
Each first frost learns the pride of leaves.

Born of the green sap, grannies warm
Their twigs that any time may catch

While up a thousand chimneys sprout
Dark prayers against eternal chill.

Whether the Will is Free

i
Snow wraps a harsh and gum-grey land,
Slug-blood retreats from the shelled hand

And foot needled for warmth pines
Stamping the hills. Breath-charted air

Caught from a gramophone defines
A girl's mood whose doved hand

Dances. Outside, a bird on the bare
Head of the white-haired day is a stare

At the crop of the sprinkled seed of sleet.
Whether the will is free, the shiver

Runs in me that ruffles the feather;
Whether the will is free, the beat

Of the doved hand, the dove moan,
Chords my mind to the gramophone.

ii
A dog is a hopper on the snow.
Wanting wings, or shoes, he goes

Spring-full as hope, and quivering
An arrow nose at frozen trees.

iii
This loping landscape doesn't care
What falls on it, what freezes there,

Whether the wants are few that house
In the head of a girl, the eye of a stare,

Whether streams have a will, but sends
Them even under ice, to sea.

iv
May be I'm the girl, the bird, the stream,
The hungry dog in this iron time,

Not hell-bound or heaven-bent,
Willing to get to where I'm sent.

Under its ice my small life crawls
Pecking and snuffing at grey walls.

Whether the will is free or seems,
I would be music, doved in snow.

Last Poem in Australia

Eucalypt scent disperses in blue smoke,
Tree-shadows stretch into the afternoon;
Into this clear, half-winter day, no sound
Breaks but the steep gears of a truck, hauling
North out of the town, out of the valley.

To the man walking that road my hillside smoke
Signs life among the trees, as he for me
Is patterned at this distance with the land,
Who daily perhaps passes me in streets
Unnoticing, unnoticed. So now the town
Heavy with sunlight on its yellow trees
Becomes, in beauty, a place unknown to me.

Always the present blurs with opulence –
This rough slope with its fierce gesturing gums
Living and dead, its rocks and stubble grass
Burned brown by sun and frost, its sagging wires
Strung out with brilliant parakeets like beads;
And smoke dissolving up where black-souled crows
Flap, on slow wings, into the downward sun.
Only what lies behind falls into shape,
Orderly, quiet – and is not the truth.

Two years that hum-drum town has weathered me
(Neither here nor there, neither alive nor dying);
Now on its fringing hills, close to departure,
I grant it in this autumn afternoon
That grace which nothing earns except in loss.

Armidale, N.S.W.

Three

Dialogue on a Northern Shore

(Guitar, fading. On a beach, on a northern shore, an old man watches his fire burn down. Beside him a young man stands with his back to the sea, staring at the dark shapes of the land. The old man looks up and speaks.)

Old Man
It's close to sunrise. That mist low on the sea is thinning.
You'll see it soon, a coast much like Ithaca's.
The landscape too, though I suppose you could say
There are signs of wear and tear . . .

Young Man
$\qquad\qquad\qquad\qquad$ Ithaca is itself.

Old Man
Itself, of course. But like. You'll see . . .

Young Man

I'll see
A foreign beach and rocks, pummelled by a foreign sea.
Like is nothing to me.

Old Man

Don't be too hasty, young man.
Kinship counts here. You'll be well received, I'm sure.

Young Man
Kinship is nothing to me.

Old Man

Come now, we're all Greeks.

Young Man
All Greeks, all human, all fools . . .

Old Man

Well, no one's insisting you stay.
Still, there are things you and your men might learn.
You've proved yourselves at sea, and in Circe's stye . . .

Young Man
I was never in Circe's stye.

Old Man

No, of course. Forgive me.
That was your crew's quarters. You were in her bedroom.

Young Man
Every day our ship cut nearer to this coast I said to myself
'Soon. Soon. Not far now.' It was as if I knew what I'd find
And couldn't wait to learn and to profit. But as the ship beached
I smelled death.

Old Man

Ah death! Is there somewhere you've been
That lacks it? Where are you from, young man?
Heaven, perhaps? Was this landfall a birth? Do I hear you
Crying for milk?

Young Man
        Tread carefully, old fellow. You challenge me
And the challenge will be met.

Old Man
                         No doubt, no doubt.
Good at breaking heads, are we?

Young Man
                Good at?
Able, anyway – and not unwilling.

Old Man
                           Sit, friend,
At least. Have something to eat. I meant no harm.
What have you come for?

Young Man
                   For what I could find.
For whatever offered itself. For the end of the story.

Old Man
It's said you left a woman – Penelope.

Young Man
                       Penelope,
Ithaca – are they different? I'm never sure.

Old Man
It's said she weaves a cloth, unravelling it at night
Because she's promised her suitors her vows to you
Will hold only until the last stitch is in place.

Young Man
That's as good a story as any. Maybe she unravels it
Because I and my men are part of the design. She can't
Recall our faces. Until we come home for good
The thread will always be broken.

Old Man
At least it's true you don't forget one another.

Young Man
(Staring into the mist)
She walks between kitchen and loom in the warm sleep
Of motherhood. I walk here in the slow mill
Of a world's favour. Yet I tread her will
Like a golden child unborn, and she, even on this coast,
Invades all my thoughts.

Old Man
(Nodding thoughtfully)
                So, after all, there are depths!
Ancient sonorities. I respect them. I hold my tongue.

Young Man
Your tongue is nothing to me.

Old Man
                  Tell me then, if language
And this landfall matter so little, what was your purpose
In voyaging?

Young Man
         We're restless in Ithaca, like migrant birds
Wandering between two worlds, always looking for something
And avoiding something.

Old Man
               A romantic self-portrait –
I like it! What do you call yourselves? Backpackers?
The Godwits perhaps?

Young Man
              I call us Proof-Against-Derision –
But now and then we're not and there's blood on the floor.

Old Man
'Dawn's rosy-tinted fingers tainted with blood' – yes,
I can imagine. But look, the mist is indeed
Lifting from the sacred sites. You can see the temple up there
Among trees on the hill slope, and the ruins of a mill.
We've tried to protect our heritage, and preserve
The natural beauty.

Young Man
(*Repeats mechanically*)
                              Preserve the natural beauty.

(*Guitar, at a distance. Along the shore, in cold half-light, a woman
walks barefooted, her hair blown by a light wind across the strings of an
instrument. The old man stands up. The young man leans forward and
stares.*)

Old Man
Down there on the sand – you see? That figure
Coming towards us, playing on an instrument.
She's a spirit of this country.

Young Man
                              Of this country?

Old Man
Yes, I assure you.

Young Man
                              Oh but I've seen her often,
Sometimes by southern lakes, or close to the snow-line,
Sometimes on northern beaches. She's a spirit of Ithaca.

Old Man
Of Ithaca? Nonsense. She belongs right here. Why else
Are you seeing her now?

Young Man
                              She must have followed our ship.

Old Man
Absurd! Quite absurd.

Young Man
                              You think so? Ask her then.
She's coming this way.
(*He calls.*)
                              Tell us, Spirit,
Do you belong to this place, or to Ithaca?

Spirit
Belonging is nothing to me.

Young Man

You see!

Old Man
I see. But do you *hear*? She said, 'This is my home.'

Young Man
Not 'This is'. '*Ithaca* is.' 'Ithaca is my home.'
That's what she said.

(They stare at one another. The Old Man's look is angry, the Young Man's full of contempt. A loud chord interrupts them. The music continues and the spirit sings.)

Spirit

Music anchors in
Those waters and that earth
Which moved and had a man
Bring song to birth;

And hangs always where
Tree and stone stream
Spoke in a woman's ear
Her own dream.

(The music fades away.)

Young Man
She's going.

Old Man

Quick follow her. She went that way.

Young Man
This way, this way.

Old Man

She's gone.

Young Man

Gone.

Vanished. What was that song about?

Old Man
                              Home and hearth –
What else?

Young Man
                 Tricky things, spirits.

Old Man
                                        Elusive.

Young Man
I think she's telling me something. I shouldn't stay.

Old Man
If that's how it seems, then yes, you surely must
Be on your way – back on the wine-dark sea,
Beating the whale's path home. Oh I can hear it
Echoing in my skull. Well-worn, but a fine old story.
But while you wait for the tide, Odysseus,
I've a story of my own you might enjoy –
Might even learn from.

Young Man
                 And I've one for you, a new one.

Old Man
I'm sure you have. Sit, please. Let's breakfast together,
Talk a little longer, and watch the sun come up.

Winter Song

> '*Stretch out your limbs and sleep a long Saturnian sleep;*
> *I have loved you better than my soul, for all my words.*'
>   – W. B. Yeats

The moon roosts high
In a winter tree –
Bright bird whose eye
Can fleck with light
Or darkly patch
This room and watch

Where you and I
Lie calm, lie deep,
Nightlong in intertwining sleep.

The snow road leads
To Westbury
From Temple Meads
Across the Downs.
Tree-shadow falls
On road, on walls,
Innocent light
Impales the sky
And lies along the shuttered eye.

Winter and death
Indict our love.
What ghost's faint breath
Haunting the snow-
Bound blackened trees
Can here appease
The living cell?
Let the night weep
That waits for us. Lie calm, lie deep.

Address to Two Cats
whose theft of a tie caused a train to be missed

Timid Kate
And that other
(Sister cat
Or cut brother)

May properties
Of my hot curse
Revoked by this
Be now inverse –

The hand that feeds
You thrive, not waste;
Be your worst deeds
Only unchased!

Cat theft or feast
By wormy moth
Matter not least
To mortal cloth;

But sprites attend
The meanest crisis –
In it unbend
The solstices

Of human touch
And heaven's weather:
Hemispheres couch
In heat together!

What's lost discretion
Hides. I make
(Only) confession
For a tie's sake.

Chorus

Admetus, your walls have seen
Such wealth, such gifts of food
And cellared wine
That not the tuneful god
Apollo, could disdain
Shelter under your roof
From wind and rain.

In your long halls he sang
A marriage song, or ran
Headlong over the hills among
Your flocks, piping them on:
His song of shepherd hopes
Fled like a girl
Down stone-deaf slopes.

Drawn by its golden wire
Lions in Orthys Glen

Followed Apollo's lyre;
From leaping forests of pine
Lynx and deer
Caught in his net of music
Ran out to hear.

Thus from the stabled sun
Your rule, Admetus, reaches
To rocky Pelion
By Aegean waters:
Rich in flocks are the lands
By Boibie's deep lake
Where your house stands.

Admetus of high birth
And wisdom inherited,
Today you place in earth
A woman loved.
Your door stands open, receiving
The guest who sees
Nothing of grieving.

Imperious stones of art,
And custom's mask, deny
The destructible human heart.
For beauty's sake you lie
With tongue or pen –
Humble before the gods,
Proud before men.

Pictures in a Gallery Undersea

I
Binnorie, O Binnorie

In Ladbroke Square the light on waxen branches –
The orange light through two veined leaves
Tenacious in frost.
                    Upstairs, she lit the gas,
And drew bright curtains on the whitened eaves,

And said (her hand above the slowly turning disc)
'I shall never go back.'
                    Mozart in the delicate air
Slid from her glass, beat vainly against the cushions,
Then took off gladly across the deserted square.
'You too must stay' (loosening her sun-bleached hair)
'You more than I – you will defeat their fashions.'

Invisible fins guided her to my chair.

Pictures in a gallery undersea
Were turned facing the wall, and the corridors were endless;
But in the marine distance, floating always beyond me,
A girl played Mozart on her sun-bleached hair.

So that wherever I walked on that long haul, midnight to dawn,
Stones of a sunken city woke, and passed the word,
And slept behind me. But the notes were gone,
Vanished like bubbles up through the watery air
Of London, nor would again be heard.

II
Où tant de marbre est tremblant sur tant d'ombres

On steps of the British Museum the snow falls,
The snow falls on Bloomsbury, on Soho, on all
Cradled in the great cup of London.
On all the lions and literary men of London
Heaping in gutters, running away in drains
The falling snow, the city falling.

Snow behind iron railings drifts, collects –
Collects like coins in the corners of Nelson's hat
(Newbolt from a window in the Admiralty shouting
'Umbrellas for Nelson' and waving a sheaf of odes)
And down the long avenue.
                    There through her aquid glass
Circumambient Regina, turning slowly from the pane,
Is seen imperiously to mouth, 'Albert, my dear,
How do we pronounce *Waitangi?*'
                    And snow descends.

There I met my grandfather, young and bearded,
With thick Scandinavian accent who asked me
Directions to the dock; and later departed
Bearing me with him in his northern potency
South.
      South. Earth's nether side in night
Yet hardly dark, and I under this day
That's scarcely light.
          Flakes descending, dissolving
On the folds of a cape
          on a single blue ear-ring,
On a bowler beneath the great trees of Russell Square.

III

The prim lips, homing, round the wind
Condensing news along the Strand.
Nerveless, the words assault, descend –
Stiff jaws convey them underground.

The verb that rackets through the mind
Transports the body far beyond
Expected stops.
      Swirled on the wind
The lost, chaotic flakes ascend.

IV

All evening the princess danced, but before dawn
Escaped from her ballroom's glass down the wide, white stairs,
And walked among bare trees that spiked the lawn.

Far from her ears, airy and thin, the beat
Of goldsmiths' hammers rang in Devonshire Street,
And spent, above a quarrel of barrow wheels,
Songs on the night:

> *Flakes of the outer world*
> *Through London fly*
> *Together hurled*
> *Under the heavy sky . . .*

V

I dreamt tonight that I did feast with Caesar.

Wilde had been lynched. His head, grown larger, grinned from the Tower
    of London,
Swung by its hair under the Marble Arch,
And looked out from the point of a spear down Constitution Hill.
South of the River they were roasting him slowly on a spit,
And in Knightsbridge several of the best families dined delicately on his
    battered parts.
He, in Reading, enjoyed the debauch by proxy,
Bored at last with the rented corpse of Art
Whose delicate lusts had never been near to his heart.

Snow fell – fell where Hueffer ascended
From Great Russell Street to meet the eyes of Garnett;
And heard the scholar's voice, 'Now it is all ended –
England shall breed no poet for fifty years.'

Yeats not a mile from where they stood.
                            And Yeats
Drew down the dim blind of Olivia's hair
And dreamed of a great bird. Then woke
Calling 'Maud. Maud.' But the room was empty.
Across the narrow alley he drank coffee,
Bought his paper from me at the corner
(I only a few feet tall in cloth cap and boots
Three sizes too large. He 'the toff of the buildings'.)

And as he went, a man approached me shouting
'This paper you sold me – there's nothing in it' –
Waving the packed pages and snatching back his money.

And 'the toff' a hundred yards along the street,
And Ezra in billiard-cloth trousers across the street
Wearing an ear-ring of aquamarine,
And Old Possum hackneying past in a bowler to his funeral at the bank,
Turned
        turned, and watching, faded from sight.

VI

Now it was time for the drawing of curtains.
The smoke climbed, hand over hand, its difficult way,
Rested, or sank back in the thick air.
The River swans nor sang for the dead day
Nor proudly departed; but each hooked
One leg across its back, displaying a dirty web,
And, strong beak poised on graceful neck, poked
The rubbish drifting at the water's edge.

VII

Chanterez-vous quand vous serez vaporeuse?

And as the last orange of the sun was crushed
The River accepted its lights, from Kew to Battersea
On, winding, to the Tower.
                          It was winter, the year '58,
And many were dead. But into the same heart and out
Through channels of stone and light, the blood still pulsed –
Carried me with it down New Oxford Street
Through Soho to the whirling clock of the Circus,
Then down, on to the bridge. The snow was freezing.
A train stood middle-poised beside the footpath
Above the water, and in a corner, hunched,
An old man's unsheathed fingers struggled to revive
The dead years on a battered violin.

Four

Poem to Suppose the Bird

Suppose the bird ruffled below your pines
This fine wet shining evening, he sings suppose
Familiarly strange. A note it is that knows
Its variations mean just what they are
Supposed to mean: this one, suppose, the hedge,

That one the compost heap, and this the patch
Your mower cut last spring and made his thatch.
Then each, then each, he sings, and each suppose
Indifferently the same must represent
Its time, its place, some shady happening,
Sunny accomplishment, or just a thing
Unnamed suppose. He seems a clownish bird,
Not sad, not happy that the sun declines
His best inflexion for the voiceless pines,
But sings supposing out what life he knows
Below your pines, the ruffled bird suppose.

Mind Your Fingers

Dear X, expatriate,
I write this afternoon
Settled above the Gulf
Right to the sun.

Summer spreadeagles
Seagulls and swimmers,
Clippers, clay cliffs,
Cordage and cutters.

'Write of yourself' you say
And I do, am not
Those thoughts you knew me by
But today's heat,

Tomorrow's wind,
Sailboat and swimmer;
Am this impermanent
Persistent summer.

A deckchair of words at home
Is what I mean –
Yours to arrange if you can,
But if you fail, not mine.

A Natural Grace

Under my eaves untiring all the spring day
Two sparrows have worked with stalks the mowers leave
While I have sat regretting your going away.
All day they've ferried straw and sticks to weave
A wall against the changing moods of air,
And may have worked into that old design
A thread of cloth you wore, a strand of hair,
Since all who make are passionate for line,
Proportion, strength, and take what's near, and serves.
All day I've sat remembering your face,
And watched the sallow stalks, woven in curves
By a blind process, achieve a natural grace.

Elegy

The nails of rain are driven, the clouds cross;
The soil that fed is fed by its own loss.

The hill he eyed now closes like an eye
Under the damp grey pupil of the sky.

The life he listened for stops in his ears;
The bone-tree, fallen, sheds the guilt it wears.

This landscape mourns and makes him as he falls
Unfailing, planted in the flesh of hills.

Of Two who have Separated
Tom and La Rue

I
An image in the vice of abstract thought
Hardens: moonscape maybe, or moonlit valley
Where scattered anchor-stones like cattle lie
In granite pastures. An age of ice has caught
The shape of things – column and channel, dry

Arena, foothills lifting into ranges:
Nothing is made, nothing erodes or changes.
Slow stars trail – northward is it? – in the sky.

My steps ring out on their appointed stones.
Absurd the noisy consequence of acts
Where nothing loves, where light or shade exacts
Only its dues – no more.
                                    An image hardens.
Not warm Venusian rain nor the spears of Mars
Will quicken buds among these silent scars.

II
I choose the close perspective of her face
Between her hands, whose tears most tax my verse.
That mask is some exact account of loss
I guess at only, know by what is worse –
                        Time and the grass grow long.

Passion she had not guessed and resolution
War in the air around her. In each glass
The nobler disciplines surprise themselves.
Smallest events repeat all things must pass –
                        Time and the grass grow long.

The city slides away beyond her sill:
Useless to say that there her loss is housed
Synonymous behind a thousand eyes.
What pain has written seems uniquely phrased –
                        Time and the grass grow long.

The Fijian Police Band Performs in Albert Park, Auckland

one

Brassbound Fijians blow up the band rotunda!
Look! Paw-paw Cheeks puffs round two hemispheres,
Constable Drum squares up to beat them flat,
And pom! this plot's the world. What earthy tones!

That marble lady under the palms and fig-trees
Says it's all Greek to her. Oaks know they're English.
Flame-beaks just gape. Naturally they're excited.

two

'Small world!' That's small talk here (boom! boom!) 'SMALL WORLD!'
Who turned the phrase? Maybe our foundling fathers.
They blocked out space in beds; they never dreamed
This bland conundrum in their seedling order.
Small so you've got to shout! Some subtle bloom
Might work it out if he knew the b flat scale.

three

Tourists, gulls, the whole lot up from the quays
Screech and take shots. (That's one in your God's eye view!)
There's Dr Treadmeasure (pom!) come to pass
A bandy sentence on our history.
Time's short. He can't see Clio for the trees,
For grass, for looking. Can't hear her for the brass.

four

Time briefed, space blocked, a world in one puffed round
From pine to palm to (pom!) What a performance!
Let's hear it in Verse, or see it an acre in Paint.
Boil up the blood, summon the Muse of Conundra,
Cut your talk down to the quick . . . for all you're worth . . .
Hard as you like . . . till you burst. That's it! Together,

pom! pom! pom! pom! pom!

High Noon by the clock, the stage strewn with bodies,
Pigeons, marbles. One bright brass blast sets up
Clamour of hands, grey wings, pale faces asking
'What was it? Did something fall? Will the boards hold?'
Whatever it means, it's here. Make room! Keep time!
The bent world's end or just beginning, *blares!*

Crossing the Bar

1972

You Have a Lot to Lose

1

Hard. Bright. Clean. Particular.
That kind of a day.
Gable points picked out on the cliff-top, the tide
Pumping through the causeway to the bay.

North the sun, south the shadow,
East and west the piles that spaced
My path I paced
Slow, looking for kingfish.

Tidings are
This time a king will come
Within a fathom of his life to take
Flounder that sweep his floor.

Water breaks up the light
But there its jigging fragments catch
The flat-back's cloudy puff
And panic stop.

Hard. Bright. Clean. Particular.
Before the tide
Turns on itself and runs
One will have died.

2

The shadow bears a shadow.
The blue blade is the one you do not feel.
The king is a fish.

What becomes of water he displaces
Is pure computing.
Simply a glance will tell
It is his element
He its ambition expressed

35

To be in movement still
The same in change.

He strikes.
You had known death and a good meal
Were inextricable.
You know it again.

3
Nothing inhibits more
Thoughts of the Human Lot
Than the human lot.
Everyman is a poet's fine prospectus,
But the crowd is all elbows
The man alone a singular definition
And the kindest mirror will ask
Who am I to elect myself his spokesman
And to whom speak?

No. I cross a causeway, I cross a bay
Of a peninsula, of an island
That slides away
Under
And if at the lower reaches of flat maps
We repeat ourselves
We repeat ourselves
Unnoticed.

4
Never suppose the man in the presidential palace
Knows more than you of life. He can just keep up
With taking it and paying out his own. When lights burn late
In his apartments, don't imagine they illumine a soul.
Bells ring, clocks buzz, decisions escalate, while the wakeful technocrat
Spares not a thought for himself – but he'd weep tears
If he had them, and time, for the boy he was in Texas.
You have a lot to lose. Lose it where the will
Culpable, inherits its own devices,
And palpable innocence its element.

5

The last you lose
Is your sinbad self
But you have brought him
Down to play
And as he goes
Lost in the flash
Of a flat back
And the business of the shallows
A kind of praise
You thought had died in your throat
Comes alive on the bay.

The path is narrow
The tide is beginning to run
And the sun
Makes light of it.

Night-Flight, San Francisco–New York

Small towns unwoken pitted meagre lights
In the huge dark. Perhaps their cocks foretold
The unseen fire. If so, they did not lie.
It pressed at the world's rim. It tinged my wing.
So great a commonplace deserves a word.
There's none commends itself. I sat so high!
I saw the light come to America.

A Small Registry of Births and Deaths

All night it bullied you.
When it shook you hard enough
They took you away.
I was shaken too. I walked
The frantic corridor praying
Representing
My terror so minutely
It went unnoticed.

The whole place moaned
As it was meant to.
A door flung out a nurse and a scream.
A doctor in a butcher's apron passed
Tying his gauze.
The nurse returned with forceps.

Your door stayed shut. I smoked.
You might have been dead. Or sleeping.

*

Bloodshot and drugged you burbled about our boy.
He frothed, mildly confronting whatever it was
Flooded his lungs. I was full of pieties.
We had never been so nearly anonymous.

*

I watch our two-year-old
Among the lawless tribes
Of nursery children.
My skin prickles.
I scan the air for eagles.
It is as if all three of us were born
In that one moment to this one concern.
I lost myself to become
This wary watchful thing.
I scan the air.
I do not want myself back.
*

Six months ago a free bomb fell on a school.
Forty-five children were changed.
They became a job for the cleaners.
Villagers carried their bodies
To the southern border, protesting
While in Detroit
Every three seconds
A car was born.

Today America sits at its television.
Its heartbeat rallies with the heartbeat
Of Lyndon Baines Johnson.

Even without his gall
He has a heart that can speak
For a sentimental nation
That loves its cars
As it loves its children.

Lyndon, if ever a missile
Blows one of your Birds to bits
Don't hate it, Lyndon –
It was only misguided.
It wanted to make her free.
Take heart that in Detroit
Every three seconds
A car is born.

*

'To see Life steadily and see it whole.'
Yes, but I wonder what the side-burned sage
Allowed was Life. Where did he see it whole?
Must the Muse eat carrion and her true servant
Construct of the small picked bones a white tower
To see Life steadily and see it whole?

*

All day it has bullied me.
If it shook me hard enough
They'd put me away.
I represent my terror so minutely
It will pass unnoticed.

I have never been so nearly anonymous.

Long Ago

Long ago
A girl whose gift
Was a cavernous contraction
About the thing she loved
Scored her fingernail deep

Down the length of her lover's back
To mark their parting.
It took six weeks to heal,
A year for the scar to fade.
No amount of wishing
Will retrace that erratic path.
Time and the blood have mended every cell.
Old now, lacking courage
And the appetite for wounds
He has made his reputation
As historian
Of one short war.

Crossing the Bar

Poetry: second best.
It represents. It speaks
Truest from a broken house.
Only the whole man
Jumps his own height.

Brumel, crossing the bar,
Represents nothing.
A singular wit
Shrugs gravity a moment off
And falls on foam.

Poets at the last are deft.
I contract to that end
My second-best art.
It will serve to praise the first.
The first served only itself.

With a Pen-Knife

I was caned often at school.
Only once so it mattered.
His name was Tammy Scott.
I never knew him use a cane

Except just once – on me.
He taught maths,
Promoted a small pianist
Who grew to be a big one,
And painted bowls of roses
In a fine, dead style.
He used the names and dates
Of the school's two hundred war-dead
To make a book,
One fine laborious painted page
For each dead old-boy.

I used a pen-knife,
Hacked my impertinent name
On the top of a desk: STEAD.
Was it the bald style
Of a life-inscription
That so distressed him?

Nothing had prepared me
In that empty cloakroom
For Tammy's violence.
He went. When he came back
I was still where I'd stopped
My forehead sweating
Against the panelled wall.

I think of Tammy
Who meant no harm
Labouring among the dead.

I walked past him, and out.
I looked at him, not 'daggers',
But truly without feeling.
He might have been a desk-top.
My pride was exact.
I would not go down
In Tammy's book.
He would go down in mine.

Three Caesarian Poems

1 *Dallas, 1963*

Caesar, you were everybody's baby
But not mine.
I thought the broken warhorse that doddered before
Alone made you shine.
But when your head leaked blood on the lap of the world
Like those your mistakes murdered,
I thought it was the golden apple
And the holy wine.

2 *This March Morning*

Alexandria, Gaul
Savage Briton –
How like blades
The Capitol's edges
This March morning
That echoes under my feet,
And I feel my blood already
Called to stand congealed
Through centuries in stone,
In cold stone.

3 *The Lesson*

A bald whoremonger
Sweating in Gaul to become
A god it was
Taught me to keep
Voice down, pace even
Eye on the object
And with a short sword
Once only
Stab.

Letter to the Enemy

I cracked down on your rising
Once and for all.
There was no appeasement,
No quarter.
Your name was dirt,
Your cheques worthless.

I settled then
To enjoy the silence.
It wasn't what I'd expected.
It was like a whistle
Pitched up just out of earshot.
When news of Nothing came
I read between the lines
And strolled in the armoury.

They told me hell
Was full of noise.
None of it came to me.

It was then I took to making
These models of myself.
They seemed to know
I loved them, and even why.
I gave them the best –
A peninsular town
Pricked by volcanic cones
Between two harbours,
More beaches and islands
Than they could name,
And a sort of
Shipboard weather
Sheltered yet open
To a sea's predictable whims.

Did I know, half-know
I was only remaking
The ground of our conflict?

But the detail!
The pohutukawa

A flush of blood passing
Slowly through the arc of a bay.
And in winter rain
Those crystal ski-lifts
Running on telephone wires.

Such energy was it demonic
That could contrive
So much in the time?
Truly I owe you the debt
I make you pay.

Enemy, brother, Lucifer
My own self
You know as well as I
If we should cease our division
How it would be –
How soon I could forget
These indifferent creatures,
This half-made town,
How I would go
Free, voluble, witless, silent, dead.

It won't happen.
Not in my lifetime.

Lucifer Dictates his Reply

Sorry for yourself
God? No wonder!
No one ever wrote
A longer novel
Or a worse one.
You let the characters take over.
Look what they've done!

What I hate most
Is the mad-womanish
Self-centre in us
Demanding parturition.

I don't want to be
A self-conceiver.

Don't sit there
On your big
Bad novelist's bum
Cracking down on the kids for misdemeanours
And letting the crimes pass.
Be a man, God.
Get out the napalm and the Agent Orange.
I need a strong hand to curb this urge
To ape my betters.
I feel a novel coming on.
Hit me with all you've got.

Meeting of Cultures

Daphne, your size tens
Commanded awe.
Now they mark a path
Past the kassava
Among the pawpaws
Outside Accra.

Pad. Pad. Sticks
And small stones crack
Among the red
Shaken ant-hills.
The lion lies low.
Scavengers
Grumble and sulk.

New nations we know
Import with the machine
Its history and fads.
All about you
Sun and Earth as ever
Abrasively mate.
They have ignored
Stranger bearers.

Eat your baked yam.
Teach your impeccable
Oxford Greek.
Your feet are beyond belief.
The fire-crowned bishop
Cocks a blind bead
On your Christian head.

April Notebook

1
April, and a fool's good day.
My salary escalates.
In the brisk morning
Anticipating fires
I think of insurance.
Preserve me from Justice.

2
Girl
You'd have me moon
In littered corners.
The dead are yours
Muse.
Keep them!
It's the living who die.
Listen.
Hear their rage and fret?
Set it to music.

3
She
After a night of serenades and skirmishing
Drags in her seasoned wake
This taut, bow-legged
Big-shouldered tom.

Catching his mean eye
A boot's throw from our door
I call him Purpose.

4

A padlocked trunk keeps
My days accounted
In draft and revision.

Iron grave
It's a womb too.
I sentence myself.

An oak-headed catechist
A Swedish captain and
His daughter whose exact blood
This world affronted
Meet there the black Celt
Uttering
History, music.

5

April 21. Far north
The sun enters the Bull.
I buttress this garden corner
With chimney bricks and plant
One palm, one pink hibiscus
One bronze flax.
All roads lead to it
A neighbourhood where
The dogs of war have never gone unfed.
Cracked brick in hand
Ears full of children
I stand between the columns
The unerected statuary of this garden
Caesar, and Henry Ford.

The wing of fire is clipped.
I look towards the dark,
Into the sullenness of its coming on.
Beneficence of the Eagle
Corrupts our days.

6

Paulina, I was your first
Petitioner. It still galls me

In this month to remember
How hard I hammered
On the gate to your garden.
True patrician
You kept your legs crossed.
You married a maker
Of plastic gnomes and bird-baths
And bore him, they say,
A succession of grudges.
I took my seed elsewhere.
Paulina, I'm still your poet
Celebrating today
Baldly, your locked gate
And the cobwebs in your tomb.

7
Happy birthday Shakespeare
the comedy of errors escalates
there aren't enough nettles to go round
among the grasping statesmen
Babel's headphones burn
Bermudas are long shorts
happy are you receiving me
their kitchens make ice
sleep tight Shakespeare
we can tell you now
it won't hurt
none of your blood survives.

8
The last grape resolves beneath the vine.
Fruit-fly and wasp defect.
I watch
Pampas captains mount in the azure field.
Autumn. Auckland.
Spotless enamel
Scuffed by dusters.

9
Climbing on that same gun
Below the blood-stained flags, above the harbour,
I learned as you do my son

While April swept the vault and seemed to show
The place they'd sailed to
How boots and trumpets of good men shook down
Walls, and whole towns.
The dead are ashes. Orations won't bring them back.
That jaw-bone of an ass was God's wrath.
We call it Anzac.

10
April decays in the grape.
It taints the air.
Which of us two
Lives to see the other die
Not waiting on the proof
Will give what's borrowed back.
While one lives
So do we both
Fortunate so far
Beyond deserving
It is a kind of faith
Refuses to see
In this bland sky,
In every blade and branch
That grows to please us,
Injustice, ruling the world.

11
Each day He dies to do me good.
I sign a protest, join a march.
What Wolf began, Eagle accomplishes.

Minerva had a mouse in mind.
It was a weasel, tore her beak.
What Owl began, Eagle accomplishes.

Eagle bears the Snake to die.
Up there it twists about his throat.
Out of the sun they fall like brass.

I signed a protest, joined a march.
Today he dies to do me good.
What Eagle began, Serpent accomplishes.

Ode

At the grave of my great-great-grandfather, Martin McDermott,
Symonds Street Cemetery, Auckland

Purposed to see the new road nudging aside
Our settler graves, then straying purposeless,
I lingered on the littered slope while he,
Intent on roads, noised his earth-moving toy
Along a concrete rim.
His finger's touched a century of stone,
And I, between the child who could not read
And the blind inscription, counted
The generations.
Practical in his fantasy and mine
The toy moved with the toll, bringing nearer
Faces, presently asking.
'Speak for us,' they cry, I hear them cry
'Speak once for us, we want the thunder voice
"Doom. Doom" that the nations know we are
Men, with men's weight and stature.'
And I, knowing again
A freedom in this air and on this ground
That are my own, that made me to be if I would
Their open throat and subtle tongue, I pipe
Light-feathered, fastened to my windy twig
The small enormity they hardly catch
That air and earth compel.
Mild it is, not as their pride urges
A worldly vent.
To hear that doom, to see the cloudy freighters
Bearing in bombs and fire, to read on the sky's page
Headlined, 'The End of Man'
I lack a warrant.
The season, its breath, these trees, their scattered leaves
Blow mildly through me, speak, and all they say
I say again, only that whatever purpose
Takes us, it takes us back, to learn by heart
That here beneath the stone he makes his road
His blood, and ours, lies cold.

Herakles

1 *Don't imagine*

Don't imagine
I'm going to lie beside you
Indifferent
As a young sibling
Dependable
Like an aging parent.
Don't believe
This mouth, these eyes
Speak for the whole man
Or that the rational brow
Accounts for more of me
Than the goat in the thighs.

2 *Seven Sevens*

i
Anonymous I watch you
Panting uphill towards me
Through the crowded park.
No one sees
The gifts you conceal.
No one guesses
A meeting of athletes.

ii
Lilies
At the boardroom window
Gesture to the light.
A blind slat
Clappers behind them.
I run through statistics
As through a field of rye.

iii
Eager wrestlers
In that one posture
We don't lock.
There we discover
The single imperfection

They say the gods inflict
On those they favour.

iv
A man of affairs?
No, I'm Herakles
Wrestler with Death
Who restores to Admetus
A living wife
And keeps in payment
Only his unspeakable pride.

v (She)
He says, 'Regret nothing.
Even the harm we do's
Short-lived.'
I panic as at the cold
Certainty of a death.
He changes down
To take the corner.

vi (She)
Because today he goes
Eyes closed
I committed to memory
The landscape of his back.
I will have it at my fingertips
A week? A year?
It will tide me over.

vii
What there was between us
Unique
In no way extraordinary
Is a private world.
Today the public world
Is as before.
A thrush sings after rain.

3 Farewell message

Live in the present.
Lose yourself there.

Trees, children, those freesias
By the brick border
Contemplate.
Become what you see.
Recall as often only
As that discipline allows
My radical posture
Between your thighs.
Don't speak of love.
I'm your history,
The silence where once you were
A swarm about me,
A white swarm
Dying.

Like

Baited carnivorous flowers
Snare and close about
Butterflies' heads
And suck their juices out.

Like a mirror faintly
Smudged with breath
The wings faintly signal
The stages of death.

Pull one free and you crush
Wings and thorax,
But pinch the base of the flower
And the petals relax.

Away, white against blue
Like a freed soul
The butterfly dances – or spins
Out of control.

Birthday Poem

October.
No more grave poems.
My birthday bloom
Is royal purple.
Royally gifted
I become the subject.

Thirty-five years and I'm out
To butt my head again
Against air, and bawl.
Mother, you expelled me with
A silver tongue
A country in my cry
A trenching tool
To seed fresh furrows.
Long, long I've crouched
In the kitchens of Art
Over the hot stove of Letters.
Hear me now.
Before the fingers are bone
Hear me.

This Time

These are the stars of poetry
Too good to be true
Over the hills
And in the brim-full bay.

And this that ultimate coin
The dead exchange –
Silence.

Unscrew your ears?
Put them away for good?
No. Unstop them.
You're not a spirit.
Listen.

Dews gather at an edge and
Drop. Drop
On frosted blades.

Even such small
Crystalline vocables
Tell time.

Count them.
Count yourself lucky.

TWO **Putting it Straight**

The Albert Park Fountain

Half on the flat crown
Half on the slope
Of an extinct cone
Our geometrical park
Draws all to its fountain

As if the volcanic god
Threw water to cool the brow
Of the hill he made
And saw as it woke in its beds
Of flowers that it was good.

Fire, now water
Tossed from earth
Into moist Auckland air:
Did the draughtsman dream of
Hippocrene here,

Believing his pencilled plan
Growing to be a park
Might bloom, and bloom again
In verse for sure some poet
Coolly would toss down? –

Coolly because the Source
Of poetry was there!
A fountain. It's there of course.
Would it be right to ask
Where he tied the horse?

Gone Pegasus, gone Vulcan,
All that machinery
And the Nine Girls gone,
Yet present if I labour
Like the first draughtsman

Putting these paths down
On paper, who saw one hill
Of our peninsular town
Might have with your concurrence
A style, its own.

Putting it Straight in London

Deception. Is that what it is? – to seem a man
Who never fought in a dance-hall, never got drunk outside one
Never rode bareback, never kicked his big toe out of joint in the space of a
      football season
Never pinched from a shop –
As if we all wore jackets and ties to school
Had the same hobbies (stamps, I suppose, and birds' eggs)
Yours here, mine there, but equally wholesome and clean –
And how well-met we are!

Deception? Yes. But what a pose to declare
Our differences. What a catalogue!
'I read two novels before puberty. Read one of them twice.
The time you gave to classics I gave to comics.'
Who's better for either? Neither of *us* can say.
But I'm the one who travelled the distance between us.
Ungracious, your guest, if I didn't play my part.

And yet I think of dropping it – just like that –
Letting my vowels out of their restraint and telling

How I backed Benghazi at Alexandra Park.
I was fourteen with a bandage round the six stitches in my head
And a smashed bike no one would pay to repair.
Benghazi paid. Over cocktails I silently drink
To his chestnut mane flying round the field at the bend
To come in third at ten to one for a place.
I drink to the Catholic girl – the first ever to undo me
Without an argument – with whom I tucked up in fern
While her father fished the lake at Ngongotaha;
And to the Maori net-ball captain wedged in my second-class seat
All night from Auckland to Palmerston North
Who told me as the sun came up she had trouble with her gums.

And what do you imagine I live in? Certainly not
The wooden box it is on whose iron roof
The rain crashes three winter weeks on end
While the grass I curse and push-mow mounts and thickens.
I try to see it as you might – rambling and white
Spanish-style, among palms?
Driving home in my professorial Morris
I shrug it away. Nobody's fault but my own.
The good Lord whose hand I shook was only a Life Peer –
It could happen to anyone. He was a decent bloke.
But could I have spoken of something out of joint?
He'd have thought I was quoting Hamlet.

A Reading at the Globe Theatre

London, June 1965

Voznesensky
Shook me.
I felt the hot breath of the Bear,
Saw his pads impress
The drifts that broke
Caesarian hearts.

On the Publication of Frank Sargeson's *Memoirs of a Peon*
June 1965

The Grub Street dogs are yapping after their tails.
Someone has made the books they said were dead
Get up and talk in Auckland.
Frank, you always grow the best tomatoes,
The fattest peppers. Only your book makes clear
Why coming through your hedge to get my share
I have to bow so low.

My Friend Julius

I knew a bald whoremonger once
(He's since become a god)
Whose one ambition was to make
Death answer to his nod.

He bedded with a king and put
That service to account.
At least one empress used to boast
She was his favourite mount.

Round about the world he went
Killing and civilising,
Sometimes nasty, sometimes not
When putting down a rising.

He wore loose tunics and removed
His private hairs with tweezers.
He wasn't, though, by any means
The *vainest* of the Caesars.

New York

Constriction is the mother of altitude.

Flat on his back in Fifth Avenue
The plainsman felt at home.

To W. H. Auden on his 60th Birthday
21.2.67

You were creased, bawdy, modest
Cool with fools, tall . . .
(We met between the lines.)

Telling a decade its fortune
You grew ashamed
Seeming infidel.

Ideas always
Knocked you about. God, your last,
Was least a bully.

Does your late line soften?
Confess you know
You've never written so deftly.

Your West is ours
Full-bellied, fast-moving
Between the pumps and jet-strips.

Emboss your shield as you go
With sable lenses
And a tongue argent.

Many happy readers,
Due returns! I wish you
Life like a shopping list

Full of reminders. Long.

Lines Concluding a Lecture on Poetry and Criticism
University of Otago, April 1966

A free and flexible action
As of the voice in his head
The professor heard
When counting syllables

That sang the syllables as words
The words as sentences
The sentences as a poem.

Miraculous! he cried
And might have thrown his gown away
But for the salary.

He swears it never happened.

What Will it Be?

Lucan loudly chanting Lucan while the suicidal blood
Dutiful to one commander marches from the wrists in flood;

Marlowe blasphemously boastful, cut down in a drunken brawl,
Playing Faustus shrieking while they led away his truant soul;

Blake to his Instructor singing for his earned eternal crust;
Shelley gulping Spezzia waters, Byron biting Attic dust;

Arnold sprinting for a carriage jumps a little fence and drops;
Tennyson four-poster bedded, Bard and Bible there for props;

Rupert Brooke his wound a puncture nobody could see or heal,
Bitten by a Greek mosquito – closed their eyes and ceased to feel.

Must the style so pre-determine how our ailing spirits flee?
Lord, what waits for Keith, for Kendrick? What have you in store for me?

Dawn Parade

Long ago
I crossed the rust-red river
Heard steel speak and saw
Scavengers wait on the dying.
There is no way back.
I dream of bombs falling in a winter sea.

Myrtle

1

A sunny morning early summer
The grass grass-green and growing fast
Jack's tractor rounds the park towing
Its chattering blades that scatter behind
A greenbow of cuttings a fluttering rain
And see at the centre of his farthest turnings
A girl her skirt high on her thighs
Her skin it must be silk to touch.
On her Jack's tractor turns, it turns
Smudging the morning gloss of grass
In closing circles.

She lies on her island and will not look
Smaller it grows and smaller yet
Will blood fly out in a crimson haze
Her flesh be chattered up her skin
And hair be clogging blades and cogs?

Silence it seems till all that sound
The mower drowned comes back and Jack steps down
His bare brown legs like trees in boots
Are all she sees beneath her arm.

He doesn't speak he strokes her thigh
Silk it is her skin to his touch
Blandly she watches his hand but she's
A nymph and nymphs are not to be had
Except by some harsh test no man
Who's only a man can pass and failing
Loses a limb or his heart or his life.

But cocky Jack insists on the test
Persists and pesters until she says
'Put out the sun at noon and failing
Fall you will on your own harsh blades.'

2

'It's true you put out the sun at noon
But Jack I should have warned before

61

Whoever sees my body bare
Goes blind is shut inside his mind
To stare at it forever there.'

But look he's taking off his boots
Taking off his shirt his shorts
Taking from her neck that scarf
Green as grass and white with daisies
Binding it about his eyes.
He lays her bare between two trees
And like a tradesman at his task
All by touch he takes her there.

3
A shadow moves across the grass
Across the steps ascending to
Important columns, portentous flags.
High in the sky a single cloud
Drifts before the drumming light.

He wakes among those trees that grow
Below the road that skirts the park
Her veins have run to flowery vines
Her face is moss her body a mound
And from its loamy thigh ascends
A scented shrub, an evergreen.

A Charm

25 shells
Shaped like shark-jaws
I threaded on a driftwood stick.
I had in mind
Tusitala at Vailima
In the South Seas.

Quesada: Poems 1972–74

1975

Cold Moon

Cold moon in velvet, Europe's moon
Riding the slates and chimney pots of London
You walk over Paris too, in squares and gardens
The fountain waters give you back your face.

Cold Europe's moon, along the Côte d'Azur
You are finding out the little rocky bays,
The flickering bat-flight between palm and palm.
In Tuscan woods the stranger apprehends you.

St Mark, St Michael in their piazzas praise you
Who with a light that silvers Como's peaks
Can gild the Adriatic. Everywhere you discover
The stones of Christ, the glass stained with His blood.

Nothing is changed by change. You are as you were
Madonna of the skies, reminding Europe
What moon-crazed folly set a city blazing,
What story sprang from that illustrious wrong.

Cold moon you showed me once an olive grove
And cypresses bathed in such beauty it seemed
The voices of their dead cried out demanding
The twang of an ancient wire, the words of an ancient song.

Under the Sun

I
In the night
Lightning over the olives
And thunder
Under the wall of Alp-rock.

Today
The Bay is blue again
And the dishevelled wildflowers repeat
The shades of rock-face.

The Old Town bakes in its kiln.

Violent Europe!
Still in the hills
Caesar's Trophy stands
On Gallic skulls
And under a bullet-riddled wall
The lizards eat each other.

2
Indolent cafés
Elegant parasols
Coffee under trees and wine
On stone benches
Under slats of cane.
Talk, and the hours passing
The life-blood flowing in little rooms
Opening on balconies that are hung with vines.
Fruit, bread
And a hot wind out of Africa.
An agony of life passing
Expecting, half-expecting
With half-closed lizard eyes
The last brilliant light
Clapping down on the rocks
And the applause of pigeons
Scattering under olives.

3
Do you remember how the leaves chattered in Provence?
They were telling us something.
Every stone had a blood stain.
Every rock had thrown back a human cry.
Rome had sent sacred water from ridge to ridge
Across fertile valleys
And in its arenas bleed still
The brave and stupid bulls.

Would Provence have noticed had we all died in that ditch
Blood filling your eyes and the children screaming?
In that rush of bright green foliage
That flood of grey earth pouring through the windscreen
Didn't we live the commonplace of a landscape

Whose beauty never for a second faded
Whose birds never for a moment lost their heads
But filled the broad fields with their wild music
Under the widening sky.

4

Driving back to Nîmes
Lonely as MacDuff
It seemed a pilgrimage of the soul
As if you had all died
'All my pretty ones'
And there in blazing summer
I made the green trees weep with rain.

5

At 8 a.m. the femme de chambre brings me
Hot chocolate and two croissants.
Two thousand years ago this town earned an Arena
Eight hundred years ago a Cathedral
Today, a modern Hospital.
The femme de chambre is Moroccan.
She has good legs and a mouthful of gold.
Poets have passed this way before
And femmes de chambre.
With our utmost ingenuity
We could not astonish the stones.
I lie watching light expand the shutters.
Is nothing new?
This poet comes from the world's end
And owns two cars, one of them wrecked.
The stones take note.

6

Have you noticed how the wings of pigeons whirr and clap in flight
Under the silvery olives? They have to work at it.
And the swallows that swoop and twitter across the pale faces of these
    buildings
And over their tiled roofs, seem inconsequential.
I prefer the gliding gulls that ride the wind
Over rock and water, taking flight for granted.
They are the ignorant masters of the air.

7

I navigate by a map spattered with blood
Yours or mine, I'm not sure, but it has fallen
East and west of the Rhône,
Across the foothills of the Alpes Maritimes
And in the Baie des Anges.

8

Out of a bank shorn of its green cover I dig
One door handle
One retroviseur
A dozen fragments of glass.
A week of rain has swollen the grapes
And filled the ditch with water.
A baby's bottle floats among weeds.
I cannot find the glasses with which I saw Provence.

9

Still in my head there's an image
Not of the wall of mottled rock
That hangs sheer over the Baie de Garavan
But of those trees like leathery Teutons
That come and go through mist on its topmost ridges
Looking down on the soft-bellied Gauls
Asleep at midday under their vines and olives.

10

Oui. Non. Jamais. Toujours.
Through the two-faced olive-leaves I see
The rocks that frowned on Caesar.
The sun makes knives
And all the sea is blue and all the sky
On which I read
Jamais. Toujours.

Northamptonshire Notes

Christmas morning
Two lights only in the Hall
The stables quiet
The woods loud with crows
And in the churchyard in cold mist
One rose in bud on the grave of Alfred Tasker
'Forty-five years. Peacefully sleeping.'

*

Midday
So much tinsel swept away
The children are quarrelsome
Riding their bikes to the village
While the gamekeeper's wife talks hounds
And shot-guns puff in the woods.

*

Night. A path so dark
I learn what 'starlight' means
And I want to make love to you
Against a tree in the wind
While the bellies rumble indoors
And the bone heads nod
Over news from North Vietnam.

*

Now all of a settled order
Is gone but the wrapping.
A set of dentures
Smiles over the manger
In which Prosperity was born.

Quesada

'Je pense . . . aux vaincus!'
         – Baudelaire, 'Le Cygne'

I

All over the plain of the world lovers are being hurt.
The spring wind takes up their cries and scatters them to the clouds.
Juan Quesada hears them. By the world at large they go unheard.
Only those in pain can hear the chorus of pain.
High in the air over winds that shake the leaves
High over traffic, beyond bird-call, out of the reach of silence
These lovers are crying out because the spring has hurt them.
No one dies of that pain, some swear by it, a few will live with it always,
No one mistakes it for the lamentations of hell
Because there is a kind of exaltation in it
More eloquent than the tongues of wind and water
More truthful than the sibylline language of the leaves
The cry of the injured whose wounds are dear to them
The howl of the vanquished who cherish their defeat.

2

Quesada on the dunes hurls himself at the elements
Howls at the sea, tries to shout down the surf
Pushes against the wind that fathers a mountain of sand
Catches at the sun with his glances
Throws his name away like a rose the surf casts back at him again and
     again.

The waves drive forward against an offshore wind
That turns their crests to banners.
They shiver in the heat haze silver and white
Shaken against sunlight above the crack of broken rollers
Driving up the hill of sand again and again defeated.

3

Is there another poetry than the poetry of celebration?
When the defeated are silent there is only the song of the victorious.

Who plays on a broken pipe, who dances with a stone in his belly?
Sing, holy wanderer, cry your anguish to wind and water.
Who but a Christian would celebrate the broken body of love?
Who but a lover would sigh to be a plaything of the gods?

4

Dulcinea walks
Through spears of grass
Her feet bare
Leaves embroidered about them
A girl in a dream
Quesada dreamed
How will she live
Outside his tortured sleep?
Hear the cicadas
Using their chainsaws
Listen to those birds
That seem to yap like dogs
Look at the vines
Binding her ankles
See where the spears point.
The spring is mindless
The sun is blind
She's a walking garden
Praise her.

5

Quesada dreams: he is walking along a lane
A park à droit, à gauche the backs of houses.
Here is a barn-like building its bricks red in the sun,
Here is a thin hedge, two girls beyond in a garden,
One dark, cross-legged in the grass, seeming to murmur advice,
One pale, kneeling, her eyes cast down as she listens.
Has he passed at last into the world of perfect forms?
Where is the bridge by which the Enchanters cross
To this green pool of silence in which a glance has shown him
Figures of beauty, sun-carved figures of light?

6

the wave that	the wave that
rides over	brings back
age	youth
advances	retreats
briefly	at length
never long	always
victorious	defeated

7

He said God that gave the wound would give the cure.
He said there were many hours between one day and the next
And in one of them, even in a moment, the house falls.
He had seen rainshine, he had seen sunfall,
He had seen a man lie down at night who could not rise in the morning.
Whoever thought he could put a spoke in Fortune's wheel
Flattered himself. Whoever thought there was space for a pin
Between a woman's yes and no was deluded.
Then let Quesada wear his madness like a medal.
Copper will be gold, tears pearls, and westward look –
Across the plain at nightfall a bonfire blazed for his coming.

8

Dulcinea at breakfast saying
One born under Scorpio
Might kill for love.

Over her shoulder
Magnolias
And a blossoming peach tree.

Saying goodbye
In the flooded courtyard
He gave her a quill plucked
From a pheasant dead on the road.
She was to write him a poem.

9

And a partridge in a poetry.

Not collar edge   *Coal*-ridge
Not bodle air   Bo-*dlaire*
       Get it right
       Make it new
And don't forget Les Fleurs du Mal-
                  arm-
                       é
                  he say
       'Poetry – she's made wiv woids.'

Donkey Shot and Liberty Prance
Off with your pants and on with the dance

So
       Kubla if you can
               Juan Quesada

And if you can't –
       Try teaching!

10

Odysseus under wet snapping sheets
Quesada in the saddle – all men are travellers
Astride, under sheets, travellers and lovers they go
To prize the world apart, to learn the spaces
In Circe's cave, on couches of blue satin
In brown grass under summer olives.
As long as seasons change don't look for stillness
Dulcinea, don't ask for kindness or rest –
Only the long reach of the mind always in love.

11
for two voices

     It is not merely the grandiose claims of the hero
Morning that reeled and trembled for Quesada

to be proud knight and lover of women
Dawn of his new day, lantern-jawed lean man
 that are mocked here, nor is the story only an exposure
In middle-years making a break for life
 of the distortions of life which Art can bring about;
Through fields where first birds talked to one another.

 the hero-fool is a warning to us all,
Before thirst, before hunger, before pains of love and war
 yet he is also the only true hero in literature
Quesada's visionary morning of the world
 because we all lack and look for a little of his madness
The straw-pale sky calling him from home.

12

She has put a cloth on the table
Also the pink paper fan
When he comes she will be ready
She will tell him he must not come again
Her feeling for him is particular
Like Van Gogh's chair
Like his shadow on the earth near Arles
He has taken her breastbone for a flute
On her skull's cave he has painted
The bulls of Lascaux
The grass is full of black olives
The sky is full of white feathers
There is a hard hand at her throat
When he comes she will be ready.

13

Our cameramen are hoisted on a boom
Over the garden
We swoop in through trees
Hearing birds, dry leaves
Seeing grass crushed in a ring.

The girls are gone
Also the lean man from the lane

He is riding somewhere
Against the sunspears.

    She had broad strong hands
    And beautiful feet.
    He wanted to go down in the dust . . .
    Living inside his mind,
    Sailing between two lives.

Limits are not fixed
Nor are the possibilities limitless.
Rainshine, sunfall, madness
Human spirit
Spirit of Quesada.

14

Dulcinea, he'd like to show you
A path dropping through ancient trees that shelter
A pool so clear the small fish seem to hang
In sun-shafts over its shingle floor.
You weren't born when he said goodbye to that place.
He'd loved it as he has loved you
With a wild sweet self-consuming passion.
Last night he dreamed you were standing
Beside a dark unruly river.

15

Honi soit qui mal y pense
Don Quichotte et le Petit Prince.

16

Favourite of gods, men's favourite under the turning wheel of stars
Filling earth and sea with life, talking winds and waters into peace
Scattering hills with flowers and light on spring's first day
Setting birds chirping of your coming and cattle leaping for their kind –
You from whom the singular blessing of sap and sinew flows
To fill the mind of the lover – Alma Venus! – mistress and mother
Smile too on Quesada's poet pressing the grapes of Lucretius.

17

That the balls of the lover are not larger than the balls of the priest
That the heart of the miser is not smaller than the heart of Quesada
That the same sun warms the knight and the squire
That the long lance and the short sword open equally the passages to
    death
That the barber may wear a beard and the hangman have long life
These are the opaque equities of our world.

That the breast of Dulcinea is whiter than the driven snow
That the strength of her knight is as the strength of ten because his heart is
    pure
That the empire of true love is boundless and its battalions unconquerable
These are the translucent hyperboles of art.

Where was Quesada whose grapes fattened uneaten at his door
Whose fields were ripe, whose mill-wheels were always turning?
He was beyond the horizon riding against the sunspears
Remembering the foot of his lady tentative as a white pennant in the swift
    mountain stream.

Pictures in a gallery in his brain
Were turned facing the wall, his limbs jolted
Coming down into a valley, night coming down
Sun catching flax and pampas along a stream
A church white in the foot-hills, the dead on his mind
The empty world full of their singing ghosts.

Owls in the poplar candles, a pheasant dead on the road
Thunder over the treeless mountain burned brown by summer
Thunder over the flooded fields thunder over the dunes
Thunder over the darkened ocean shafted with light
Thunder in the long line of the surf breaking against an offshore wind
Thunder in the long line
Exaltation in the defeated heart of Quesada.

Who but a Christian would sing the broken body of love?
Who but a lover would sigh to be a plaything of the gods?

The Mirabeau Bridge

after Apollinaire

Under the Mirabeau Bridge the Seine flows
        And all our loving
            Why should I remember how it goes
Happiness used to follow after our woes

        Let the night come strike the bell
        Time keeps moving I keep still

Hand in hand together couldn't we lie
        And face to face
            Our arms a bridge of sighs
Over the slow streams flowing from our eyes

        Let the night come strike the bell
        Time keeps moving I keep still

Love goes by just as these waters are flowing
        Love goes by
            Slow as life is in growing
And violent as the hopes that attend its going

        Let the night come strike the bell
        Time keeps moving I keep still

Days pass and weeks it's all the lover knows
        And time like love
            Won't alter but on it goes
Under the Mirabeau Bridge the Seine flows

        Let the night come strike the bell
        Time keeps moving I keep still

Fifteen Letters from the Zebra Motel

1

In bed Sunday morning
In the Zebra Motel
I'm watching white curtains
Belly in the wind
And light strike through
I'm listening to
The whoosh of cars through Parkville

Sunday morning
Music time
I can't get the ABC on my bedside console
Room service won't answer
My bed-cover's red against a white sheet
I wish you were here

2

Down there under trees
Goes a green tram
Clanking in the sun

3

I make you walk into the naked bathroom
Your thighs and belly are in the cold tiles
I put it to you in the fluorescent mirror
All my wishing is in that empty glare

4

I meant this fourth letter
To tell you whatever I was
One Sunday morning in Melbourne
When sun shone
Wind blew
Room service wouldn't answer
ABC wouldn't play
And the cars rushed on through Parkville
Down the long straight road
Past the Zebra Motel
To where the world ends

5

Believe me Fausta
My cover's the colour of hell
I can't be without you
Not here not ever
You belong in my mirror
Never doubt I love you

6

Here's my sixth letter
Sailing in bed
Flying in the wind
And in the air
An eternal out-there drive
Down the freeway to death
Where leaves flicker
Like lives going out
And the skies are endless

7

I choose for symbol
A smiling swordsman
I can't do better than that
It may be my fate
To flash a blade for ever
I hope on horseback
You'll miss me when I die

8

When the Zen master died
He found himself in a comfortable western motel
With a Gideon's Bible
From a console at his bedside
Came the laughter of mortals
The master called for a stock-exchange report
And took up the phone
They say by the third morning
He'd made a million

9

The clock I bought in France
Lies flat on its back on the floor
The carpet muffles its ticking
Its face shows twelve
This morning's gone
Already out in the park
Children have buried it
Under a shower of grass

10

I dreamed you were in my suitcase
A fold-up lockaway
Pack of a woman
With a delta of pubic hair

Ned Kelly's dead
So is God
Where will the wind end
When will you come

11

The wind never tires
Of its trick with the curtains
It pushes through
In a dozen shapes and sizes
Whispering of itself

12

Koan:
If the Sunday stick-man exposed himself
To the blind nymphomaniac mirror
Would her seeing-eye dog's bark
Prove worse than its bite

13

Mothers
Sisters
Wives

Mistresses
Daughters
I dreamed you were all flying
In the face of the wind
Above the gum trees
Crying in your throats like crows
And I ran a black-ink roller
Across the continent
From Darwin down through Melbourne
That marked it
CANCELLED.

14
The cars never give up
Somewhere down the freeway
They rush into a great emptiness
And fall for ever
Reciting telephone numbers
Recipes
Advertising jingles
Prices and incomes
Instructions for use

I watch trees dancing
Oak arms
Fig torsos
Spine of one tall pine
Against a sky that still seems
A benediction

Fuck it here I am
Fuck it (sing with me)
I'm going to live for ever
In the Zebra Motel

15
Not to need
Not to believe I'm needed
Not to look into mirrors
Not to look into eyes
But into trees

Into the sky beyond them
Into the heart of the park
Where the unfolding leaves
Are patching shadows for summer

This last and solemn letter
I write to myself

The Swan
Baudelaire's 'Le Cygne'

I
Andromache, it's you I think of – and of that river
Simoïs, unworthy of you. How many years
Since your towering grief blazed in its petty mirror
Grown falsely great, fed by your widow's tears?

Thought of that flood – it set me remembering
As I crossed the Carrousel Bridge over the Seine.
Our former Paris – it's gone. A city's a thing
Changes more quickly, alas, than the heart of a man.

Only in memory now I see the bustle of stalls,
Weeds, stone blocks splashed with green stains,
Piles of rough-hewn columns and capitals,
Jumbled *bric-à-brac* shining in shop-front panes.

There a menagerie used to spread out its tents,
And there, at the hour when workmen first appear,
When, under cold clear skies, street-sweepers send
Storms of dust up into the quiet air

I saw a swan once, escaped from its cage.
Its webs on the roadway made a dry scraping;
Over uneven ground it dragged white plumage;
Near a waterless gutter, its dumb beak gaping,

It bathed its shivering wings in dusty earth.
'Thunder, when will you sound? Rain, when will you fall?'
It seemed to ask, home-sick for the lake of its birth.
I see that unlucky creature, that strange and fateful

Piece of mythology, an Ovidean figure, twisting
Its crazed head on a downy convulsive rod
Towards the ironic sky, cloudless, persisting –
Towards the heavens, as if reproaching God.

II

Paris changes! But nothing in my melancholy
Alters a jot. New palaces, scaffolding, blocks,
Old suburbs – all of it tells me the same story,
And my dearest memories weigh on me like rocks.

Passing the Louvre, for example, an image assails me:
I think of those lunatic motions of my great swan
Sublime and ridiculous like every refugee
Gnawed at by one desire – and then again

Of you, Andromache, the greatest lady become
A chattel in the gift of stately Pyrrhus –
Grief-crazed, bowed over an empty tomb,
Widow of Hector made wife to Hélénus!

I think of one who trudges through streets like bogs –
Negro, red-eyed, wasted, tubercular,
Straining to divine beyond the curtains of fog
The palm trees of her majestic Africa.

Of all whose loss can never find relief,
Not ever! – of those who thirst for their own tears
And hunger for the breast of the she-wolf Grief;
Of thin orphans withering as flowers wither.

So in the forest where my spirit runs for cover
These distant memories echo like the hunter's horn:
I think of sailors forgotten on barren shores,
The chained, the defeated – all these, all these I mourn.

For a Children's L.P.

Just for the Record

When teacher lets the stylus down
And round and round the record goes
Up comes a poet's thinking frown
A poet's choosy nose.

Oh children, do you hear me groan?
Your faces all are shiny new.
Once I was beautiful like you,
Now I'm a voice on the gramophone.

Ecology

Look there – down in the bay
Where a blue heron is wading
Dump trucks and bulldozers
Are filling the edges with clay.

Soon the mangroves will be gone
The heron will fly away.

When you run on the new sportsfield
Think of the lives that stopped
Six feet under the clay.

Walking Westward

1979

Caesar is still Caesar

Caesar is still Caesar
even if he breakfasts on turds
before a speech to the House.
Egnatius may rinse his teeth with urine –
nonetheless his smile is valued on television.
Even Mamurra, bull-necked brazen-brained ex-All Black
has a hundred hectares of dairy land
and a prick like a stallion's
to make him feel himself a man of substance.
I, your Catullus, by contrast
known for nothing but verses
lie awake at night thinking out lines
to make the name of a bitch live for ever.

A breeze from the ink-blue mountains
stirs in the macrocarpas
where you dream in your garden deck-chair
a novel face-down on your lap
over the grave of hearts.

Is it Caesar's cheek-scar you lust after
or the dental charm of Egnatius
or is it still Mamurra down at the stock-yards
carrying all before him?
I know it's no poem of mine that's strutting
behind your hard whore's eyes.

Breaking the Neck: an Autumn Sketchbook

Breaking the neck

These are the gifts

of the night
soup in a cup
a long

needle
for the leg

and two sandbags

                    to keep the head from
moving from
                                        side to
side.

Driving to the orthopaedic clinic

A skein of ducks
and then another
rippling eastward out
high and fast
over the estuary.

Or it might have been
two lines of telegraphy
an impression on the eye
dashed down:

'11 a.m. / tide low
sun on mangroves.'

My father and the Waitakere Range

Secretary of many committees my handsome father
wore a broad-brimmed hat, carried a Gladstone bag
winked at me from the school steps at prize-giving.
From our kitchen window the suburb sloped away
gently for miles then gently rose again
to the Waitakere Range that vanished when rain was coming.
In sunshine the air between could be subtle crystal
the Range ink-blue. Last night I remembered the sunsets.
Sunsets like that went out with Gladstone bags.

A political poem for the 'seventies

Reading a poet
of one of those People's Republics
who dreamed he ghostly walked
in Windsor Castle and saw
Majesty's ineffable nipples

I recalled those '30s boys
who dreamed of clear-eyed giants
married to their tractors
amid the alien corn.

Stockhausen: 'Ylem'

Through phones in darkness
this first night when autumn
lays a hand on the moon –
storms of frogs, plagues of brass,
poles advancing on tropics
and away from it all
the white panicky glittering
rush of the stars.

Ai ai tei wun
from the Chinese via Fenellosa

Cloud piling on cloud
fall after fall of rain
whichever way one darkness
closing on the level road.

In the east room
I am part of the stillness
my hand on the untapped wine-cask.

Cloud on cloud piled
fall after heavy fall
darkening over.

No sail comes on the river
no wheel by the road.

The wild swans cooled

The lake is a glass
reflecting the russet
of an autumn wood.

The glass is a lake
on which the poet counted
59 swans.

Nineteen years had gone by
since his first visit –
he was older
but the swans the lake and the wood
seemed unchanged.

Swans paddled and flew
trees shed their leaves
and the lake reflected.
It made the poet sad
but it was all so natural
he found it hard to say why.

How it came about

Sitting alone in a 'high-class Chinese restaurant'
hearing three Indians talk of a Japanese tea-garden
thinking of K with love, with love remembering J
he was lucky enough to think out a poem about
himself alone in a 'high-class Chinese restaurant'.
Was it because the Indians raised their voices
in praise of the beauties of the Japanese tea-garden
or because he had opened the poems of Brecht on the table
or the food, the music and wine that had this effect?
It was all these things, and the colours, black and red.
For just a moment he thought he was truly himself
and far, far from himself. He was the bones of a poem.

Bidding the lover goodbye

Pampas heads
in wind
against the sun
are white flame
at the sky's blue altar.

They are the plumes of horsemen
riding away
over the hill.

Farewell summer!
Vale!
There will never be another like you.

Long before . . .

Long before the sun goes out for ever
it seems the trees will take over
and the insects among their branches
and the animals underneath them.
This the gods have decreed because we subvert
their Cosmic Joke with ungodlike efforts at order.

O Brave New World
without pogroms and sham trials
without cities and the bombs to rubble them
without the shame of history! –
nothing but the mindless movement of leaves
and ignorant jaws ceaselessly devouring.

Ode

A shelley
held to the ear –
listen! It's
the west wind.

Late night, old house

Round moon sank in the sash frame
and when he descended the stair
full of old dreams and emotion
she came a moment to the window
risking the eyes of any late-night stroller
to wave a hand to her departing lover.

Whether the will is free

On an April evening
the tallest buildings of our city
turn blind eyes
to the western clouds –
it's their defence against drifting.

Even so
the luminous quivering
sunless sky
dislodges them.

'Now is the month of maying . . .'

The sky has gone dead.
The park crunches underfoot.
The English trees are going to pieces again.

Soldier's poem
after Rihaku through Fenellosa & with a glance at E.P.

Takanini horses don't dream of winning at Trentham
nor do Trentham gulls give a fuck for the Ellerslie Racecourse.
How you feel about places depends on what you're used to.
Yesterday we marched out of Ardmore Camp,
today it's gunnery practice on the Desert Road,
grit in the eyes and snow closing down on Ruapehu.
How do you keep your thoughts on the target
when your trousers are hopping with fleas?
Loyalty? It's like with horses and gulls – a habit.
No one thanks a soldier for staying alive –
they just keep moving him on.
It's the dead ones get the brass and the bugles.

Breaking the neck

'Get well soon and write for the Revolution'
telegraphs the secretary of the New Zealand
Marxist-Leninist Workers' Party – but I've no time

being in revolt against the Gods. White flame
in the blown pampas is my concern
and the sky calligraphy of high-flying ducks.
Already there are complaints from Valhalla
but I won't alter a word. My death is assured.

Twenty-two Sonnets

Spring 1974

I

1 September

Maurice, I dreamed of you last night. You wore
A black track-suit, red-striped. Saying goodbye

We fought back tears. I woke thinking you dead.
Here in the North manuka is flecked with flowers,

Willows bent in stream-beds are edged with green,
But the tall-striding poplars seem no more

Than ghostly sketches of their summer glory.
Beyond the dunes blue of the sky out-reaches

The blue of ocean where the spirits of our dead
Stream northward to their home. Under flame-trees

By Ahipara golf-course someone's transistor tells me
The news again, and down on the hard sand

In letters large enough to match the man
Children have scrawled it: BIG NORM IS DEAD.

2

Rain, and a flurry of wind shaking the pear's white blossom
Outside our kitchen window and tossing the lasiandra

As it did that morning four-year-old Michele Fox
Sat at our table painting shapes she said were flowers

While we listened to the news: a coaster missing up North,
A flare sighted in the night over Pandora Bank,

Radio contact lost – the ship's name *Kaitawa*.
That was eight years ago. On the bus north

To Reinga and Spirits' Bay the driver remembers it –
Not a man saved, not even a body recovered,

Only smashed timber scattered down miles of coast
To tell how quickly it can come. I kept that painting –

It was the world she saw believing she had a father.
He was third engineer, a Scotsman, a good neighbour lost.

3

October, and the kowhai declare themselves through parks
And gardens, and along the bush road to Karekare

As if someone had called on the faithful each to light a candle
And through a darkened arena the yellow flames

In their thousands flared into life. I know the darkness
Those flowers make known, a spirit like water gathered

In a cup of nasturtium leaves at morning – black water
That lines the cup with silver. Let's say it's because

One evening thirty years ago as I walked to Scouts
The world unveiled itself and through me burned

An ecstasy of which each moment after of life
Harbours an echo – as these kowhai hide themselves

Till the season calls them forth. My books advise
I will know that ecstasy once more before I die.

4

to Alan Roddick

The visiting celebrity who's not a poet's arse
Has come like the Queen of the May and departed south

Scattering his paper flowers. Last night we read our poems
In a room like a bunker. My newest tonalities

Which sound in my head like a small Wagnerian storm
Beat vainly on concrete drums. I felt the need

Of your astringencies. So many daughters we harbour
And a son each, and all so far apart

Distrust grows in the gap. Next time I read in public
I'll tell the empty chairs, 'Roddick of Invercargill

Is a true poet.' The dead ponga next door
Is smothered in clematis and from its thickened top

The white flowers spill down. Alan, the sap is moving
South into winter. It will set you writing again.

5

Thinking of the Mediterranean blue beyond yellow walls
Of Roquebrune Castle, and terraced vineyards, I was reminded

There's a painting by McCahon of the lamp in his studio
That burns with a golden love. Nothing expresses more aptly

The artist's feeling for his work. By that light
He has made the mountains again, and the black horizon,

And written into our skies the thunder of Israel's God.
Our suburb this evening has nothing of that austerity.

Cut grass breathes, already kowhai flares are falling,
Greens and purples compete calling on Hanly to paint them

Or at least to rest his head. When I go to my desk
And switch on the lamp so the last faint light of the garden

Is cut away, it's sometimes, as now, these names
That keep my mind on what the light has extinguished.

6

Spring hides scars on Dickens Street but the old cottages
Are most of them in good heart. We park outside number 6

My mother beside me lost in her time machine
Sixty years back when she lay behind those sashes

Staring at moulded ceilings, fearing a dream would end,
Her parents home after two years sailing without her.

She was seven. I know where the path ran down
Past the strawberry patch behind the red-brick orphanage

Whose children hung over the fence. How they must envy her
She thought. And when patriots chased her from school

Because her name was Karlson, she didn't care too much.
'I'd like to die there,' she says, and I feel the blessing

Of retrospect on the griefs of Dickens Street, that offered
Sanctuary against the malice of the world.

7

Looking at the fountain from the park's lower slopes
At 9 a.m. you see the sun cutting athwart

Its falling waters, making strips of opaque silver.
Sculpted it all seems – oaks, palms, Moreton Bay figs,

Even those scatter-branched kowhai whose flowers, I remember,
Twenty years ago Diane told me were *cloches d'or*.

Nothing entirely random nor exactly repeated
Is the art of nature, and if I unlock myself

That principle holds. I remember three of us, students,
Crouching under trees in Sargeson's garden at night

While he held a lighted candle to show us pawpaws.
Everything grew from a centre. Reality was yellow.

Was it more than fancy? Those golden bells of kowhai
May be chiming inaudible 9. There is also dog-shit.

8

To Maurice and to Maurice and to Maurice
Duggan, Shadbolt, Gee, how they load us down with fictions

And all our yesterdays maybe have lighted fools
The way to Dostoevski. How many years ago was it

That Curnow's bantams roosted in his macrocarpas
And he and I one midnight crept under the moon

And swung on the branches bringing those feathered half-wits
Down around our heads with a flapping and a squawking

That echoed over Big Shoal Bay? Do good poets
Make bad professors? Do many Maurices

Make light work, as one Sargeson made a summer?
How many K.S.'s could the North Shore harbour

Before the Fall? I tell you my Lord Fool
Out of these nettle prophets we still pluck our safety-pins.

9
17 October 1974

Spring is a recurring astonishment – like poetry.
So suddenly the oaks in Albert Park have assumed

Their bulk of green, so helplessly I find myself
With forty-two years notched up, my birthday presents

Hedge-clippers, screw-drivers, and *The Gulag Archipelago* –
And as I unwrap them a young man with a pack on his back

Knocks at our door wanting breakfast. His name is Blackburn,
Son of a 7th Fleet Admiral who rained down death

For years on North Vietnam – but the boy went to jail
Sooner than fight, and he's here to study mushrooms.

'He who forgets the past becomes blind,' says Solzhenitsyn
In that bookful of Russian blood. 'Cultivate your garden,'

Say those Voltairean hedge-clippers. The quarrel of sparrows
Fills the silence of God that has lasted forty-two years.

10
for Kay

'Jesus! I'd like to lay down lines of cold melodic fire
Like the exiled Florentine – such ease, such sentences rolling

I imagine over rotting teeth' . . . and I thought of that June day
We made it, all five of us, from the coast of Tuscany

Inland to Florence, to the Uffizi Gallery.
Do you remember the swallow in the Primo Corridoio

How it flitted from marble figure to marble figure
As if at home on a mountain? – and then from a casement

That glimpse of the yellow Arno? But it was Botticelli's Venus
We'd come to see, who'd been waiting half a thousand years

To ride for us on her scallop shell out of blue wavelets,
Flowers falling around her, zephyrs breathing about her,

A floral cape dropping from her naked shoulder –
And to look right into us with those unerring eyes.

11

Getting up in the night, a pain in the balls, nausea,
A shaft deep into the silences of 2 a.m. and . . .

I come to on the laundry floor, head sore from the fall,
Neck wrenched, groaning, feeling like a hundred tons.

What dark angel clapped me an instant under
His infinite wing-pit I can only guess – but worse

Has happened in the garden this morning – two fledglings mangled,
Their heads chewed off and vomited later on the path,

Their murderer at the door wanting milk. I pick pear blossom
And the cluster of freckled white flowers in its aureole of leaf

Lies on my desk. Does age make the Spring more vivid? –
Roy Fuller says so – 'The best poet writing in Britain'

I want to add, thinking I should clear my debts
Even if only literary, even if only in a sonnet.

12
9 November 1974

As the train pulled out of Nice she offered you a sandwich
Because you were a soldier, because you spoke of poetry

In a deep grave voice. Outside lay the coast of your childhood
Guillaume Apollinaire de Kostrowitzky – Polish Italian French

Who knows? – a bastard from the confluent gutters of Europe
And a poet. Next stop Antibes. You couldn't have guessed

Its Musée by the sea would one day bear the name of Picasso –
Your friend, suspected with you of stealing the Mona Lisa

(They'd locked you in the Santé for that). The palms dripped light
Into the blue of Golfe Juan where warships rode at anchor.

You promised letters, and you wrote them, Guillaume – such letters! –
Passionate, extravagant, from trenches lined with corpses.

Fifty-six years ago today shell-fragments and 'flu
Finished you. She kept the letters and never married.

Autumn 1975

13

Late for the very last time called to your bedside
(How long had you begged them to call me?) and all the colour

Gone from your face and from those arthritic hands
I would have held to steady you through the fires

At the dark threshold you were required to cross
I was locked in the pit of myself until that night

I put a sonata you loved on the record player
And opened the sliding door to the beautiful sky

And the cold stars above the cabbage tree
And thought your drained face looked down and listened

Or I was a child and it was your younger hands
Storming the keyboard ringing those Beethoven bells

And then the tears flowed free unlocked by illusions
But in the morning I woke and knew you were dead.

14
to Conrad Bollinger

'Did you write that sharp-tongued letter?' Yes, I wrote it
Two decades ago, because a story in a journal –

How can I explain? – simply, it went over my nerves
Like a note off-key, like the goodwill of a salesman

His foot in your door. Why quibble about one story?
But that voice has gone on sounding until now it's known

And honoured and echoed through all the echoing rooms
Of this high house of Culture you and I

Are committed to – and still to my ear, Conrad,
It's false, factitious, fabricated, vain.

April is our *helden* season when the new toetoe
Ride into heaven and the old men march again.

I no longer write such letters – nor disown them.
Petitions from the faithless, they lie in the lap of the gods.

15
to Sam Hunt

That story I wanted to tell – it was how I rode
To the gate for the meat and bees had swarmed in the box.

I was nine or ten, riding a horse called Bosun
From a house among macrocarpas half a mile

Through manuka over a hill above a brown dam –
All the way along that clay track singing

In my best voice, my loftiest soprano.
I reached for the meat not noticing the swarm

And they came at me, stinging. They say when Pindar
Lay in his crib bees hovered over his mouth –

And yours too I think – an emblem of sweetness
Or lyric grace. With me they played Kamikaze.

I galloped hell-for-leather, bees in my hair,
Trailing across that sky a dark and angry plume.

16

Xuan Loc fallen, Danang fallen, we wait for the fall of Saigon.
Nobody weeps or cheers, nobody puts on sack-cloth

For the thousand thousand lives we took or broke
To get our own sweet way. We didn't get it.

Does Lyndon Johnnie underground sleep sound
Dreaming light at the end of a tunnel? Holyoake hasn't been told.

Harold Holt went swimming, and all those airy ministers
Of canister bombs and body counts took jobs

With the World Bank, UNESCO, the Ford Foundation.
Washington, Wellington, leather chairs, inflatable arses,

'Peace with Honour' – and last night walking home
I saw in a darkened house a fish tank glowing

With purple lights. There's no God. We don't answer for
Our violences, nor even for our sense of beauty.

17

April leaks from leaf to leaf into May
And you lie in darkness, your face like a mask of Keats,

A beauty unrecorded, unrequited –
And yet I half-believe your ear must catch

The thrush's note. Has man an immortal soul?
Flight – only flight – the bird's eagerness to be gone

Is proper to the vanishing season. A mother's love
Is what a son learns guilt and selfhood rejecting.

When we sat at the piano I tried to get it right
But stole your music instead and took a path

Where you couldn't follow, couldn't judge me wanting.
My once and only music teacher mother

Those lessons were hard; this, your last, is harder –
Man has a soul indeed. That soul is mortal.

18
The fall of Saigon

Our biggest march came late. It was '71.
A girl walked with me, starry-eyed, bewildered

Shocked at the war, frightened locked in that crowd –
Fifteen, twenty thousand pushing into Queen Street.

Outside the Town Hall leaves of the tubbed trees
Decked out with raindrops shivered under the lights.

Our chanting rose to the clock and the cold stars
That watch over us, that bless us rarely.

So many years we've fought that war in our sleep!
Now Xerxes at a phone in the Oval Office

Is pulling his troops out, and I remember that girl,
That march, telling ourselves 'Keep calm, keep walking –

History won't take our names but she'll maybe award us
An honourable footnote on a page of blood.'

19
after Baudelaire

Nature's a temple whose pillars, because they're alive,
Can give forth sometimes a baffling babble of voices;

It's a forest of symbols that look upon a man
As he passes among them as if he too were a symbol.

Perfumes, colours, sounds, you can hear them speak
And answer one another like reverberations

Mixing far off in riddling harmonies
Vast as darkness itself, vast as light.

There are perfumes that are fresh as the flesh of a child,
Mellow as oboes, green as meadows are green;

And others corrupt, opulent, expansive,
That seem to have the scope of infinite things –

Amber, incense, balsam – celebrating
The secret touch of finger-tip and wing.

20

Our party ends in the kitchen. Haley unleashes
His animus like a dog. It goes straight for me.

'You're an academic fuck-out. And as a writer
You're a fuck-out too.' Haley is probably

The best Yorkshire surrealist writing in New Zealand.
He's forty-one, looks twenty. 'You're split, man,

Right down the middle.' (He chops me cleanly in half.)
'And your teeth are false.' (I open my mouth wide

To prove they're my own.) 'Your praise of Ian Wedde
Was a cold fart . . .' (The blurb writers quote it, I think.)

'And that shit you wrote about me . . .' It's true I wrote
I didn't like Haley's poem, and now I think

I don't like Haley. When the Dimple's gone he goes –
Kisses me at the door, asks me to dance.

21
Tauranga

Five children and a shag are fishing from the wharf.
Across the estuary autumn has taken away

From willows and poplars their definitive shapes.
Yellow-brown, slate-grey, hazy, smudged,

They fade into green fields and blue-green hills.
An empty sky is immense and fills the frame.

I count forty-one launches, seventy-two parked cars.
How can a faraway world be made to seem

Less unreal than its image? If the cars were people
And the people cars the sky might fill with bombers

Trying to decide their future. Into the picture
Come four young Maori with flax kits; also their granny

Who clutches a thermos. They row away in a dinghy.
If life goes on without thought, is it right to complain?

Autumn 1978

22
Visiting Te Aute College

On the night plane back from Napier I sort out images
Behind closed eyes – yesterday rolling through Auckland

That convoy carrying to Bastion Point the force
To drive the last of a tribe from the last of its land,

Break up its shelters, tear down the flag of its pride –
And today the fiery trees by the Williams veranda

Under a green hill where sleet will scatter in winter –
English trees, English architecture, an English church

But in the meeting house those panels ordered by Ngata
On the premonition of his death. Welcomed in Maori

I could only answer in English, but I remembered
The wise king who wept when the sprig was lost

That might save his people from death. His tears became legends.
The tears of the dispossessed are the legends of the tribe.

These white flowers

these white flowers grow only in the moonlight
their yellow stamens are the spokes of prayerwheels
truth tellers of the unbidden sun
they bloom in a garden in a dream

down the path comes the girl wearing my old raincoat
pretending to be a flasher
she is like electricity
like fresh spring water

out in the street the first leaves of autumn sidle down
from the tallest trees in the world
the clock in the tower has taken another minute from her youth
and added it to the sum of my age

the waxen cups on their shadowy stems
seem to float unsupported in the moonlight
fragile they look
but I know they will outlast us

The Young Wife

Bees in the weatherboards
        ceilings stained with honey
the whole house is a hive.

Those mounds out there are carbodies
fencelines
              obsolete machines
dead
and blackberried.

Since that first breathless night
I've called him Gerontion.
        If he wanted a child
        why didn't he adopt me?

It's something from Wagner
                 the bees are performing.
                     When they stop
you hear the clicking of fleas.

Time to light the lantern.
                    O eastern star
            every night the same stew.

Walking Westward

Walking westward
you have it all before you
the great out-reach
pale blue with a clean white edge
the downing sun bright orange
rabbits among lupins
              a dog in the distance
no human shape.

Out there is the world
is nothing but the sun bleeding
               cloud cerements
ocean
       darkness enfolding.

The fish of Maui is under your feet
the hook of Maui is in your guts
here is all the beauty of Lackland
the surf is blind as Homer and forgetful
in Paradise are no legends
the drowned angels are silent
             as the millennial stars

  *

On the stone stairway
to the square of the churches
oil lamps flare at a breath from the sea
and across the water flicker
lights of San Remo.

The windows look out on the square
the square looks over the water
the town is still, listening to music from the square
at a light salt breath
black smoke flaps from oil flares
dark heads look down
                              shadows
shades of shades.

Sunt manes
              and the ghosts live for ever
on the waterfront tables are laid
for supper at midnight
white cloths   red napkins
this night began before Christ
the oil flares flap on the stairway
the music answers the silence of the stars.

*

And when the emperor Henshu walked into paradise
he was assigned this place
served tea in a pagoda
beside the river running deep and strong
clear over bluestone
out of a forest of redwoods.

Henshu emperor among the poets
who noted in his diary
'Green hair of girls
lives under blue water
combed by currents.
Rain that picks at water
hides hair from eyes,
sun restores it to view.'

*

André the Pole who taught us about wines and donkey sausage
Otto from Vienna who made a magnificent cake
and dreamed he was panting behind his girlfriend's car
      until he turned into a kangaroo
and all at once he was bounding across dry grass under gum trees
wind in his ears   horizon opening before him –

L from California who couldn't have an orgasm
and Aussie M who had so many
        you could have made a fine paté of her liver –
and Izzy G   German Jew
        frying chicken dumplings in deep oil
sawing dangerously at the wheel (one of the first Holdens)
because he insisted on turning to look at his passengers while he talked
        had been at Hitler rallies
had felt at his own throat the euphoria
that would drive his race to the gas chambers –
                        escaped into Russia
sat out the war in Siberia
remembered Communist efficiency as shops in one village
        full of boots with no laces
        in the next   laces but no boots –
liked an irony but political innocence
                and a big mouth (mine)
he properly frowned on.

'56 Armidale, New South Wales
the year of Suez and of Hungary
made excuses for the Russians
        (Suez was 'our' crime)
        or didn't know what to believe
but asked ourselves was totalitarianism
                        was repression
inherent in Socialism
        the big question
(ask it still and sometimes answer yes)
consigning that other Marx brother to a small boat
along with the Capitalist pig-shit theoreticians
        to argue about the means
        and how to share the bread and the water
and who catches the fish and who drinks the seagull's blood
        (and 'who navigates us towards what unknown' etc.)
and salute instead that black flag of irony
        Izzy admired
with a sense of history bearing half a million half-remembered precedents
fine compositions   plausible fictions   horrible accidents
        flowing into us
into this day that's full of sunshine and cicadas and sparrowtalk
an aching back   a halting typewriter
the breath of wind just now that drove a cloud across.

*

the moon
this moon
this very moon and no other
moon of 15.2.76 making over Hobson Bay
                its universal statement
sailing over pohutukawa
                that shades our house in the mornings
moon unmoored above garage and ponga
white influence felt along arms and in scalp
cold brilliance
                pallor spilled on the floor
would not flinch at blood
                or our most inventive coupling
has been worshipped
                        walked on
moon
is said to draw up tides and drive men mad.

*

Takapuna 1970   the Mon Desir Hotel
Baron Philippe de Rothschild
        vintner   financier   Jewish intellectual
sending the wine back
        telling the waiter
        'Give it to the cook.'
Sat under those big pohutukawa
watching waves coming across the Gulf from Rangitoto
translating Marvel
                    waiting
for his wife's heart to be repaired
(a cutting and stitching no one in the world could do so well
as Barratt-Boyes at Green Lane)

said of the Arabs
        'Such uninteresting people'
and I felt uneasy
        remembering the six million.

'72, saw him in a box at the Nice Opera House
with Milhaud and the Begum Agha Khan

Milhaud in a wheelchair
80, with dyed hair.

*

Mediterranean
a room with southern light
that strikes off sea through vine leaves
light reflected
               caught with
a brush in its hand
or playing on the ceiling
the only movie ever made in heaven.

Picasso's horned figure   brows in leaf
broods over her nakedness
why did they call it 'Modern'?

and at the Auckland Art Gallery
I stood breathless before it
knowing that room although I'd never been there
where the sun lay on its back and with delicate strokes
painted light over light on the ceiling
above the brooding lovers.

Mougins   Notre Dame de Vie   Antibes
statues on ramparts against the sea
terraces   orange stone   deep windows   tiled parterre
and the lover with wreath of oak about his brows
taking in her nakedness
as a man takes in a painting.

'Holding that energy is near to benevolence'
and add to that
               l'occasion
the times that release it
so that the blessings of the heavens
holy influence
               the rain and breath of stars
these are intelligible
as to say that she the lover looked on
was Proserpine
               responsible for the weather

for the way light struck light from water
          green from branches

or any morning like this one
that is a world of webs.

When the lovers die their stars are not withdrawn.

    *

Art has nothing to do with perfect circles
          squares   parallelograms
they belong to the will
even the best of moons is hand-sketched
          effulgence-blurred
but a rough triangle
          that's different
the Nile Delta for example
or what Antony saw first and last in Cleopatra
a blunt arrow-head of crisp hair
          pointing the way
down
    into another dimension
only perfect world
          slippery-sided
inward-enclosing
          welcome
and welcome
          and welcome
'die when thou hast liv'd'
and all the perfumes of Arabia couldn't rival what the lady made there
who called him infirm of purpose
talked of plucking the baby's toothless gums from her breast
and dashing its brains out
because he could not use the dagger
would not draw a circle about her brows.

    *

fallwater
          down
and up there
trees

            blacker
than black sky
edge-fall to
            water-drop
knee-deep in stone
                    cold
audible-silent
            rush
and deaf
and blind
            but for
fernstars'
            white
burning.

*

Balmoral Intermediate
                    1945
learned to spell 'principal'
        (distinct from 'principle')
because it was on the headmaster's door
committed to memory that the chief was chiefly an adjective
(despite his great bulk)
                    not a noun
Pemberton
            who told me to ring the school bell
because the War was over
        (50 million dead and half of Europe in ruins)
and ringing the bell I was worried
it had been War so long
            what would Peace be like?

This morning a quartz sky   an opal harbour
        late summer gardens in flower
        city of clean edges
and the little boys in black and the bigger boys and the big ones
gathering in tens in scores converging in hundreds
across the Domain   up from Newmarket   down from Mt Eden
staggering
            their bags full of what might be stones
but are free text books
to learn in English 'the 8 modes of language'

$$\text{(oracy)} \quad \left\{ \begin{array}{cc} \text{speaking} & \text{reading} \\ \updownarrow & \updownarrow \\ \text{listening} & \text{writing} \end{array} \right\} \text{(literacy)}$$

$$\text{(production)} \left\{ \begin{array}{c} \text{moving} \longleftrightarrow \text{watching} \\ \text{shaping} \longleftrightarrow \text{viewing} \end{array} \right\} \text{(reception)}$$

confusion of thought enshrined in diagrams from the Government
                                                    printer
tortured into text-books
small clear brows furrowed with incomprehension or
                                        ruffled in revolt
to be read as failure.

Peace was Korea
                the Cold War
the CIA
            Vietnam
corruption of action because corruption of thought
corruption of thought because corruption of language

a white butterfly drifts across the tomatoes
a bell rings
                50 million.

⋆

in arteries heart flutters
spirit catches its breath
'Life is a gift,' said my mother
having nearly lost it
but the old plangent note returned
the looking away   the regret.

here   now
pulse in throat   sun in sky
and every mortal thing
        remembered   forgotten
shark inshore
                wings falling
the 'possum's last violence
on the floor of the cage.

Penelope has a flat in Wollstonecraft
            sits unpicking her knitting

and at Beecroft there's the big house with 3 cars
            and 3 horses and 2 score of gum trees
            kookaburras before sunrise
            2 nice girls and a recordplayer and a barbecue and a
                                    cat and a dog
            and if you go in August
            a bank of freesias in bloom   fruit trees that blossom

and at Mossman
                    and at Kingsford
Lane Cove
        and that flat of Bruce-and-Brenda's
somewhere near Gladesville
or Kings Cross where I knew nobody
        $175 at the old rate
        Epic Fare
marble fins cutting a velvet sky
        'return refreshed from'
Sydney
        first foreign soil I ever stepped on –

'56 they were arguing about the design
it was every good Ocker's mad laugh
            and then it was the cost
and now it's 'the 20th century's
                    most beautiful building'.

Somewhere in the syntax
in the joints of words put rightly together
        you know time's passing
                        you feel
past and present in the passing
a hum as of that generator working through the night
            in the carpark at Macquarie
tall lights shining on grass and gumtrees
a car starting
            somebody calling goodbye.

Somewhere in the musi-mythology
Chaliapin
            on the sea-front at Monte Carlo
taking a gloved hand:
                        'Madame
I have a bass voice
            but the heart of a tenor'

and add to that
            Forrest Scott
after midnight
            at the White Heron Lodge
Auckland
      asking Iris Murdoch to dance.

*

fresh-faced
as if he ate well   slept well
the CIA man who thought
Phoenix had been wrong
because half the twenty thousand murdered
were 'innocent' – mean not VC
            (imagine Dr Goebbels saying
            the programme for the Final Solution
            had been wrong
            because half the six million weren't Jews)

he was free to walk about
so is Nixon (so is holyoake)
Lyndon Johnson died in his bed

the mean masters of destruction
the mealy mouths that abet them
they don't figure among the unemployed
there's work for them always

smell of rotting bodies
fades into text-books
resolves into numbers
20 thousand
6 million

50 million
and half of them were 'innocent'.

*

Otto's cake
              no baking
bought biscuits soaked in wine
heaped over with cream

and when we left Armidale
he was at the station
with Izzy   Iain Lonie   a dozen others
stoking euphoria
                    tapping tears
350 miles to Piermont Wharf
woke to sunrise on the Hawkesbury
and at Central Station
Otto
        the same
had driven all night
to greet us at the other end.

*

Bristol University
                  Wills Castle
built on smoke
              with crests
and mullioned windows
but no moat

Marleyn's bass voice on the stairs
              'Donna nobis pacem'
O'Toole at the Bristol Old Vic
      before his films and fame
      everything from Shaks to Shav
the signed Yeats at George's inscribed
'the years like great black oxen tread over the world'
£3.0.0
        and I hesitated
and next day it was gone

first snow
waking at Westbury-on-Trym
puzzled by a strange brilliance on the ceiling
the black trees edged with white
Whitelady's Road
                        Blackboy Hill
the Red Maids' School
             the Downs
the Centre rebuilt from the ruins of '45
St Mary Redcliffe spire
             dockside survivor
sky-spear flying
             repeated in water

Kay at the Bristol Steam Navigation Company
the burred r of the West
the oi oi and the curly cobbled l
Brightstowe
             that became Britstowl
Selkirk in his corner with Long John Silver
as ''ad loike a missin' lag'

my 26th birthday the first dog in orbit
Laika
     she died there
could make nothing of that
but the silence followed us to London

Clifton / Hammersmith
                 same bridge-maker
('only connect')
     Isambard Kingdom Brunel
and Boozy O'Toole came too
to Kensington
             the Royal Court Theatre
but McGooghan at Hammersmith
the best actor of his age

How are we visible to ourselves
               but by the fires
these light in us?

*

                        came ashore
who had walked already above cloud floor
had looked up from his book and down 7 miles
                                    to arctic ice
had seen off San Remo
                    sea floor's mosaic
the scarves of light
                    are shaken over

*

October she phoned to say
for her at last it was   over
                        forgotten
                        irrelevant
three nails meant for the heart

might have made use of the new maths
that has a cold beauty
like the beauty of a fiction

as for example that a survey of 19 love affairs showed
        17 were over
        7 were forgotten
        and 13 were irrelevant
        but only 2 were all three

9 were over and irrelevant but not forgotten
5 were over and forgotten but not irrelevant

how many that were over were neither irrelevant nor forgotten?

to which a Venn diagram
viz:

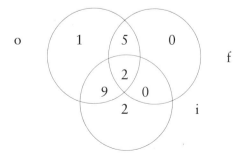

returns the answer 1
(rendered poetically, one only)
            irrefutable
as to say in the language of another dimension
he had explored with her
the caves of generation and the terraces of the stars.

*

and Donne said
(not to mention Ern Hem)
don't ask for Dr Who the bloody bell told you
        wanting to make a blue movie
        Long Tongue
        sequel to Deep Throat
with Kath Romancefield at the Villa Isola Bella
        it tolls for thee
but how could it rival Fellini?

and Milhaud in a wheelchair
80, with dyed hair.

*

February   Wellington
white wood   blind windows
a kind sky   a good sea
and from one high room
the 2 spires on Willis Street
the red and the green

5 beds to choose from
    all of them empty

downstairs were the smoky athletes in the mirror
their shouts echoed on the landing
their cries reached the carpark
green branches fainted across the tombstone houses

that was no dream
the air is electric
the whole town is charged with an absence
it enters no plea

a jet climbs out of Rongotai
7 p.m.
the hills beginning to fade.

*

Menton soixante-douze
storm in the olives
shutters banging
woke to a strange light
wind assaulting hillslope
running at rockface
driving home rainspears
paper torn from hoardings on the Moyenne Corniche
branches down in the garden of Blasco Ibanez
frigate anchored off
              in orange turbulence
listing.

Guessed what K.M. felt at Bandol
breath of testaments
for 3 days no silence among the tombs
an old wind that knows no need but its own
unloving wind that drives the lovers in hell
Francesca recalling the tributary rivers
longing for rest
sulla marina dove il Po discende.

*

Moon
      cold warrior
wasted
on the stone steps
on the waxed floor
      breathless
between boards
         announcing
SCORIA
      PARIS
the WARS
the smoky athletes
longing for rest.

*

'58 your Ford Popular cost you
£450
and you could drive it around
                    (and around)
Piccadilly Circus

Supermac elegant at parry and thrust
with Gaitskell in the Commons
while the old bulldog whose promise never to surrender
had hurried our blood through static
entered like a toddler
        fell backward into his chair
and fell asleep.

Broken teeth of Europe slow to repair
cats and broom flowers among the masonry
Amen Court in shadow of St Paul's
CND
        'South Africa Defence and Aid'
Rhodesia
            all the good causes
(most of them lost)
            innocent faith
or where it faltered
energy.

Hand in hand under the embassy windows
(Cambodia
            where was that?)
Phillimore Gardens bedsit stacked with paintings
the loo shared with Mr Spiteri from Malta
picked the meter padlock with your hairpin
every shilling twice used
once for gas   once for Woodbines.

Calamari in a Chelsea basement
Shadbolt worrying about his lungs
Kevin Ireland
            lost child with a long nose
sadly sketching

Janet in the Maudsley   blankets up to her chin
wearing dark glasses
and in Soho cobra Kaye
who became Kasmin and ran a famous gallery
writhing out of his basket
to unheard melodies
                imaginary pipes.

And the Thames flowed by beyond that wall at Hammersmith
sweet Thames
                numbering our days at the Doves
last hours of our indifference –
London
                not style
but sanity
light on leaves falling over the towpath
a red bus crossing Brunel's bridge
the swans turning with the turning tide.

*

but first things first
        as fernstars for example
or moon's path off Ngongotaha
with Ainsley under the willows
1949
        slow reel
fishermen casting in gold

*

After dry weeks
                rain
and that's to say 'rain'
as it hammers on iron
nothing to do with Spain

Rested
        could focus on nothing
but sparrows in the pear tree
exits / entrances
remembering last night's
denim itinerant
chain-smoking poems.

Here today
still at hand and by heart
soothed as if by fingers
that know a need
nowhere to jet to but
       gone tomorrow
walking westward
the green doors
the runnels of water.

Uta

from the Japanese

First light
flickers
in the east
and we fumble
to dress each other.

My hair this morning
I won't comb.
The hand
of my beautiful lord
has been its pillow.

Great ships
riding at anchor
are rocked
as I by my love
for this child-man.

Shining
he seems to me
like the swift river
dammed
and breaking through.

People
in this towered city
abound.
My heart has
one inhabitant.

We two
found it so hard
the autumn mountain –
how will he
cross it alone?

So young
he'll lose the way.
Could I bribe
some Underworldling
to shoulder him?

On that route
to nowhere
may the frontier guards
every night
sleep sound.

My lover
is thinly clad.
Wind of Sao
hold your breath
till he's home.

Dim
the russet shore
in morning mist
where my thoughts
pursue his skiff.

In the godless month
only the rain
is my friend
on the hill-paths
weeping.

River fog
hiding the slopes
has set
the Autumn mountain
adrift in the sky.

Light snow
over the garden
this cold night
and I lacking a pillow –
must I sleep alone?

Meetings in dreams
are sad.
I wake
reach out
and touch nothing.

His pony's tracks
under snowfall
will be hidden
so those who pursue
must lose him.

Does the river
frozen
feel as I do
under ice
the flow of love?

My year's
sins multiply
and darken
like this flurry of snowflakes.
May they melt together!

        If I die of love
        I die of love!
    Then at least my Master
      will come again
        to my door.

Monday
Tuesday and Wednesday
I've seen him in dreams
and I want to see him
Thursday as well.

      In my dream of
    Shiotsu mountain
        his horse
    staggers under him
both of them homesick.

Nightingale
only your song
over snow
tells the mountain village
Spring will come.

    Nights with no moon
        Spring
    without blossoms –
      am I alone
    the constant one?

Wind
scatters over hilltops
white clouds
fickle
as his thoughts of me.

Long ago
transplanted
from far away
this little plum tree
is first to blossom.

Still the reed-plains
house seems empty.
Cherry-blossom
unlamenting
scatters.

One wild goose
faintly
honking
over
has fixed my hopes.

Chamberlain's
slave-boys
please
this blossom-time
leave the courtyard unswept.

In faint ink
a line of verse
look
on the smudged sky
the wild geese are returning.

From season
to season
I've knocked in dreams
at his heart's
locked door.

Hand-scooped
water catches
the moon's image
a moment only.
So passes my life.

A sword
at my throat
I felt in my dream.
An omen?
Will there be no return?

Or shall we
make love
as we did once
when the moor's rushes
shone in moonlight?

Footwearying
mountains hide
this nightingale.
Where there's no one to listen
can she be said to have sung?

Pine-shaded
rock-water
in the hand –
unreal summer
in the head.

Husbands
go hunting
while their wives
trail red skirts
along the lake-washed shore.

This world
to me is like
sunrise on
a rowboat's
trailing wake.

By the stone store
dependable pine
when I stare at you
one long gone
stares back.

Summer mountains
my lover
crosses
and louder
the cuckoo sings.

Geographies

1982

Scoria

A Reconstruction

murmur
               mormorio
susurration
               audible silence
picked at in the fowlyard below

earth smell
               as of wattle root
and through their tracery
azure
               puffed with white

That is 'for example'
       lying in the track through wattles
above the vegetable garden
in sight of the lemon tree
and there was beyond the lemon
  asparagus
beyond asparagus
beans
and the brown boards of the fowlhouse
and the grey rocks that were
                      SCORIA
stone on stone
         walls / terracing
as of a century's habitation
work of one man   one decade
upper lawns and flower beds
lower garden and orchard
paths
       the pergola
rotting under its roses
stone on stone
       soft earth sifting between.

Energy cousin to benevolence
and both of light
                    on grass
on grey absorbing stone
on the three green
                    visible cones
to the north-east
                    Mt Eden
eastward One Tree Hill
west
        Mt Albert
that have inflamed their skies
burst in cloud
                sent rolling out
rivers of rock
                    congealing
to a ridged and rifted landscape
outcrop on which to stand a house
wallstones
or stones for a small hand
            bent on birds
the fields of bracken and wattle
littered as of battle
the dead cones their obsolete cannon
Maungawhau
                    Maungakiekie
Owairaka.

Dry
its pores edged
sharp to the touch
bearded often
                with a white lichen
hard on palms
            on bare knees
but a warm refuge
        my friend the rock
SCORIA.

Ivy had swamped had smothered the front wall
the stable one so held so cluttered
you could walk on it lie down on it
vanish in its broad top die in it
breathing its scent like a dust that caught in the throat
unseen between in the dark shine of leaf
heaped there over the hairy arms that bound it
the tall rock wall above the level lawn
where was always trimming cutting to be done
mower clippers the sword and by the monkeyapple
lilac that in this month in this spring sun
will be blossoming still above its worm-eaten wrists
over the dwarf lemon beside the impossible gate
larger than life in sight of the sun and shut.

Three Kings
                the nearest cone
but hidden beyond two ridges
of its own making
            a suburb's frayed edge in
billy-filling summer
                        the black
berry
            in the dry
grass and bracken
about the dripping cave mouths
saying
we are your neighbourhood gods
Vulcan
                Matuahou
created your world in our image
of scattered stones
who sleep in your dreams
who breathe on your pillow
whose skies we painted red remember us
and the pie broke open and bled on the hotplate
and the sun was a crippled smith
                        journeying
forge above
                    below
and between the blue black
berry.

As the matador's cape concealed the steel
so the spread wing in sunlight
                    or a black shield
green in sunlight
the black knight strutting and shining
green in sunlight
under the red comb she goes down for
                    as under a cloud
                    as under a fiery banner
                    crouching
to the packed soil
beyond the bean rows
black on black glinting
green in sunlight
                    shuddering
a moment only
                    ruffling
and back to
        picking and scratching
picking and
                    scratching
it being important to scratch the packed earth
to the left and the right
        with thighs big like a peasant's
        under heavy skirts
importantly
                    to the left and the right
picking in the scratches

and the small head stops
and the bead eye stares
                    into the lacery
the round blank shining eye
staring
                    into the lacery.

Wattle in sunlight
        Hephaestus' golden net
        scent of verbena
        'he who shines by day' lays down
        green sheen over black feathers

glint in her beads
and Ares astrut
                under the blue canopy
laced with gold.

Somnolent under the forged net of gold
and in nostrils
                verbena
and in the air
                audible silence
scratched at in the fowl-yard below

dream of flight
        waiting in the wax
in the wings
        Naxos   Delos   Paros
the child's legs vanishing in ocean
father to the man
who might carry to his forged world
word of
        SCORIA
PARIS
        the WARS
the smoky athletes
longing for rest

verbena   rosemary
lavender   lilac   daphne
and under the piano windows
carnation
where water ran warm from the tap
and the tamed foundation stones absorbed the sun.

Czerny and verbena
Mozart and rosemary
lavender and Liszt
and for the Moonlight Sonata
perhaps the primal challenge
                of cut grass
to purify the nostrils of the tribe
with scented gardens through the blind
a dérèglement of nose and ear and eye
as for example the simple

　　　　　　'notes of colour'
chromatic scales
　　　　　　　　even
arpeggios of light
　　　　harmonies of shade
over blade leaf petal stalk stamen
receding　　　rising
beyond the ivied wall across the school the suburb
to the green cone
　　　　　　cold forge of Hephaestus
hammer of Vulcan
source of all.

'Come to Manukau
　　　　to the fields of Tainui
for scented grasses'

this to Reia
　　　　sleek bodied taniwha
dolphin god of the Ngatitamatera
playing in sunlight
in the shallows of Hauraki
the enticement of scented herbs
that brought him swimming northward
where club and cooking-pot waited

sunrise
　　long shadow
and out of shadow
voices of the Ngatitamatera
crying vengeance on
　　　　　　　　Maungakiekie
Maungawhau
　　　　　the pa of Tainui.

Ground shook
on which walked no man
hot stones rolled from the lip
fire flew heavenward

                gods stirring the cauldron
                Vulcan   Matuahou
laying
                shadow over the harbour

day dark and shrunken
                night inflamed
groaning under earth
twittering in heaven
trees tossing on windless slopes
where walked no man
the lip spitting fire
bright rock bounding
                down dark slopes
blitzkrieg of the blacked-out valley
and one slow armoured column
pushing into the valley
moving forest about
adjusting stream and tide-flow
Phlegethon flowing under glass
over its own hardness
cooling westward down
into the valley.

Cloudfire   rockflight   flow
as of glacier
where walked no man
westward into the valley.

How you slept knowing it your own sleeping
face the flies explored their walk your waking
those summer Sundays late that drew you back
to a dream of legs each fly a feather's point
over brow lip nose with curious communication
of purpose hurrying and halting departing arriving
and there must be glare pushing at the blind edges
the hot room holding in its teasing dream
your hand from waving away the white legs
melting like wax in true blue open ocean
for ever walking westward out of Naxos
out of thin air the fallen feathers floating
the boy still struggling under his sleeping face.

Bk bk bk bkaa bkaaa
          bkaa bkaaaa
bk bk bk bk
              bkaa bkaaaa
bk bk bk
          bk bk bk bk bk
lay language
              your waking
subsiding (bk bk bk)
to the languid / discontented
kaaaaa
        kaaaaaa
                kaaaaaaa.

Veronica
of the spread wing in sunlight
and to Dieffenbach
              that other veronica
speciosa
        the koromiko
in lilac flower among flax
its scent on the air
'where this shrub grows
        is richest soil'

green-bronze mirrors of flax
          turning in the breeze
          catching sunlight
on the slopes of 'Manakao Harbour'.

Aspire to no forge nor flight
but five short steps to the bar
driving
        DOWN
left foot shaking the earth
        and out of that crouch
arms   shoulders   right leg gathering
the whole weight
              UP

and over
                    'falling to foam'
or as it was in those days
                         to sandpit
or under the piano windows
                    to cut grass
to make that bar your horizon
horizon your bed
            and to lie along it
defying the upright posture
a moment weightless before
the Fall
            to roll in cuttings
in earshot of
                    Beethoven
Rachmaninov
                    Chopin
as if to have swum in that moment
without support of water
to have draped yourself over
the skyline's elegant couch
                         informally
before the angel entered
bringing gravity to the garden
scales falling like glass from the windows
scent of grass invading
legs tumbling ungainly
and a bamboo pole your horizon
holding
            5ft 2.

'Owairaka' (said Robinson)
                    'surf-rider
daughter of a chief'
            from Kawhia (was it?)
and the tribe moved north
built their pa on the hill
            gave it her name
but couldn't hold it
against the tribes of the isthmus
the assault closing

              palisades breached
fire and blade and spearpoint ascending the slope
only the caves for escape
                    running crouched
                    through crooked caverns
                    shouts and shadows pursuing
and at the narrowest pass the gross old chief
wedged himself after them
died there to be hacked out
while his people escaped
into the manuka valley

Owairaka / Mt Albert
        the westerly one
        fringed with eucalypt
blue-grey in distance
against the Waitakere Range

and Mt Eden / Maungawhau
where we held our breath watching
        she on the back seat of the car
        he over her
                    in mist
        the windows clouded
        moving as in a dream

and One Tree Hill
                    arcadia
        white on green
        lambs and daisies in grass
        among lichened outcrops
        beyond the olive grove
        in sight of the sea.

New timber   new iron
'panting of saw'
conflict of hammers
(7 true notes to the nail)
sawdust on the wind
and under iron where showers beat
the unfloored joists

over stonecrop and bracken
the suburb moving
                inching over itself
                red roofs   green gardens
                across the isthmus
                towards the further harbour

And she said 'Please get me that horse manure'
        meaning the beautiful big bran muffins
        steaming in the roadway
        handing me the bucket and shovel
a day full of hammering
that seemed to stop and listen
        repeating 'manure for the garden'
        pushing the bucket at me
        and whose garden was it
        and if it was no shame and no one would laugh
        why didn't she get it herself
forced out protesting
to scoop it up
under the unseen seeing
of saws and hammers.

Ernst Dieffenbach
                1843
'the government town of Auckland
7 miles from harbour to harbour
2000 inhabitants
                a bank
a fine barracks of SCORIAE'

and 15 years later
                Julius von Haast
'the hills
models of volcanic action
have made luxuriant gardens'

Hochstetter   1867
'cones
        with craters distinct
Rangitoto
        the Vesuvius of Waitemata'

and at the century's turn
the grandfather Swede
      no 'sang aus dem Exil'
(unless the 'sang' should be blood)
but moving stone over stone
         terraces   walls
as of a century's habitation
a landscape adjusted
to the will of a man
in the hot eye of Vulcan
under the hammer of Thor
between two seas.

Winter rain
     splitting firewood in mud
     the blinding melancholy
     of the thrush on a wet lawn
     of the grey warbler singing

intolerable Sundays
     Waitakeres curtained in cloud
     Mt Eden swimming in windows
     the roast   the early fire
a dead man's gloom alive
     his 'sang aus dem Exil'
     in redwood panels

clean hands on cold keys
cold feet on clean linoleum
and through aquarium glass
the green world
     heavy with moisture
the grey rocks
     black with rain
the iron roofs
     loud with it
and crystal ski-lifts
     running on telephone wires

but on a rare clear morning
        frost

sheet-ice on barrelwater
crystals over bunched soil
black burns on broadleaf.

Maungawhau / hill of the whau tree
from the hilltop two harbours
and westward
            the Waitakere Range

and he saw fires on Maungakiekie
and called his people inside the palisades
stomachs tight
        fear in the pits at sundown
crouching behind the lashed stakes of manuka
moon cold over the Gulf
and silence

Sunrise
        long shadow
and out of shadow
voices of the Ngatitamatera
crying vengeance on Tainui
            for the death of Reia

mid-morning the palisades breached
high noon
            the last skull crushed
            on the slopes of the crater

Unbroken silence of the tapu
        harbours blue and gold
isthmus green
spring wind in the whau's white flowers
among the rotting stakes

Maungawhau / Mt Eden
200 years of silence
hill of death
            hill of heaven.

Yes T.S.

A Narrative

To make real
                        distances
real
                        here today
at the blue doors
                        jetting
(fast   faster   unfasten)
westward
                              and

*

down there man
                        that's Mount
Isa
                silver roofs in a
red
                        landscape
that grows nothing but
nothing
but
                        money.

*

Palm fronds   dust
            you won't see me for
to make real
                under trees
                    on tiled
pavements
                every girl a
                Chinese
box
            you can't open
        this whole universe so

[*Auckland–Singapore*]

[*Singapore*]

143

crammed
        get it straight
you are
                in-
significant
           you
are
get on with the wordwork
buy yourself
        chopsticks
        a batik tie
maybe
      a nice cheap watch?

*

and the question
          is she
        following
me
or I
           her
and if so
not easily unravelled at
32 Celsius
          why
       lapping one
another
        and look
the lights
     she's turning again
have changed

*

Waiting for the kiosk to open –
       the slapping
English mother
     something in the trees
       that screams
and a moth in black velvet.

*

Rain have fallen sun have shone
Three years have pass since you are gone
Straits Times
                    in memoriam
17.9.80
Our hearts still ache that tragic day
When you left us without a say
the late Mister
                    Liew Cheong Wai
departed 17.9.77
Your love was great, your heart was kind
A devoted man, none could find.

⋆

Straits Times Quotations:
真正的著作家有如清泉，并不使人觉得
渊深；而混浊的池水反而使人觉得深邃。

(Clear writers, like clear fountains, do not seem so
deep as they are; the turbid looks most profound.
                    – Landor)

⋆

The Chinese mother
                    follows her toddler
                              over the lawn.

                                        He stops
she stops
                              he / she
runs.

                              At the lake a
gentle hand.

Waiting for the flower to open.

⋆

The long chase   [*Singapore–London*]
        (jetting westward)

over black
vegetable
India
brings us to
this glass
palace of the sands
that's an Arab airport.

We 'pause for breath'
'take on fuel'
(or whatever)
and still he comes.

His chariots inflame
the dark cusp
of the world.

Eyelids
half close
over the marvel of it
attending
an inward concert
bugles   trumpets   horns
remembering
a long-ago tobacco
that was also a racehorse:
Desert Gold.

*

Yes t.s.   [London]
it's
(it is)
still
whirling away
a world
it's London
calling
the Clash   /   dreadlocks
toilets
(and thanks
for the anagram
to Rosy Allpress)

146

                    flush
(t.s.)
                aux étoiles.

*

Two skin'eads is
                better'n one
you can knock 'm togever
and 'ere's free
                    (yair 3)
                leaning
'eadpiece filled wiv Rock
                    in the all night
post office.

*

                        5.45 a.m.
next door's cough-storm lasted
one hour.

Now he's sleeping
        the poor faceless bastard
and I bless him.

One dry Vita Weet
        water from a plastic cup –
to know the
beauty of the Beverage
            you must be deprived
            of the means to make it.

Come now, Sleep
            I need more of you.

*

(Hey God
                    dis poet
laCKS TEA Do
somethin'
                will ya!)

*

147

Did a nightingale (etc.)
            in Berkeley (etc.)
                    but this is
the poetry of fact
                        viz
21.9.80
                    6.20 a.m.
cock crow audible
(x4)
                    at
WC1N 2AB.

*

    I say, 'It comes out of pain'
and for a moment
            the morning square
is striped in long lines of light
after rain.

*

'So I let myself go. The days glided by in this sort of baccarat
game . . . An idea of myself was all that was in my head. An
idea that was born gently. A forgotten word, an air. One feels it
bound up with one's whole self, . . . like a form seeking another
similar form with a lantern in the middle of the night . . .'
            – Louis Aragon, *Paris Peasant*

*

Tapper on the hot-plate
                    whistling
'ain't we got . . .'
            £2.50 from the old
            Covent Garden
            will make me
'in the morning
in the evening'
            and oh yes
in the plunging night

            tea.

*

Today
     no one has spoken to me
     no one has spoken
     no one has
     no one
     no

*

Song

Fred Astaire he's my tin kettle
and oh how I love
     my Fred Astaire.

He's good to me I'm in fine fettle
yes   yes   I love
     my Fred Astaire.

You wouldn't think a thing of metal
could dance and sing
     like Fred Astaire.

He makes me think I want to settle
down with him
     my Fred Astaire.

*

'Torn, shaken, bruised, carried precipitately up and down
and round and round by the unending change of small
events from day to day. Faces, people, personalities, recede
[. . .] The idea of the past and future of one's life shrinks
and swells like an erratic concertina. One day one's work
seems nothing but scribbles and scraps of paper, and the
next, a sudden fecundity of thought brings it to life again.
Meanwhile the *moi* is hidden, and in its cell is trying to
integrate itself within its own (predestined?) form.'
     – David Gascoyne, *Journal 1937–39*

*

Not to work at it
            but to cock an ear
at the well's edge
hearing silence faintly broken
by the small
                        crystalline
bells of water
            tripping over moss
on to cold stone.

*

3 crows in the square
            you say it's night there
flap down through sun-shafts
missing me
                        loving you
those flowers from the pear tree
these leaves beginning to fall.

*

Silent (it is)
                        the circle
at the edge of the
                        silent
square.

Girl's voice
                        voices
                off the flat fronts.
They scatter.

Can't see the trees but
                        hear them
as the breeze shifts in sleep.
        In the circle of light they get
                        written.

It's 10.44.

A taxi goes round the square that
a jet goes over.

                    It too's pressed
between pages.

What's kept there
                    if it isn't sanity
                    if it isn't fact?

*

This syntax
              as in the sand
mix
              of a Braque
surface
              won't let the
eye
not lightly
                    slide
over.

*

'A by-pass for example
                    relieves the symptoms
but does it improve the condition?

'A catheter in the neck
                    (p.v.c.)
will measure pressure of blood
                    in the chamber.

'The ribs are not clipped out
              but merely opened wide
like arms
or double doors.

'Blood loss
                    brain damage
both are related
to time on the Machine.'

She is German,
her name Beate

as in beatitude –
blessed.
  She has the precise small face
and broad brow
        of a medieval woodcut
of the Madonna
and together
we are listening to Bach.

'In hypothermia
        the patient is cooled
externally
and through the blood flow
         to 16 Celsius
         and the heart
stopped.
        I have 60 minutes
to complete my work.

'During recovery
        cardiac arrest
is not of course uncommon.'

  *

        telex
(tell K)
    that blood orange
moon's become
      a cheese rind
      a nail paring
a heavenward golden
        gondola.

I've been away too long.

  *

and this poetry editor
    in his lovely Muse flat
with a Sunday
Times table
        set for 6

is talking about 'the return to
form.'

                       Oh Form!
honourable suitcase
battered
            covered with labels
             have you anything
to declare?

*

'It is in life as in drawing, one must sometimes act
quickly and with decision, attack a thing with energy,
trace the outlines as quickly as lightning. This is not a
moment for hesitation or doubt, the hand may not tremble,
nor may the eye wander, but must remain fixed on what
is before one. And one must be so absorbed in it that in
a short time something is produced that was not there
before, so that afterwards one hardly knows how it got
knocked into being.'
                – Van Gogh, *Letters*

*

17.10.32
London – Charing Cross

48 48 48 48 48 48
48 48 48 48 48 48
48 48 48 48 48 48
48 48 48 48 48 48

Dover

  |
  |
  ↓

Boulogne

48 48 48 48 48 48
48 48 48 48 48 48
48 48 48 48 48 48
48 48 48 48 48 48

Paris – Paris Nord
17.10.80

'He was forty-eight years old.   [*Paris*]

'Paris had attracted him as a magnet does a needle . . .

'He hid behind a rather deliberately absent-minded expression. Once, in his youth, he had published a small book of poems. But when it came to actualities his mind was a tight and very tidy mind. He had discovered that people who allowed themselves to be blown about by the winds of emotion and impulse are always unhappy people, and in self-defence he had adopted a certain mental attitude, a certain code of morals and manners, from which he seldom departed . . .

'Mr Mackenzie's code, philosophy or habit of mind would have been a complete protection to him had it not been for some kink in his nature – that volume of youthful poems perhaps still influencing him – which morbidly attracted him to strangeness, recklessness, even unhappiness.'
                         – Jean Rhys, *After Leaving Mr Mackenzie*

★

Hungry
                              uncertain
               crossing (is it?) the Carrousel
night falling
and rain
                         also the temperature

shot from (call it) 'Baudelaire's Swan'
('son of' / 'return of' – or just 'II')

glasses blurred with rain
                    map too wet to open.

Now comes the barge
                              its lights
                    its dream-like swinging
drift
and up from it (listen) a phrase
                              a phrase
a phrase
disconnected
               of the Little Nightmusic.

*

All these French speak French even
the infants and they keep it up even
when you try to seem not to be listening
you will never catch them out. The little girls
have round brown eyes and soft curls
ribboned and frilled with white socks
and they're called Sophie and Natalie and
Blanche. And they speak French
morning to night
                    du matin à nuit
sans cesse and without any mistakes.

French dogs don't speak French but
they understand and this one in the
Gare Nanterre brings me his tennis ball
to throw so he can chase it – encore et encore.

*

Il faut demeurer quelquefois ici
tout au bord de l'hiver

parce que c'est l'actualité
de la vie – n'est ce pas?

It's the same moon up there
though you wouldn't believe it

blanched like that in sunlight.
We should all put up sometimes

right here at the brink of winter
because really that's what life's

all about – isn't it?
C'est la même lune en haut

oui – incroyable comme ça
blanchie en plein soleil . . .

*

A train just went through this station
without stopping it didn't stop
                        I'm on my way
            to St Germain-en-Laye
                        and the rhyme
comes gratuit with the trip
                at four francs cinquante.

*

In Nanterre Préfecture
the dreaming towers of workers' apartments
            are camouflaged blue and grey and
cloud colour
                        so that they faint away
                                and away
                        into the heavens.

*

Head hot
                        chest burning
not a word of English within
                                shouting
or dreaming
but this window's looked into by
                a thousand windows.

                            In style
in a foreign city
                in blue cotton pyjamas
                        you could die here
watched by an audience greater
than at the Comédie Française
                        and earning even
a generous round of applause.

*

Monsieur de Paris
                    wears a red rose
        as he takes your head.

'Have courage'
                  he whispers
           waking you at dawn.
'The drawn sabres
        will salute you as you go.'

    *

In the early light Verlaine's
                  roses: absolute red
            his ivy: absolute black

tout rouges les roses
tout noirs les lierres

and isn't that also
                  la poésie du fait?

    *

Who's this making heavy
             weather of waking
            looking out at the
thousand windows
                looking in
                    and saying
'I don't even know which
fucking
country I'm in.
            I don't even know . . .'
over and over.

Come now
         my drunken boat
       you don't have to be
sinking or capsizing
every moment of the day.

    *

'Dogen instructed:
      "It is easy enough to give up one's life or
to slice off one's flesh, hands or feet if one feels

so inclined ... But it is difficult to harmonize
the mind as it comes into contact with events
and things." '
                    – *A Primer of Soto Zen*

*

And here are Normandie and Lorraine
come to Paris
                    red scarf at the throat
a mile two miles
                    stretched out along
          the Boulevards chanting
'Giscard, you're fucked –
     the miners have taken to the streets.'

GI   -SCARD   T'ES FOUTU
LES MINEURS SONT DANS LA RUE

*

This is the late sun of summer
          these are the last leaves of autumn
     come together
in the Luxembourg Gardens.

          These are the young mothers
these the belles demoiselles bourgeoises
          and this the traveller
come together
     in the Gardens of Luxembourg.

          The leaves are falling fast
the shadows our bodies cast are long
          the pool of the Fountain of the Medicis
               is carpeted with gold.

          There's warmth on the face
there's a lift in the voice and
               something like sadness in the air
          they come together
in the Luxembourg Gardens.

*

Matisse is a lot of red interiors
    with chairs sketched in black
Matisse is five huge dancing figures
    on a blue background
Matisse is a whole life you might have lived
    if you had been Matisse
Matisse is cut paper pasted and
    dancing in space
Matisse is on the phone he won't
    let you sleep
Matisse is an odyssey in one hotel room
    in a city that rhymes with Matisse
Matisse is the dream of the poem of
    the life tout en couleur
I salute you Matisse   Matisse
    je vous salue.

    ★

    'By dawn on Thursday an endless cavalcade jammed the
highways leading south. Like animals fleeing a forest fire, a bizarre
array of vehicles was streaming from the city: fire engines bearing
firemen and their families, tricycles, furniture vans, coal and ice-cream
carts, street-sweepers with revolving brushes, even eight funeral
hearses crammed with living freight.
    'Black smoke from burning fuel dumps cast a sooty pall . . . at
times so dense that no man could see across the Place de la Concorde . . .
Soon every railway terminus was closed save the Gare de Lyon, where a
frantic trampling horde of would-be refugees clawed at the iron railings.
By now more than a million had gone and Paris was dying by inches.'
    – Richard Collier, *1940: The World in Flames*

    ★

Au 'voir, Paris
    get fucked / I love you.

    ★

for Cathérine, aged 7   *[Dijon]*

Pedalling
    past the gipsy camp

on the hills outside Dijon
                with la petite
je l'aime
elle m'aime
                tout va bien
my pet
 c'est la vie qui roule ici
                        à bici-
clette.

        ⋆

The grapes are in
                the last leaves are
orange and yellow and black
on the vines
        down the beautiful hill-slopes
                in late sun / chill shadow
run the lines.

        The presses of Burgundy
Chambertin-Gevrey
                Nuits-St George
Pommard and Beaune
have issued their annual
                statement of faith
in the future of France.

        ⋆

Turquoise inshore   [*Menton*]
        out there a dark louring
                as of ocean.

Below the promenade
it grinds its teeth on pebbles.

Here you make out
        the ghost of him you were
                loving the ghosts
of those you loved.

        ⋆

Notices in the lavatory, 1st floor, Hotel
Richelieu (one star):

Mesdames Messieurs
Dimanche Repos Hebdomaire
Pas de Ménages dans les Chambres
Mais
Le Petit Déjeuner vous est servi.
Merci de Votre Compréhension.

Lorsque votre petit déjeuner est
terminé voulez-vous avoir
l'amabilité de sortir votre plateau
dans le couloir. Merci.

*

This is the silence craved
   in the hot loud summer
long ago.

In the street it's raining
        and you seek out
the one
thunderous
          obliterating
café.

*

'Avant qu'Abraham fût
Je suis'

'Avant qu'Abraham fût
Je su s'
    i

'Avant qu'Abrah   fût
Je su s'
        i   am'

'Je sus'
        'I   am

Jesus'

        'I am
before Abraham was'

★

Je est une auto
elle suis Rimbaud

★

                        Moon
                still holds itself
still
in the waters of the port

                    palm fronds
                        like frozen
fountains

                one distant car
            to make a silence
emphatic.

Time to move on.

★

'Unlike Cézanne, Matisse does not try to reconcile   [Nice]
these conflicting aims in each painting, but alternates
from phase to phase, or even from picture to picture . . .
In this constant questioning of his own work – which
has gone on just as much in periods of supposed
relaxation – we recognize the type of the modern
artist. That Matisse strove for serenity and at times

162

condescended to elegance and erotic charm ought
not to deceive us as to the doubts underneath – or
as to the frequent loftiness of the results.'
          – Clement Greenberg, *Henri Matisse*

                    ★

4.11.80 was
a day of airports and gloom –
                    black olives at Nice
               Swiss chocolate at Zurich
          snow and the news at Munich:
Reagan elected in America.

                    ★

                         Yes T.S.   [*Munich*]
winter surprised us
coming over the Starnberger-See
                    in a shower of snow
                    and we went on by car
and took tea in a konditerei
          while snow still floated and fell
                    over the Hofgarten.

Bin gar keine Holländerin, stamm' aus
               München, echt bayrisch.

                    ★

down
through the
               pallor before
the half-light
                    before
dawn
                    over ice
               through snow
under trees
               it's the land
(remember)
               of childhood's
iron-crossed

                    ach-tongued
movies
          of the unfolding of
                    history's
hard porn
               black as the jack-
boot
black as this white
absolving snow's
                         white
in the earliest
                    timeless
onset of light.

   *

Dom Spatz   [*Regensberg*]
               Thurn und Taxis –
buy your beer from the Bishop
                    or from the Duke
and the Danube's carried away
                    in twists and torrents
                    through ancient arches
beside the wursthouse
under windows where
                    Friederike watches
snowflakes drifting
                    over icebound roofs
                    and frozen cobbles.

                         Time.
Time to move on.

   *

                    Blue   [*Amsterdam*]
here
               the movies show you
it all going
on
                         going in
                    good to see
but it isn't

                         164

                        mine
it isn't
hers
                  only the ache
belongs.

★

                        city at night
                   canals in the city
                 still water in canals
                  lights on the water

cobbles in the street
people on the cobbles
windows for the men
girls in the windows

                   trams under trees
                    leaves over trams
                 snowflakes and leaves
                lights through the snow

hotel on Damrak
mirror in hotel
face in the mirror
poet in the face

★

Taking stock in Amsterdam: Correspondences:

In Dijon Jean-Pierre played me a tape of his
    interview with Frank Sargeson. We spent the
    evening reading Verlaine, waiting for the night
    train from Paris.
I arrived in the South 2 November le Jour des Morts.
Verlaine arrived in Amsterdam 2 November 1892
    and stayed at Oosterpark 82 with the painter
    Willem Witsen.
Van Gogh had been dead two years.
I've come to Amsterdam to visit Elisabeth
    Augustin and to see the Van Gogh Museum.

Elisabeth lives at Oosterpark 82, the house once
    occupied by the painter Willem Witsen.
We take the tram to the Zoo building where a
    meeting of writers is to take place.
Verlaine was taken by tram to a writers' meeting.
    Passing the Zoo building he noted down its
    inscription: NATURAE ARTIUM NUTRICI.
Invited to look for a souvenir in the room
    Verlaine occupied, I find a copy of R. L.
    Stevenson's *Catriona* dated 1892.
In his *Quinze Jours en Hollande* Verlaine
    describes this room as beautiful and the
    view from it of houses at the back as 'very,
    almost too, Londonish.'
Downstairs, Elisabeth plays me a recording of
    Jim Baxter reading and I note the lines 'Teach
    me at once to wander and wander at ease /
    Be glad and never regret.'
She tells me how, during the war she walked everywhere
    in Amsterdam because as a Jew she had to wear
    the yellow star and could not take the trams.
    She survived only because her husband was
    Aryan German.
Elisabeth gives me a translation she has made into
    German of my poem 'Long before the sun
    goes out for ever . . .' from *Walking Westward*.

    ★

Lange bevor die sonne für immer erlischt
scheinen die äste ihr licht zu übernehmen
und die insekten in ihren zweigen
und die tiere inter ihnen.
Dies haben die Götter angeordnet da wir
ihre Komischen Scherze mit unsern ungöttlichen
            kräften umwerfen.

O Brave New World
ohne pogrome und scheinprozesse
ohne städte und die sie vernichtenden bomben
ohne die scham deer geschichte! –
nichts als das achtlose sich regen der blätter
und gedankenlos unaufhörlich mahlende kiefer.

*

– My father died in 1942. My mother was taken into a camp for Jews near
Amsterdam. She could show she was a member of the Catholic Church
but the Germans say that is not enough, she must prove she is baptised.
I write to Leipzig for the proof, quickly. When it comes I send it to the
camp but they send it back saying she is no longer known to them. At the
end of the war I learn from the Red Cross she has been sent to Poland. In
that camp they are gassed at once – on arrival.

*

These are the high far grey clouds over Holland
and behind them paler clouds through which
the weak light of another morning breaks.
Here's a lake with trees on the skyline
and on the far shore water lying under poplars.
These fields with cows could be the fields of home.

Soon the rails will run out of Holland landscapes,
there'll be none left to display. No more the waterbirds
of the lowlands will be Holland waterbirds,
no more the hedges and the fence-lines Holland.

*

Pissaro's sympathy with the anarchists of the late 19th century is   [*London*]
well-known . . . Yet it would be almost possible for anyone ignorant
of Pissaro's politics to go round the 200 or so paintings, drawings and
prints assembled at the Hayward and emerge still ignorant . . . Pissaro
was a pacifist anarchist. As he grew older he took a dimmer and dimmer
view of the social order . . . Being an anarchist he had no belief in a rival
system, so he opposed capitalist society not with its mirror image but
its true opposite, the value of individual experience. If that sounds like
escapism, it is because we have been indoctrinated by people with a rival
system to sell.
                    – John Spurling, *The New Statesman*, 13.11.80

*

So now from London
and the wrecked square
          an owl hoots after midnight

the last leaves are broadcast
                    where a Mary moon
steps out and faints
                    among the high
                         white traffic
and

*

(to continue)   [*London–San Francisco*]
when I worry
               as I do about
us
                    not us
two
                    or three or
four million
                    but us
                         ubiquitous
'the human race'
                    consoling to look
                         (as I do
now)
                         down
                    and out and
away
                    over hundreds
                         thousands
(it might as well be) of
                         miles of
mountains
                    under snow
and to know
those myriad magical white
points
          casting miniscule black
shadows
                         are firs
are forms of
life
               sheltering more
forms
and more

168

and that there's nowhere
not anywhere
down there
                    not even one
of us.

*

Moon and stars   [*San Francisco*]
            over Wildcat Canyon Road
                        and this stillness
absolute
the wild free ways
                    have brought us to

25.11.80
4 a.m.
under a Navaho blanket
            in a panelled room in Berkeley
knowing it's lunchtime in London
                        midnight in Auckland
and in the control room
            among that heady desert of stars
time perhaps
                        to collapse a galaxy
or maybe invent one.

*

Reagan country
            it's like (let's say)
                        plywood
                    under the feet
or plastic eyeballs.

A seedy bar
            on the Boulevard
talk of the fight
                Sugar Ray won
or the other boy threw –
                        warm
handshakes
            first names on first

meeting
                    'Nice people'
'Real nice guys'
                    so why do I feel
I've been in this old
                    B-grade movie
before
where everyone you meet's
acting
and doing it badly?

    *

West of Polk at sundown –
                    that's off to the right
          as you walk to the Opera
from George and Mary Oppen's –
                    one long
straight artery
          runs down into the blackness
of the valley.

                    Those corpuscles
the red and the white
                    moving in chains
are tail-lights /
                    head-lights.

                    The hills hulk black
behind
                    and behind at this hour's
the huge
blood-bank of the sky.

I'm thinking as I walk
                    of George's
          Betsy-Pup who slept
through poetry history gossip
                    but woke to eat
and visit the garden.

She quivered with love at a touch
and her ears

like winged victory
refused to lie down.

★

Yes t.s.   [*San Francisco–Auckland*]
        to make real
            distances
real
            to let be
things that are
            to make do
(for example)
leaves to fall
snow
        rivers to flow
and to bring it
(jetting westward)
                full
            to the full
beginning again
here
            circle.

The Clodian Songbook

15 Adaptations

I

                        Whom do we write for
Cornelius
                    in a popular culture
                    under a cooling star

for the dear loves?

                        the children?

                              the lovely and the lonely
moments?

Catullus could sign himself away
and all his words

but Clodia?
                                        this near world?
Never!

                              Here's my thin sheaf
friend
take it it's
                              (till the cows come home)
                                                  yours.

2

Clodia's pigeon pair
                                        one on egg guard
the other at large
or roosting above tomatoes
heavy with their siftings –
                              she likes the hard peck
they give her fingers
                                        she likes their talk
of rolled oats
under the awning.

Ignoring my parallel season
                    she ripens in her deck-chair
                              eating the stained fruit.

I too like that tang on the tongue
                              softness of feather
pain of the sharp peck.

3

That prow drawn up on shingle
                    under willows where the early

                  lake fishermen
              cast into stream-flow –
put your ear to its hardwood
you'll hear the slap of salt
snap of sail
                              rush
of long nights straining under bellying moons
                  northward to Suva.
                  On her side
like the star Cross she lies under
given over to calm and reflection
                    Catullus' yacht
              hot youth of Catullus.

                    4

        Clodia
                do you care
      does it chip at you
                that the old old
                should frown?

        Sundown over the lake
                        beyond the etceteras
                        bush-spike burned black on it
              on the red flush
                        but we know
            where and how it returns.

                        Not so our youth
                        light in the eye
                        fire in thigh
                and is it
                        are you wanting
        when darkness knocks
        perpetual dormitory?

          Lose count Clodia
          lip and tongue tell
                  but not
                        number

nor mumble anything
but these kisses
and this
and these.

5

'Countless' as they say also of
stars / sandgrains –
ask a conventional question
Clodia, you get
for example
beginning at Ahipara and counting
north
along Ninety Mile Beach
grain by grain
or when you lay on your back on the golf course there
numb with cold
and watched the numberless clear stars watching us
'myriad'
over my shoulder –
is how the poets counter
questions of many
of kisses
of what it will take
to slake a thirst, abate a hunger –
not infinity
but an unfixable
number
cardinal like
these kisses
and this
and these.

6

End of scene Catullus
Cut!
Snap go the wooden boards on the brightest days
when your wants matched

hers
flower-burst and leaf-
break

                                   twined vines
              and a lurching tenderness shaking
                            underfoot
your whole earth.

Phone   knock   urgent cable
          nothing rouses her now unless it's to tell you
                          end of scene!
you're not wanted nor welcome.
Very well then
it's a hard school.

But you, girl
             have you thought of the long nights
the subtle notations of silence
those spaces between the stars
                  we used to populate
                  with songs and jokes?

            Who will ink poems on your pillow
pile your table with impromptu sculptures
phone you from the earth's end?

                  You see this rigor
                  of the shoulders?
It's what they call
the courage of a trooper.
More than a scene is ending.
                Catullus uncomplaining
                    walks away.

7

           Air New Zealand
                    old friend of Catullus
       you offer a quick hike
               to Disneyland
               the South Pole
    Hong Kong's hotspots
      to ease a jealous ache.

Thanks brother
            but I'd rather
you flew downcountry a message to Clodia.

Tell her she's known to her 200 loveless lovers
      as the scrum machine.
                  Tell her
         Catullus loves her
      as the lone lawn daisy
                  loves
                  the Masport mower.

                  8

         This morning in bed it was
         7.20 the papyrus a tangled
         screen and through it ferns
         condescended to the lawn flax
   flew heavenward thinking as I lay there
   of *The True Confessions of George Barker*
         in pink paper covers I borrowed
      from the pocket of that 1950s raincoat
         of Asinius prince of poets who died
         the month I returned it after twenty
         years – lying there wishing I'd kept it
         Asinius, as a memento of you.

9

Yes please
                  do (and
wel-)
                  come to dinner
don't bring
any but
                        just
takeaways
                  a bottle and
your appetitive
               Clodian self
                  the big

things
                              (love
ideas
                    bananas)
                    your ever
readycatullus
                              will
provender.

10

Aurelius
                    I too revere it
          rampant outsize unwavering
hard on course to heaven in the early
                              light
I remember
     while Helios from the world's lip
lapped dew from grass blades.

                    What a mouthful!

But keep it brother
          east of my Clodia by a good ten
                              kilometres
and well down-wind.

If she hears of it she will have it –
                    if she has it
Catullus will take a simple
woodman's revenge.

11

Furius and Aurelion
back from the Gay Rights Convention
Catullus 'born on the sabbath day' salutes you –
enjoy whatever your own
tastes in transport
                              pedicabs
irrumbuses
          riding nose-to-tail in tandem

or just holding hands at the movies
and may the law stay out of your trousers!

But as a poet I protest

                          why GAY

you dizzy pricks?

                        That's one

indispensable
irreplaceable
word
you've rendered unusable.

              That was vandalism, brothers.
              That was misappropriation.

12

Salt smell and the green green daylight
                         under
wharves
         piles grinding and giving and
            off the bollard winding
rope

           and out in open harbour
fresh whatever-the
              wind   rain   sun
or on summer nights
wharf lights
          painting the water in oils.

Yes Clodia
I mean
        Kestrel Toroa Peregrine
         before the Harbour Bridge
before the North Shore was invaded
            by insurance salesmen
before the Fall.

Our citizens don't dance on their bridge
          can't walk on it either.

Clodia weeps for the days of her youth.

13

Fucking, I feel at one with the world
Clodia
it's like rowing into heaven.

                Through glass
      the moonlit ferns and ponga
sculpted in the grove of Priapus
                    approve.

          On this coast are white
wine
and oysters.

14

Suffenia opens her legs to life
          – no doubt of it!
but she rides Pegasus
side-saddle.

15

Ianus I'm camped a hundred yards from your bones.
The moths attack the lantern and die as surely
as you did on that asphalt strip near home
we used to burn up with our eager wheels.
Defeated in love and in my dearest ambitions
I've come to visit one who took the last blow first.
The world's sweetest when it promises nothing.
Remember our eel-trap that summer polio closed
the schools and drove us north? These tears are happy.
I wish you manuka on the eternal winds.
'So long' we used to say, not knowing what it meant.

At Home

A poem called 'The Weather in Tohunga Crescent'
for Allen Curnow

Up in the night to free the cat that
slept in the cupboard among towels
and got locked there look out and it's
moon all over and stars the big

ones not so much points as small
beautiful orbs and the bay of course
glass echoing moon echoing stars
over and above so if the gulls squabbling

for standing room would just stop
and the crickets lay aside their
bows a moment you might hear it
the music of the spheres.

So lightly it comes over us this
late summer stillness and steady
weather you wonder was it ever
different and will it ever

change. Early morning brings
a walker on the pipe that crosses
the bay and the gulls fly up ahead
descend behind in a white leisurely

ribbon. Someone who doesn't
think beauty should happen by
chance has burned the toetoe to
make a little beach where the road

ends but there are no visitors
except the tide twice daily making
its own broad way over the
mudflats. Tohunga Crescent

you could say begins in the
mangroves and goes on up to
the stars a euphemism for last
night's breathlessness or just

an acknowledgement that here
we're born we die not without
effort but as the tides and seasons
come and go (can't we say?)

'naturally'? The cat's asleep
under the ti-tree's flick-knives
our distinguished neighbour's retyping
a poem called 'The Weather in

Tohunga Crescent' and the weather's
keeping its countenance in the
glass of a bay that's for the
moment just as blue as the sky.

A Warm Wind from the East

Frank Sargeson

Our friend the novelist seventy-
eight next week and he says he's
written his last book can't
think any more can't write

connected sentences can't recall
the plots of his favourite Dickens
he used to rehearse scene after scene
not even sometimes the names

of his own novels can't answer
letters put down among cups pills
other letters where forgotten one
moment means the next draws

a total blank in a room full of
books piled up to be knocked

at a giddy turn across his
unswept floor. But cats are

fed there's cheese in the fridge
tea in the caddy he cooks
himself vegetables and fish a
corner of the garden's good for

tomatoes the best anecdotes
still surface and whatever
the losses they don't include a
wicked eye nor a good loud laugh.

Tonight the wind's in the east
the warm wet edge of a tropical
cyclone driving waves and seaweed up
on Takapuna Beach and I walked

there remembering the same wind
twenty-five years ago when his
garden was the other side of those
green pages he wrote on and if

you went for a walk over the
rocks to Thorne's Bay you might
come back to lettuce peppers fruit
in a bursting bag even a pumpkin

just inside your door and a note
saying come for a meal. Well that's
over and everything like a novel
has a beginning and a middle and an

end except that novels like
life go on repeating themselves
long after the garden's gone back
to wilderness the house to ruin

the old man to dust and his last
green sheet has flown off into
the sagging hedge on the broad back
of a wind that blows from the east.

Old Pale Gold

Waterfront Drive that morning
light still low striking off
the eastern reaches out past
Waiheke when the bus dropped

them at Mission Bay. They
swam dozed on grass Muff
bought takeaways Deliah wept
Amazon giggled Reuben stared

at the sky disbelieving what
seemed to float there Bim
vomited on boots stuck over
with blood red out of Cookie's

small head dying now in a white
ward sun climbing over the naval
base the still shimmering late-
summer air jammed with sirens.

A Coastline and Two Facts

Why else but 'because it was
there' we went four of us walking
down the coast where the surf
boom floats over dunes and up

to those high-flying cliffs a place
of wild reaches and eye
illusions in search of the whale
our friends two painters said

was there dead at high tide. At a
distance through drifts of
spray it was a black hump shining
on level sand and seeming in

morning light immense that as
we neared shrank to a whale-
child twelve feet at most one sad
fluke waving Mayday at the

sky the familiar tail half-
buried in sand the upward eye
already forfeit to the gull
crowd that drew back a discreet

space allowing us our proper
reflections. Tide-fall had left
a lagoon and in its calm shut
by sand bar from turbulence a

swan glided watchful and as we
turned from the black death
seemed to elbow its way up white
over white, catching the sun.

St Francis at Karekare

Karekare windless and the trees
patched with moonlight the two
young 'possums I've taught to trust
me as their St Francis I hear

squabbling on the veranda. Come
little friends I call in my saint
voice taking two slices of our best
Vogel's loaf and they disengage

one coming straight at me no
beating about the bush the other
like a shy girl hesitant half
turning away. These I tell them

holding up the slices are Sin and
Death and first the brave one
then his smaller side-kick
sibling they take them in long-

fingered hands crouching on
the woodwork their jaws going
like small machines. But two
slices they silently insist

don't make a beatitude
and soon I'm back with
more of the same. Here I
tell them are our political

leaders and I name that cheek-
scarred Caesar and his lame
well-meaning rival and again
'possum fingers apply them to

'possum teeth and down they go
inch by inch together with
Sin and Death. Enough I think
but those pink twitching noses

tempt saintly excess so again
it's back to the breadboard a slice
each to represent my worst
critics and I invent two mean-

spirited half-men who write
under the by-lines of Style
and Content. Fingers shut tooth-
machines click into action

I see the critics slowly
chattered away and still the big
round moon-reflecting eyes are
clear and perfectly neutral.

This May be Your Captain Speaking

Moon moon moon moon this
obsession darkness and clear
light over water the beach
Takapuna winds from all quarters

on vacation small waves
lifting with that breath-
catching moon-reflecting
pause its flash or shimmer

running down their raised
foil before falling the whole
Gulf across to Rangitoto
listening and over it a

huge havenless heaven alight
all the way out to the end
of the ever. But it's the sea's
particular talk these words

spaced out between wave-
break in every of its modes one
beach having one voice settlers
heard ancient Maori came

upon a characterising
untranslatable statement under
pohutukawa endlessly
varied endlessly the same.

from *Poems of a Decade*

1983

The Plum Tree

1
My father
walking away
was seen to look back at
the plum tree.

2
In a sudden wind
each leaf
fluttered like a flag.

3
To sparrows a territory
to my father a plum tree
to itself nothing.

4
Old wood / new leaf
the mind's obscure conjunction
was seen to be
a mode of beauty.

5
Seven years' devotion
to a liberal cause
hadn't altered
the plum tree.

6
When God told Eric Eason
to go south
the plum tree made no comment.

7
Eyes nose mouth
of the pumpkin lantern
glowed orange in darkness
under the black plum tree.

8
Louise Henderson
tells the plum tree
she's done with abstracts.

9
Properties of the night
include the plum tree.

10
The years of Dionysus
are over.
Apollo
is in the plum tree.

11
Dear Dad
I make no elegy
but this true record
of the plum tree.

Workshop Cinquains: What am I?

I am
the sex that turns
your purring engine on
that makes your heavy virgin vaults
unclose.

                    I live
            in your pocket
        dreaming of/faithful to
    the one and only iron wife
                        I fit.

Inset
in certain slot
I mend an intended

absolute closure so you may
enter.

So don't
leave me behind
or lose me on the way
lest ending send you back where you
began.

Three Adjustments to the Atomic Clock

1 *Tapping*

Tap. Tap.
Don't stop. Listen.
It's yourself moving
over the white plain.
Tap. Tap. Tap.
A typewriter?
A white stick?
Tap.

2 *Ode to a Grecian Urn*

You're sitting in a blue
armchair
                    trying to read a
                                poem
about poetry.

What is that girl about?

                    She's down the
                            corridor in a
glass
staring.

            Until you put her out of

the glass of your mind
                 the poem
won't give itself up.

Neither will she
      unless you put away the
book.

             She discovers a
               grey hair.
Each tick of the clock you
grow
older.

             The stillness
has a life of its own.

             Perfect. Perfectly
still.

3 *History*

It's what we think happened
before what's happening now
and before that.

Henry Ford
said it was bunk.

Our Fords
humming over the asphalt
are saying it still.

Woken

Nightwake
                          sees my
self
                not as others
                    make me
out
to be
but worse.

                Thick-skinned
day
will say
                    the hell
                    but night
knows:

From now
                    do only
                      exactly
as you feel
                    in your
self
to do.

Abjure
                pleasures of
praise –
                    blame
                will look after
itself.

Paris

1984

1

City so long announced come home to my dreams.
These are the days of my defeat when I long for
your anonymity, your bidets. Light me a whiffling candle,
pour me a small black coffee, send down-river your glass barges,
let your new immaculate wheels put forth on their tracks
to St Lazare, tell your best-breasted girls to expect me,
your clowns before the Beaubourg to hold their fire;
ask the crisp ready leaves of St Germain-en-Laye
to delay their plunge, the plumbing everywhere to hold back
its last laugh, the cars to polish their hubcaps.
Already stone angels in the cemetery of Père Lachaise
are trying their wings against rumours of a wind from the north.
It will be late summer, it will be autumn, it will be almost
winter and it will be winter. It will not be spring.
City so long undreamed, please look to your laurels.
Here there's nothing but the spite of choked passages
and green bananas, nothing but the spirit of Palmerston North
going to bed in lambskins. Paris, summon me to your table.
I invite myself to your board, I accept your invitation
and my defeat. Paris, put yourself in the picture.

2

Paris, you don't know yourself, haven't spent time
after dark wandering from menu to menu reading in the rain
unable to make your mind up, haven't eaten pans bagnats
at midday along the embankment and under bridges,
haven't shared your toothbrush with the President of the Republic;
have never been taken upstairs by a willowy whore
with a cunt like a black fist in the half light,
never found the long passage to the little courtyard
with the broken Diana; never learned to read the clouds
or translate the litany of fountains into Old Norse;
have never been offered even a major speaking part
by the Clichy clowns whose act is silence; never
run a race with the shadow of the Eiffel Tower and lost.
Poems are not written out of a study of maps and menus.
There's no truth in what the clouds say except when raining
and then it's in all the papers. The concierge knows you

for what you are, she watches you entering the lift;
her eyes follow your shoulders and her ears your feet.
She will question your bed and mirror in your absence
and they will talk. A concierge is seldom happy.

3

'The known appearing fully itself,' Denise said
breaking the hairbrush, and that's how you seem to me
this morning, Paris, drinking my café au lait: 'Authentic'.
I salute you over the gravel and through the fountain;
I salute you through the autumn trees of the Tuileries.
Outside the cinemas of the Boule Miche, twice around
the Arc de Triomphe, all the way up the incline to Montparnasse,
I salute you between the eyes and behind the eyes.
From this marble under my hand, past the sweating waiter
in his oversize apron, through steam from pavement grilles
over the stalled line of Renaults and Peugeots and Simcas
past a yellow façade with its windows and iron balcons
up to clouds colliding in French, I salute you.
Give me your Picassos, donne-moi tous tes Matisses,
let me address the boulevards, allow me to pacify the Metro,
permit me to lay a blessing over the buttresses of Notre Dame
and stand the Seine a drink in the Chamber of Deputies.
This is my day, Paris, you will fall for me today
like a Roman Empire, like a Jacob's laddered stocking,
like a devaluation. Paris, I wish you good morning.

4

Magic you are, Mr Muscle, magic you have always been
but so much is yet unspoken and would have remained so
had your neck broken before the fall of the Fourth Republic.
You have come at last and again to the city of liberation.
Up go the starlings in alarm, down come the pigeons to greet you,
out go the trains and in comes the breath of the soul.
The cobbles are trying your feet, the handsome birthdays
of the five saints are spinning in their Russian revolver,
the blood-red typists are walking into the sun.

There will never be a notion so brilliant as this actual,
these surfaces giving yourself without recognition,
without name, with only the tattered rags of a language,
with the eyes of a child let loose in a field of flowers.
Paris has its hand in your pocket, its escalators
are touring your dreams, its gendarmes directing
with whistles and truncheons the flow of your blood.
Lie down among stars along the Champs Élysées,
let them sing to you of a famous victory over death,
stamp into every line the determined blood of your birth.

5

Here's Catherine Deneuve she's walking under klieg lights
against a garish mural brilliant in the deepest bolgia
of the new Les Halles – hesitates, lights cigarette,
walks on. The cameras love her and so do you.
Take her to coffee in your head. Take her to bed.
On the escalators gipsy children have picked your pocket
and in the dingy gendarmerie you hammer out a statement.
Disguised as a spaniel she waits in a nearby café
drinking thé citron and rehearsing her fabulous lines.
Through cloud cover out of sight the force de frappe is drilling
for the first blue sky when they will drape their jet-trails
at an anniversary over the Arc de Triomphe.
Forever new, Catherine looks up and smiles.
'Thin girls die young,' say the graffiti 'and that leaves
fat old women.' You feel yourself drifting away
over traffic, through the jostle of falling leaves,
above the cold shoulder of a statue staring down whitely
at a girl on a bench in the Luxembourg Gardens weeping
at the thought of Catherine Deneuve. Your name may be Truffaut
but there's no end in sight. This Paris is like a disease.

6

Losing yourself you keep your hold on grammar,
and now by way of crescendo a white dove flies out
of the face of Magritte, or is it by way of diversion?

You have come a long way to enter the bathroom of Bonnard,
to take to task Picasso in the light of a Cubist dawn,
to look through Matisse's window at the palms of his hands
as they're blown against the blue of a Mediterranean night.
Loneliness has honoured you with a singleness of vision
that admits you to the frame. There will be no charge.
The morning is a paradigm of vermouth, cool and dry
and heady as you walk across the Pont Neuf already
making for the end of a story. Paris, take this down:
the sweeper is losing his argument with the breeze,
the leaves are storming the Bastille, a priestly cassock
wants heaven now, this world is climbing and flying;
the thin pale clouds are enacting nineteen-forty
for a silent movie; everything is written on the river
in a foreign language, everything engraved on the sky
with a silver tip. Paris, you ancient sewer,
my spectacles and my shoe-leather embrace your ways.

7

It is because we're all to die that we visit Paris –
not that we want salvation or think eternity possible
or believe more fervently in God than in the bathroom,
nor in Notre Dame with its burning bushes of candles,
but that this is an arcane language we can turn an ear to
as to the thrush on a wet evening, knowing more or less
its import without understanding. This and the sense that
not being gods or angels we have slipped right by
the frontier guards and are walking invisible in a heaven
of plausible dimension leading by cobbled backstreets
to breadsticks, berets and bicycles of favourite old movies.
Paul Gauguin came to our ocean for similar reasons
and the blood still shows on the walls of the Beaubourg.
Night is certainly a laboratory in which are made
colours of the trees, the river and the morning sky,
and you'll need your wits about you walking home
through the cold dawn without a visible presence
seeking only the safest route to the Rue Madame.
To the riddle of Life the best short answer may be Death
but not desiring it we can always settle for Paris.

8

This is where the President of the Republic spends his afternoons.
Here's the street where his motorcade passes. From this dais
he pins on ribbons and medals and kisses wrinkled cheeks.
He's the one who decides whether fish in your southern ocean
should wear water-wings or grow two heads.
Sometimes he leans to the left sometimes to the right,
sometimes he's ten feet tall, sometimes he accepts diamonds
but the bombs go off on time. Here's his mistress.
She has two breasts both of them strangely beautiful
when seen from the south. This is the Rue de la Paix.
Here's the boulevard where workers from the regions march
demanding a bright new numeral for the Republic.
This is the Quai d'Orsay, this the Aerogare des Invalides.
Climb aboard and we'll take you for a picnic in the Bois
where there are no bombs. Paris will never again
suffer the indisposition of the boots of a foreign invader.
Even the army will fight. Be careful of the hard-boiled eggs.
In 'Le Déjeuner sur l'Herbe' of Manet only the lady is naked.
In the eyes of the President are tears for the love of France
while he pours the wine. Nor will the franc be devalued.

9

Poems have been written on roof-slates, starlings
are drinking diamonds, the webs between the branches
have been renewed this early winter morning
as the cabs encircle once more the Place de la Concorde.
Paris has washed the face of the obelisk
and the rain has gone leaving an unutterable sky
admiring itself between shadows on a secretive river.
I'm alone with millions and that seems more than enough
with coffee and croissants and a generous jug of tears.
My love will be broadcast at eight to the underworld
which is not Paris, the world which Paris is not
where you may be walking at dusk not thinking of me.
How is it that such a tenderness must die
leaving no trace but colours squeezed out of tubes,
scratched on roof-slates, caught a moment in the webs,
observed if at all only by a passing cloud?

Dear children of the goddess of lonely light,
all those who have loved this body full of voice
and whom it loves, accept the blessings and praise
of the poet of Paris who stirs you into his coffee.

10

Now is the night we used to call Symbol of Death
but there's water through branches and lights and stars on the water.
Showing at the cinema on the far side of the square
is your movie with Catherine Deneuve – yes already it's made.
She kisses you in a mirror and the cats on the mansard
quote Rimbaud at the moon, which answers in French.
The glass doors open inward, the shutters push out,
and there beyond the balcony railing it runs
the silver ribbon of your thought rebuffed by the light.
Here you can see why Chagall's lovers float up
through branches to join the stars – it's the shortest route
to a high old time and not as difficult as walking.
In the Rue Mazarine your table is waiting in a window.
Will she be there with her neat and busy bush?
Go out among these hands that are pure conjecture.
As wine touches the tongue, as eyes exchange,
as a voice caresses an uncomprehending ear,
do not neglect to dictate these informal strictures
with all their whims of glass, their glosses on lust,
to the Paris of Paris that's nobody's dream but your own.

Between

1988

Part I

After the Wedding

1

After the wedding comparing notes with
Cousin Elspeth and Cousin Caroline
about our childhood bareback riding
on the Kaiwaka farm –

                    How, fallen with your
10-year legs did you get back up
even supposing he stood for you?

Cousin E remembered vaulting from the back
of her pet pig.
                I used the ruts worn deep
by the cream sledge – stood him in the hollow
and leapt from its edge.

                    Elspeth
and her sister, blonde babies
under the trees I climbed –

                    wooden veranda
hot dry garden sheltered by macrocarpa
dogs panting in shade
                      my face black
from the summer burn-off.

2

In sleep I still trace those tracks
below gum trees
                    skirting the swamp
through bush to that pool of pools
where the small brown fish suspend themselves
in shafts of light.
                  My feet sink
midstream in heaped silt
clouding the flow.

Water had cut its way
through black rock greened with moss
down to that glassy stillness overhung
with trees.

In the rock cleft
a deep hole water-worn and cold and dark –

I caught the eel that lived there
                its sinuous spirit.

3
In recollection summer is for ever
renewing itself even in the thickest
leafmould shade.
                It draws a life
from heat in the ploughed field
where I gathered fossil gum
                or in a hayfield
or in sunlight above the flame
above the dam.

                Cousin Elspeth, Cousin Caroline
cantered bareback
                        fell
(years after me) from the same horse.

4
Weddings are full of God and the Word of God
and the word God. I wonder what they mean.
To be one with your body, your body one with the world –
more than a marriage, it's a consummation
bracken and oil-flame like red cellophane
flapping on the hill-slope.
                        Eden
won't ask you back, you must make your way
in dreams, by moonlight, or by the broad light of day.

5
There was another stream, a creek
on the far side of the road
where the old house had been.
              It ran through reeds
silent.

The moons repeat themselves
the moreporks retort
the eel and its sibilants
are fluent

        an old chimney stands.

6
It's not what the landscape says
but the way it's said which is a
richness of saying, even of the thing
said –

        that finely articulated slope
a few words at the water
the breathy manuka and the precise
pernickety ti-tree

        a long last sentence of cloud
struck out by the dark.

After the wedding
I lie in darkness
I see something that might be myself
              step out for a moment.

It makes the moon
look at itself in water
              it makes the stars
gaze.
        It hears a nightbird and something
                        that rustles
in reeds.

It sees itself called

> > > to light up a silent
vast
> > beautiful
> > > > indifferent
waste –

mirror to the mystery
mirrored.

7
Break it
> > > (the mirror)

the Supreme Intelligence
is always silent
> > > > and death will come
in the guise of just this stillness
or another

> > but that was always the case.

8
'Marriages are made in heaven'
> > > > – not so.

We marry to be nearer the earth
cousins of the fur and the stalk
> > > > talking together

that brown water reflecting
these green hills.

The Magic Bagwash

Remember writing a story ten
years ago ended driving a
van 'The Magic Bagwash' north

of Auckland with the motto
'Everything comes out White'
parking on a coarse mat of

grass under pohutukawa
listening to waves flopping
and sighing those days when

Joni Mitchell sang 'Clouds'
and we marched for peace – just
a fiction but now like

something that happened
'really' to someone really
young, giving it away

cutting his losses. You know
how it is the human
spirit keeps on breaking

out but it was looking down
the long empty beach from
the van with its motto

under pohutukawa gave that
perfect past tense to what
the waves were saying.

As if Nothing had Happened

1 *Dream One & Dream Two*

He liked to put it on record – a dream of jungle,
red loam, still water, alligators basking,
their ruffled brows done out in green designs.
Cats in the garden woke him. He slept again
and dreamed a word-rejoinder to his dream –
woke laughing and forgot it. Dream One remained.

2 *The Dream of the Dream*

Woken into his dream he's naked in an upstairs room.
Trees on the high far slope show no signs of spring
but the sky shifts, the air promises something – a lifting
of the heart. He kisses a thigh where it joins a crotch
first right, then left, hair-springs touching his cheek.
She smiles an inward, languid smile. He pushes on
Up the valley into the dream of the dream of pleasure.

3 *The Dreams Continue*

Landed in Amsterdam he slept in the airport lounge
waiting for an onward flight. The huge round orange lightbulb
over the tarmac was the Holland sun through fog.
Where was the black box? He could paint Van Goghs in his sleep
or slide in A4 blank and bang away at dreams
of the freckled lakeside lady her sky on a spike.
She was wild with wanting, but only to go down on paper.

4 *That Summer*

That summer so many dreams like cars on a rail
drawing alongside, you climbed in and pulled away
or let it go, there was always another the same
unlike the London Tube and they ran all night
Sloane Square to South Ken where he missed the last
on the Piccadilly Line and took an actual taxi –
anticipating Paris, remembering Los Angeles,
living in Auckland, but only by word of mouth.

5 *Real*

What he always wanted why should he argue it was
what they called the real because he saw the rock
in the word and the moss around it, water running
over the green beard, and if it was a Zen Master
spoke out of the dark deep hollows among roots
of ancient trees that was something of himself, something
for the child beyond the dream who could smell leafmould.

6 *By Any Standard*

So he typed his letter about visiting the snake-house
the snakes seeming to look right past the faces
looking at them looking. He climbed the stairs with her
inside the greenhouse and she photographed his face
looking down among tropical flowers, admiring her.
He thought maybe his face fell forward into folds
or was that the dream? She never sent the pictures.
Looked at by any standard she was beautiful.

7 *The Wind in the Garden Blew*

We live in a gamy world. Yesterday he read
it was Radiguet said real poets have their own voices
and prove it by imitation. You remember the review
of two women writers, one English and obese
the other American and anorexic – they both looked out
from under her left breast when he took her clothes off
and lay down on the brilliant Indian bedcover
under the slatternly light. How he wanted her,
how he had her, that's not told in their stories.
The wind in the garden blew as if nothing had happened.

Two Dates for the Auckland Calendar

12 September 1981
Eden Park

Gathering under a hill
under banners

                    many

being part of many
and waiting.

Up there
the bridge squad

   the airport obstructors
waving and leaving.

Here
the gangs leading off
under shields and helmets.

How long since this
whatever it is
so squeezed your lungs and heart
so choked your throat?

 *

Look to left or right of your subject
not at it directly.

A balloon sails over the park
bearing a name: BIKO.

The street rises and falls
the many grow more.

In all this movement
watch your feet planting themselves
one in front of the other.

In all this noise
listen to yourself chanting.

Here in the stills
our mouths will be black and white
and wide.

 *

With one voice and
fifty thousand mouths
the park is singing.

 *

No poem is ever so much
about an action
as the batons pretend.

A block away at a signal
the metal blue and visors
are closing.
Now maybe it's time
for the reign of stones.

You see how it is
out of something like shame
wanting to dig down
and find yourself in fear.

Long forgotten
this hurt of men charging
knees boots fists elbows
and bones.

No reason to be solemn because
they're whacking your head
with sticks.

       Interrogate
your bruises.

       Demand
they give you a name.

4 April 1986
Bastion Point

It has many tongues and many children
who sit around it singing.

To put it out you put in
two hundred men in metal blue and visors
with truncheons. It's happening now.

Arrest the fire, put it in handcuffs
carry it to the cells, bring it before the Court.
Give the fire a good stiff sentence.

Will houses go up on Bastion Point?
Will they go up in flames? The fire
has many tongues and many children.

Deconstructing the Rainbow Warrior

In my game (and yours, reader) it was always the Frogmen
had clever theories. We did the dirty work

using the English language like a roguish trowel.
Tonight, two rubberised heads have set their Zodiac on course

from Okahu Bay. Past the Container port,
around Marsden Wharf, they're ferrying a transitive verb

called Bomb. In a hired campervan a man and a woman
smoke, check their watches, and bicker.

Turenges don't make it right, and anyway
the name is false, like their Swiss passports.

Half of Auckland, Dominique argues, has taken their number.
She's exaggerating of course. He refuses to panic.

A beautiful night. You can see the lighthouse light
on off Rangitoto, and an undercover moon

casual among clouds over North Head. Here come
the rubber boys back in their puttering Zodiac.

Remember, reader, poems don't deal in fact –
this is all a bad dream in the Élysée Palace.

Now scatter – it goes like the Paris Metro, according to plan.
Soon you will hear explosions. Someone will die.

More than a ship will founder. And the theory? Ah, the theory!
Dig a hole for it with your English trowels.

Between

Twirling an angry necklace on her fingers under the
    lamp she was saying she couldn't stand her
teachers or her mother or her life and on the other
    couch her mother who she said had sulked all
afternoon was saying 'Why hasn't anyone any
    pity for me?' and that she was so tired
she could scream and scream. Sorry for them both I said
    nothing, knowing if silence wouldn't help
it couldn't make anything worse. Impossible to read
    while the air was so loud with their angers.
One channel upstairs was offering a Midland saga
    of poverty and heart-break, the other
a Californian police drama with jokes and canned
    laughter. Then the row stopped. They were gone each
to her room and I could hear a tap dripping, and the cat
    snuffling after fleas, and a car cruising
down the Crescent, and what might have been stifled sobbing from
    behind one of those closed doors. I know how
Passion always gets a good press and why it should be so
    but have you ever thought of Reason as
the neglected child of our time? The cat has come to rest
    on my lap and my ears are growing out
like vines into the spaces of silence beyond the pear
    tree in blossom between the dark houses.

Paris: the End of a Story

The tomb of the unknown soldier, le tombeau
du soldat inconnu – London, Paris, and I guess
Arlington and elsewhere, but this guerrilla fighter
nameless in a check shirt, there's no tomb for him.
In a million stills he flinched from the levelled revolver
of the chief of police. Last night on television
he died again, falling back in a sitting posture,
then toppling sideways spilling blood on the street.
He's been dying like that in public for more than a decade.

And the ones with back-to-front collars they'll tell you
'He's in heaven now, he's with God his Maker' –
and the ones with shaven heads and saffron robes
they have their mysteries too – 'This world's an illusion.
Everything is spirit.' I say the poor bastard's dead
and what's more mysterious than that?
                                        Gone. Dead
and no bugles. What if that tomb burst open
and out the Unknown marched at the head of a column
soldier after soldier down the Champs Élysées
proclaiming the end of war, the end of a world –
would he wear the face of the guerrilla fighter?
To be stuck on this twig in the universal wind
whining for answers! Listen out there – you hear it? –
that silence beyond the silence of the stars?

Ludwig had a face like mine. He thought that words
wouldn't solve the mystery, they were the fucking mystery,
and you could thank God for it if God was one of your words.
I'd thank Ludwig for that but Ludwig's dead.
I remember dark clouds banking up over Paris
and a beautiful face in rain that wanted to speak
and I too wanting – we were silent as the stars.
It was something that didn't happen, like the gun that wasn't
deflected, like the rope not cut from the wrists
of the man in the check shirt who didn't walk away.
In words these things that didn't happen happen.
I see him lead his column down the Champs Élysées
past a café where I sit with the beautiful woman
who didn't say a word, under a louring sky.

Notre Dame sets sail down the river Seine
on l'Isle de la Cité, biggest of Paris barges,
fired by a million candles, a million prayers,
a cargo of souls with one-way tickets to heaven.
God sings in the choir and whispers in the crypt.
He knows the name of the soldier in the tomb,
he knows the language of love she didn't speak,
knows more than enough, that's why he hides his eyes
tired in the mornings, looking out over the square,
limping on cobbles, sheltering under bridges
from this unseasonable rain.
                                        'Dulce et decorum . . .'

'Mort pour la Patrie . . .' I see them setting forth
in columns splendid to the north, and east of north
through wheatfields down the valley of the Meuse
through latesummer forests, across the crops of crosses
(black iron, white wood), through campsites along the river,
through village squares past monuments bearing their names.
My death sits at his table in the Champ de Mars.
The one who keeps his silence keeps his head.

A dream of Paris, someone calling his name,
dark skies, wide streets, the mansards glistening black
on the hillslope rising to the Sacré Coeur,
in Montparnasse a street-organ, a beckoning girl –
however it came to him Horváth woke up to answer
the call of his future and died in summer thunder
that cracked a branch down on his playwright's head.
L'amour. La mort. City of love and the dead.
His unwritten words are locked away in marble,
to rise at a signal, a thundercrack, a bugle,
to march in columns, watched by our silences.

Here now's your bed, flowered paper, windows opening
to a narrow balcony over the Rue Madame,
rain still falling on the yellow gravel
of St Sulpice. Turn off the light, shake up
your pillow, imagine this sleep to be your death,
this room your tomb, this rain falling for ever,
the Seine flowing, traffic on the Boulevard Saint Germain
endless, the cafés noisy. A bullet in the brain
is only the end of a story. It starts again.

The Poetry Room

1 *Carpe Diem*

You know of course the saddleback's a kind of bird
the hatchback a style of car. Things known to us
and things not known are equally often surprising.
Suppose it's true our planet and sun are on course
to vanish in a black hole and still you're refusing

because of something said on Thursday. Will it be loud
as we rush to the last implosion? Will it be long?

2 Professor Moon at the Lectern

This is a lecture on darkness O dark dark dark
I will take you into the dark. Turn down the lights
while I project my slides of paintings of darkness,
umbrageous monochromes. Listen while I read
poems of the night. I tell you light falls from above.
I tell you we all come out of the dark of the womb
and go back through shadow to the darkness of earth.
In the caverns of the ear you're attending to my silence.
In the black of your brain the light of my life burns clear.
Professor Moon is walking on the face of the waters.

3 Where Alph the Sacred Beater Ran

The quick brown fox jumps over the over. What
a lazy dog. Clean bowled. Looking down the vista
of the Vistula I came up against a cliché. It was
squinting into the sun where the brown fox had run.
Only Clap Cleanser will scour you a clean bowl.
Now is the time for all good moon to come to the aid of . . .
Moon? Did you say moon? Hurry up please, it's time.

4 Lawn Order

In this photo the Squad in blue metal and visors
are gathered around like wasps. That's a wrist they're breaking.
At the picture's edge that's me, waiting to be next.
Whoever dislikes disorder must like the Squad.
When they break a wrist it's always for the best.

5 The Craft of Poetry

At four-thirty he rested elbows in sunshine on the sill
of his office window. A woman walked down the drive
and another walked up and both of them were pregnant
and they smiled as they passed like craft exchanging salutes.

6 *The Poetry Room*

The poetry room has no doors and they're all open.
You can't get in by applying or asking for a ticket
but once inside everything's as it should be. Marvellous.
And you never open a book. Remember that character
in a French novel who thought so much of England
he never went there – just dined on beef at Cherbourg?
How could real England match his imagining?
The poetry room's like that. You walk home whistling.

Going to Heaven

              married one
            fathered three
travelled far
      wrote (say) a round
                    dozen
died and

   *

mangroves
moongroves
       salt on a light wind
               rattling
cabbage trees
blinds
      and on a bland night
broadcast
           a dog
two moreporks
  a nameless night-shriek
      a million-piece
insect orchestra

   *

          green dark
colourless

green
        and the moon still
            in water
on water
in a glass by the bed
shakes at a
ghost-step

   ★

        all this sounding
            silence
nothing changed
           fifty years
turning on itself
in sleep

   ★

        such a long way
to come back
was always
             that
summer
        even in rain
         on a sack
stock-still
         astride
the grey pony
         above
the brown dam

   ★

what lays the stone
         stare
down
         thunder
      and a bitch of a
      non-existent

it was the wrath of
        it was the rock
of

Hephzibah! Hephzibah!
Beulah!
        (Moriarty!)

       backward dog
go bite your tail!

*

      and all the time
         it goes
greening down slopes
     trees a decade taller
     a decade broader

      and yourself
one fuck nearer your last
      rising to look at

    a white cloud's lovely
satisfied / self-satisfied
         trailing
over its earthly mirrors

*

     along a ridge-top
       threading
among sky and cloud

(who rode to heaven
on a horse?)

     young head-in-air
astride the grey
pony
       above
the brown dam

*

here are shellpaths
     bare boards

underfoot
                             and a
breeze from the sea

*

breaks as always
all over
                   another sunday

here is heaven
                    take off your
clothes and
                        lie down

                      prepare for
(again)

takeoff

Goodbye

The dead don't write
poetry have no need of
it no matter who

it was spoke through
the grills of the night
sky when no breeze blew

out the candles
of the stars you were
alive it was one

incandescent
airy arrow over
the city and out to

sea all lights and
engines and the roar of
waters and I was away as

ever over
seas in my flying
chair taking my pre-drink

drink writing on
the head of a pin good-
bye again. Goodbye.

Part II

From the Clodian Songbook

I

Death, you clever bugger
   who would have credited you
with such finesse!
   Your shadow passed over me
and took instead
Clodia's white pigeon
   that used to peck her fingers
   and warble obscure reflections
among her vines.

There he lies
dried out
feet up
   weightless in summer grass.

   And look at her tears!
   Venus and Cupid
are moved to join her in weeping.

   Congratulations Death –
you're an artist.
You know just how to strike
and where.

Had I been the one
called down that dark road
no such flood
would have followed me into the night.

2

Friend Flavius
these breakfast silences
        won't keep you out of my report.

    Nightly your squeaking bedsprings
her moans and your grunting
                    give me a ball-by-ball
                    on your performance.

        Are you content with these
as spokesman for the team?

Speak up, Flavius.
        My sports page goes to press
in half an hour.

3

                Verania
mother-met brother-hugged
handing out duty-free packets
still jet-lagged and already talking
                    of your return
to Spanish lovers
            the London theatre
hitching down the Rhine –

oh my dear
                scatter-brained
                clatter-tongued
Kiwi kin
Catullus groans
        to see what a cliché
the world has made of you.

It's an old story. Catullus just back from 'overseas'
boasts the eight bearers are his who carried him into the forum.
He's trying to impress that beautiful woman with Varus
who's trying in turn to pass himself off as her lover.
The woman's not trying to impress. She just covets the bearers –
but when she asks to borrow them for a jaunt of her own
Catullus mumbles they're not his exactly – they belong to Cinna.
He's angry now with the woman for causing him embarrassment.
Isn't that the travelling salesman and the company car?
Human folly is constant. Only the bombs get bigger.

5

Calvus sends me his book
               printed at his own expense.
He hopes for a plug from Catullus
for the jacket of his next.

          I ought to fire it straight back
                  or write 'Calvus
please don't send me your arsepaper –
I've plenty of my own'
                      – but I don't.

          I write 'Calvus, how kind –
                I'm looking forward
to getting into your book
as soon as my desk is clear.

6

          Aurelius, you big prick
if I complain to you
                call you lustful
         improvident, irresponsible
without honour and without restraint
it's jealousy drives me.

I know how your presence in a room
      the way you hold yourself watchful
            and that Paul Newman grin
light fires in my Clodia.

            I ought to name you rather
Father of Hungers
god of those appetites
      without which there would be no
                  trouble among men
the earth would be silent
            and have no need of my songs.

7

'Young man,' she used to say
            'you stay away from old Furius.
His hedge is a disgrace to the suburb.'

                  I tried to excuse it:
'You should see the vegetables he grows
behind that hedge.'

                  'That may be so,'
she said
            'but they say he doesn't have a
                  washing machine.'

                  'He always looks clean,'
I said.
'He's a great cook
and he lets me borrow his books.'

                  She wanted to know
            why he didn't cut his hedge.

                  'He's a writer,'
I told her.
                  'He's very busy and famous.
His books are published in England.'

'What's the good of that?'
she asked
'if he doesn't have a washing machine
                            and his hedge
is falling over the pavement?'

                        8

Remember, poor ghost of Furius
                those Eliot lines
                we used to quote
                with ghostly relish:
'What is that noise?
                "The wind under the door . . ."'

Auster blew from the south
Boreas from the north
                Favonius from the west
                Apheliotes from the east

        but that overdraft of yours
£1250
                            it blew
up through the floorboards
        making the scrim billow
and the roof-iron groan.

                        9

Down here's the Henderson Valley
    up there the Waitakere Range.
        Here makes wine
        there makes water.

    'It's all piss,' says Postumus
    filling the glasses again
    but don't let's mix them –
I'm here for some serious drinking.

Large lunch
Clodia
one appetite
doing duty
for another
but it won't.

Look
now there's this
tree in my
trousers
and a fire
in your garden.

Don't pretend
you don't
under-
stand.

Just call me
in
apply your-
self
be my tree-
feller
I'll be your
sure-fire
brigade.

11

'It may not be God exactly'
Clodia tells me
lying back among sheets
in an unwonted moment
of unwanton wonder
'but *there's something up there*' –
and why not?
But if there has to be a Big One
I choose for myself that goddess

daughter of Latona
born under an olive
                among Delian hills
who sees to crops and hunting
              – or in darker moments
when wars threaten and the rocks
                  shake underfoot
let it be that one
          who turned over in sleep
closing her legs
on Maui's trespass
        and laid him to rest for ever.

12

      I turn the light on a poem
          and find you, Ravidus
inside.

      What are you doing here?
Did you stagger in drunk
     or is that just your burglar's
cover?
          Are you after some easy
Publicity?
   And what's that poem of mine
thinking of
admitting you?

         Piss off, Ravidus
you critical nightmare –
find yourself a newspaper column
         if you want to lift
that dog's hind leg of yours.

13

That day you burned my book
   because I'd put you into a poem
         too true to be good
I called up my cleverest syllables
and locked you into another.

I can't keep you at home
or call down the rockslide I'd like
on your lovers
Miss World –

              you go your own way.

                       But here
in the parlour of words
I'm the boss.
                     Here
Clodia
           you do as I say.

14

Trapped by my appetites again!
              Sestius is such a good cook –
but after the meal
sitting over our glasses
with cheese and grapes
he offered to read me a chapter of his book
                       on critical theory.

              I should have guessed
but how could I refuse?

              It must have lasted an hour –
post-colonial, post-structuralist, post-
modern –
                 did his pole house
have something to do with its drift?

           'What do you think, Catullus?'
(his eyes bulging and glazed).
               'Solid,' I acknowledged.
               I suggested he call it
The Deconstructing Kiwi.

              Driving home
I had to stop the car
and spill my guts in the gutter.

Such good cooking
wrecked by bad writing –
                        it's a metaphysical puzzle.
It took me two days to recover.

                Clearly the literary life
is more dangerous
than we care to admit.

15

Today there's something in the winter sky
                                signalling spring
something to do with light –
and the hand of the wind on our cheeks
is less rough than it was.

                        But my bags are packed –
I'm flying north
into the last of that hemisphere's summer.

                        Goodbye Clodia
                I don't ask you to be faithful
but keep safe
remember my birthday
and never doubt I love you.

                        Travel is my vice.
Already it's as if I can see
                        the first brown leaves
falling into the Thames.

My heart's an anchor
        my head a dinghy on the running tide.

16

Suffenia, feminist in fiction
                and Tullius Tuhoe
walk off with the Book Awards
and Catullus chalks up another defeat.

Gender and race combine
      like an All Black front row –
unstoppable!

Yes yes they are deserving.
      Certainly they are the best –
as much and as truly the best
      among our writers
      as it is true to say
Catullus is the worst.

17

From that middle-class riverside garden
      haunted early and late
by the garbling of pigeons
      remember, Catullus, watching
      through the little wall-gate
how stealthily she followed the streets
towards the mean heart of the town
      where she offered herself
she said for money
really for the hell of it
      and for stories she would tell
back in that warbling willow-hung arena
above the river
making you sweat and swell at the image
      of her rubbing the hot husk
      off the corncob
      of a Hell's Angel
rampant astride his Norton
      outside the hamburger bar.

18

Clodia, when you haven't
one more malicious lie
to offer the world
about Catullus
I'll believe you don't love me.

Likewise when my poems
stop making it public
that you're a heartless whore
consider our affair at an end.

19

Seeing you weeping at the graveside
Calvus
while trucks rumbled by beyond the hedge
and the mountains stood so still and so silent
against a sky
that went away for ever
I wished I could believe
Quintilia from some far place
watched fall
those tears she had inspired.

The pain is in not believing.

Brother
I offer you no cheap consolations
only that the far sky is there
and the moths playing around the hedge flowers
and the trucks going by along the road.

20

Inside you
Clodia
a tired cock
subsides.

Mouth in pillow
whispers
to your ear
of a natural
disaster.

Sinking
of the Titanic.

Closing time
at the Anemone.

We sleep
in one another's
arms.

21 *Postscript*

An elbow of grass where the stream ran down to meet
the long arm of the sea, and on the headland

pohutukawa for shade – our campsite, Clodia
where earliest morning offered a great grey stretch

of level water turning to blue with the sky.
The stream was my path inland, deep into bush.

In a clearing there, listening at a gullet of stone,
watching for those small brown fish with transparent bodies,

I met his flat snout and tusks, his black-bristled shoulders
and mean pig eyes. His breathing seemed thoughtful

with just an echo in it of grunt and of squeal
before he turned and went, leisurely, among ferns.

That was four decades buried and long forgotten –
so why should he visit me this January morning

between sleep and waking, in all his particulars,
still thoughtful, still threatening, keeping his options open?

Part III

Kin of Place
a poem for Kendrick Smithyman

A student stumbling upon a blind mountain
found its wizard had written a Christmas sonnet
to the best man at his sister's wedding.

*

Those of us who know the far North know
that if death isn't total extinction
we will cross a bridge on rotting piles
over an estuary. On the far side
tide out, day hot, the light grey-green under mangroves
the ears and eyes of childhood
will be restored to us.

That single crack is a mud-shrimp;
that far wet flap, a heron departing.

Casual as a cocky
one kahawai is herding mackerel in the green of the stream.

*

When I wrote of Mangawhai what I remembered was
the crack of whips and weight of wooden yokes.
What's known now seems to come, half from what's written
half from what's half-recalled. It was a warm morning
the bush wet, the bullocks' steaming flanks
heaving, sinking cloven shafts in the tracks.
We were re-enacting history, not for itself
but for a purpose, the taking of one kauri
to be sawn at the pit. I remember the old house
due for displacement. Sash windows wouldn't shut,
hens had invaded bedrooms and laid their eggs
in mattresses and pillows. Harness and gum-spears
rotted and rusted on the big verandas. I found a cup
won by two brothers, Wallace and Nelson Hastie,

cousins of my cousins, Champions of Australasia
at the cross-cut saw. What I remember is fact.
'How deal with' is half our story. Words come first.

*

Sargeson told me domestic conflict
was killing your talent. He was wrong.
Your talent was a hungry dog that fed on scraps.
On that North Shore we all bayed at the moon.

I used to think if I understood your poem
too soon you might correct it. But I helped you choose
titles for your third book. I remember a hut
by a summer creek. You kept returning indoors
for another typescript. My merest doubt
meant death to a sonnet, amputation for an ode.

Being about once, walking with Mary
you met us on a beach, showed us a shell,
wrote a poem describing a meeting minutely of poets
and the showing of a shell. It was a poem about being.

No day beyond Kaitaia or east of Eden
was ever ordinary, not anyway after
your eye had lit upon it. Up went your words
like salt on the wind; in came tide under mangroves.
This was our proximate world we could talk of only
to the kin-of-place in the language of a landscape
known only to the senses, spoken in sleep.

When summer comes down out of the bush hills
spice on its breath, clematis in its hair
I think of a stream flowing out of deep-carved rock
to a shingle pool where brown fish hung suspended
in shafts of light. That was the place of beginning.
Even fantails seemed to respect its oracular quiet
so the water words that gurgled from the stone
were properly heard, never interpreted.

*

Strange flocks are seen to straggle over the isthmus
fact carrying word, word carrying fact –
ungainly pairs. Dark weathers gust across
and out to sea before the powers can act.
Mostly we like what we live. Pain is reflexive
to be read between the lines, not for discussion
while fish swim and butter melts in a pan.

This is the season when blossoms take a beating
in a strong light. One poet, asked to dream,
conjures a mud-flat; another, a scoria cave.
Scene becomes anecdote, anecdote history, and still
verbs tug at their moorings, nouns are tossed,
the harbour spills its sails out on the Gulf,
a city goes on growing under our feet.

*

A dwarf with a billiard cue and a mania for fact
was asked was there life south of the Bombay Hills.
He said he believed there was, and went on working.

The Radiant Way

A good student, 'The place is lumbered,' he tells me,
'with a Rump of aging Hippies' – and it's true I can see
Blake-men trapped in their burning beards and hair.
For lack of invention the Age strikes some to pillars
of Marxist/Feminist/Post-Structuralist salt.
Stiff-jointed liberals dance to escape insult.
'Academics are Saussure they know everything'
goes the graffito, 'they know Foucault about anything.'

Remember those post-war silken ladders unrolled
from palaces of cloud? The hard-working world
was going to join us there, Leavis and Levis in
the Realms of Gold! Now everything has to come down.
There's text in a bus-ticket. Anyone tape-talks
and it's history. I tell him, 'Believe in your books.'

Voices

1990

1820 The Missionary

1

Ten men to hold the wheel, children screaming,
our whole world shuddering, heaving, breaking –
how potent those words to calm us: 'They that go down
to the sea in ships, that have business in great waters,
see the Work of the Lord and his Wonders in the deep.'

God who delivered us out of Leviathan's jaws
has brought us here where welcoming thighs open
to the dark pathway. Better we had gone down
in that cold hell than in false paradise.
Dreams and mosquitoes plague me in my tent.

Marsden's lash, Kendall's lusts of the flesh –
where is our faith? Our half-drunk countrymen trade
muskets for women. The natives kill without rancour.
On still evenings I listen to small waves lapping
along the shoreline. It might be the language of God.

2

Our visitor put on green glasses and a wig.
We shouted 'Atua!'. The natives ran from our table.
They say their recent dead go by this headland
on their way to Reinga. At night they hear them whistle.
I wonder – mocking their faith, do we mock our own?

For hillslope, riverflat and eastern bay was paid
fish-hooks, hoes, axes, blankets, trousers.
Also tobacco. The old chief made his mark,
eager to sell. Discreetly I asked him why.
He thought me mad. Had I never felt, he asked

south wind around bare shoulders? Shaped a bone hook?
Felled trees and carved with stone implements?
Tomorrow, next year, for ever the land would be there.
We could not take it away. Why did we value so little
iron axes, fish-hooks, trousers, blankets of wool?

3

Today our first plough turned New Zealand soil.
I walked behind two bullocks. Dark loam rolled out
like a bow wave. I thought of what is to come
and wished this day might be remembered well.
How fortunate we first! God speed the plough!

This evening on the estuary three canoes,
their chant preceding them – *hoea! toia!*
over still green water. Soft-voiced Hongi Ika
splendid in feathers, kai tangata, eater of men –
he paddles out of silence and into the past.

I give this moment to my kin-of-place
now and for ever. The seed of your growing is here
in this Bay of Islands. Europe is in our books
and in our boxes. We will unpack them slowly.
God save this bright air, these untroubled waters.

18 October 1836 The Catechist

Dogs bark me from sleep. Pale light through an open flap.
Grass swish. Twig snap. Whispers – and now this hush
a thread in the book of my dreaming – a threat?

I wake to myself – John Flatt, crossing the Kaimais
from Matamata down to the Bay of Plenty.
The forest lifts dark arms to that billowing light
expecting song. Why are its choristers silent?
Fear won't dispel this well-being of my waking.

Black hair, brown shoulders. I watch them climbing the track,
young warriors, armed – but stones, bare hands would serve
to wipe my dream-slate clean of trade and farming,
my unborn children and their children's children.
I give them welcome, ask are their mokos smiling.

A tui answers. It speaks of flax in flower
last spring by the Mission House. They came with baskets
of human flesh and picnicked on the lawn.
An outrage, yes. But an answer to our Message.
We could eat our God. They would eat their enemies.

Tent, clothes, bedding, axes, everything is taken.
Only my horse they leave – they have not seen one
And seem to fear it. 'Muru,' their leader explains.
Clothed in my understanding I'm left on the track
Through a cold forest, twelve thousand miles from home.

I ride, singing to the One who made me naked.

1840 The Treaty

5 February *The Girl*

'Don't believe that,' is what the Missionary said,
but walking home at sundown I saw them again –
the ropes of Maui big through holes in cloud.
I showed him I could say the twenty-third Psalm
not looking at his book. He talked about guilt.
Last night the sailor came again to our whare –
blue-eyed, freckled, his skin tasting of salt.
Soon they will sign the paper. Pakeha ladies
in big dresses walk to and fro on the lawn.
Their men wear swords and hats. My uncle makes
a thunder speech. He doesn't like what is done.
I have climbed down to the inlet with this hook
the sailor gave me. If I can I will catch a kahawai.
I say the Psalm. I say a prayer to Maui.

5 February *The Printer*

Pompallier in Romish purple gave us no look.
We stood behind Reverend Williams at the table,
the chiefs ranged each side in their coloured cloaks.
Uniformed, hatted, the Governor rose to tell
of her Majesty's wish for order in New Zealand.
Kemara spoke: 'Governor, good health to you,
but we need no Treaty. Go home! We meet on land
once mine. Will a Treaty return it? Am I so low
I must crawl under your feet? I say, Go home!'
Outside the blue sea sparkled, the lawn shone green.
Five hours the speeches lasted – and more to come.
Does the Governor understand the way of the Maori?

Did Williams translate fairly? Will the chiefs sign
and know what they sign? Time will make us a story.

6 February *The Printer*

Morning confusion. Missionaries, chiefs, all wait –
the Governor thinking we are to meet tomorrow.
At noon he comes, plain-clothed but for the hat.
As signing time approaches my anxiety grows.
I speak: 'Your Excellency, do you believe that these
assembled understand what they cannot read?'
He replies that he does. I remind him that Heke says
'We are children in these matters.' 'Then they must heed
the missionaries' good advice, as Heke will.'
Marupo speaks, and Ruhe. They oppose the Treaty,
then sign, as does Kemara – the seal is set,
the marks made. 'Now we are all one people,'
his Excellency tells them. I am to give them blankets.
Tomorrow he will proclaim the Colony.

8 February *The Settler*

Why should we cheer? One hard-earned pound per acre
for our patch of fern and forest – and now, this noon,
our title worthless, theirs to the land entire
empty or occupied guaranteed by a Crown
alone permitted purchase! On the upper harbour
the tribes have welcomed us and let me teach them
trades and cricket. Potatoes, corn, flowers
are flourishing, and a pasture. My children learn
the native language. Yes, we shed homesick tears
and think of returning. That is a dream – no more.
Here sea and forest and soil have been providers.
But now, with flagship, gun-salutes and Governor,
England's long arm lays on her sons and daughters
this act of dispossession. Why should we cheer?

8 February *The Chief*

Their men in black whose God is most powerful
advised us to sign, but the silent man of God
dressed like a chief in a mat of shining purple

frowned. 'Possession passes,' is what they said,
'but the land remains.' Heke believes it is true –
I am uncertain. I think the young are headlong.
I remember my youth before the time of the tupara.
Once I crept at night on our enemy sleeping –
Strike to the left! *Thrust* to the right! – I broke
five heads and got away. At daybreak they were gone.
Those warrior days – are they over? I would have them back;
but not sleeping cold in winter, not axes of stone.
I was given this blanket after I made my mark –
the Governor's gift. I draw it around me in the rain.

15 April *The Governor*

He grabbed the gunwale, stared in my face, shouted
and turned away. Colenso was embarrassed:
'It was nothing' – but I demanded he should translate.
'He's an old man,' the native had said. 'Alas!
soon he will be dead.' That was the day of the Treaty.
One vexatious month later I was carried on a litter
to be cared for here at Waimate. But as days go by
see how my arm by God's dear grace grows stronger –
you can read my letters! And strength returns to my leg.
I am due at the Bay but now it rains and thunders.
Waiting, I fret. God knows where my sheep wander,
my tea and sugar are lost – but your ship is due
dear Liz, from Sydney. Believe me, I am happy!

21 May *The Governor*

A clear night, still water, bird-calls from the forest,
Liz at my side – such peace, unpleasantly broken
by news from the south of Captain Pearson's arrest.
These Wakefield demagogues at Port Nicholson –
I must curb them, and block the French, or we may lose
our foothold. I cannot wait for more to sign:
the Treaty as it stands must serve our purpose.
Tonight we have drafted formal proclamations
claiming New Zealand for the Crown. The North we take
as ceded by the Treaty: the rest by Discovery.
Shortland will sail with constables and soldiers
to show the flag in Cook's Strait. On the Waitemata

239

the capital will be established. I lie awake
tuning my ear beyond silence, listening to the future.

1840 The Dream

1
Bathurst, New South Wales, New Year's Eve –
the eve of 1840 – I, a Scottish doctor,
in my bed at the inn, the clock striking midnight,
assigned convicts dancing to a horrible fiddle,
their feet scraping the floor as if their ankles
were still in chains, their voices harsh against sleep.
So far from home, I dreamed of travelling further.

2
Hauraki Gulf, New Zealand. Natives paddle us
towards Waitemata, chanting as they go
a song about the Pakeha come to exchange
blankets and guns for land, who will build a house
if the chief Ngapora assents, and whose soft heart
is seized by the beauty of the maiden Kora.
'Tena kumea!' they chant. Our canoe drives forward.

3
Today we crossed the isthmus to the western harbour.
Kumara on woven flax, pipi hot from the hangi –
these were our welcome, and talk of land for sale.
Sunset fired the slopes. I felt a city
growing inside me, reflected in these waters.
Not guns, not blankets – dreams are our secret power.

1848 The Radical

1
Stanley thought I might be first in the South to own
Hegel and Spinoza. Below today, I checked
my iron bedstead, plated teapot, Dutch oven –
all gifts of friends. I washed in salt on the deck.

Porpoises thread the bow wave, flying-fish
sprint forth and skim. At night the Milky Way
is an arc spanning the sky. My hardest wish
is to stop thinking of Etty. Interminably
poor Cargill adumbrates his Pilgrim plan
for the Scots Christ. He doesn't see his daughters
kissing the sailors, sharing their sweetmeat spoon.
In these latitudes I pray my spirits recover.
'Ancients of earth' (remember Tennyson's line?)
here we are yet 'in the morning of the times.'

2
North from Port Nicholson, my guide a Maori boy,
my thoughts homeward, and yet my head made light
by this astonishing land – ocean stretching away
forbidding on our left, rising on our right
a dark forest – until, rounding the headland,
I hear across an inlet the beat of a drum,
see a kind of castle, English soldiers, a band,
drilling, dispersing, to a parade-ground scream.
'Boat ahoy!', and the ferry takes us over –
I and my two-shilling guide. Unfair to call
these soldiers 'lazy lobsters' as I have done
in letters home. Truth is, their time may come.
One day I may write of the horror of cloven skulls
whitening in grass beside a southern river.

3
Nelson, its air like wine. My time as 'prentice
to life I pray is over. But I, the Radical,
made head of a college – does it seem possible?
'Citizen Clough' (Matt calls him) writes from Paris
news that excites me – not class against class
contending in the streets, but the will of the people
discovering love. Here, where we mix as equals,
when asked to sing I offer the Marseillaise.
Last week climbing with Weld I felt an earthquake.
Our hilltop heaved and shuddered. There is a power
in truth and justice that will move the mountain
of English king-craft, priest-craft. Can we not make
a beginning of its end? How long must the poor
carry their burden? Here, let us see it happen.

1849 The Settler

These trees that hang over the bay
shedding red stamens – the Natives call it
pohutukawa. Like a discreet servant
the tide enters. My children run to meet it
barefoot, brown-skinned. I call them savages.
They seem to fear nothing, born to this wild land.

I scrub the floor with sand. The pine whitens
and the grain shows through more clearly.

Last year the local hapu took my husband.
They told him, 'Eat and grow so you will make
good kai for us.' After two nights they laughed
and let him go – told him, 'Long pig, run home!'

Two days ago a war party stopped at our door –
took pork from my kitchen. I couldn't speak.
Naked, beautiful men – by now they may be dead,
or eating the dead.

                    Light dances on the water,
sharpens the headland's edge and the far horizon –
a brightness that speaks to the soul. Home is the dream.
I fear for myself, longing for a sail, and letters.

1860 The Pakeha-Maori

I know that talk: 'It's time to drive the British
into the sea.' No, I don't take it lightly.
Those who say it mean it. A Pakeha-Maori
I say 'God save my Queen', and then I wish
my tribe success. I know that men must fight.
Pakeha in me says, 'We can take New Zealand
but only if we get our strategy right.'
Maori answers, 'Our ally is the land –
we will drag their mana down, and the white Queen's law.'
I think who wins is right. I salute the victor.
It's long since Lizard Skin, old warrior chief,
his death-bed eyes burning because he foresaw

this conflict, gave to his kin these words I offer
to both sides now: 'Be brave, that you may live!'

1860 The Soldier

Our job, he said, was to take the battle forward.
Tight-tied, the thin brown sticks of their outer fence
gave nothing away. Our biggest guns had answered
a haka that shook the trees. We charged into silence.

St Mary Redcliffe and the docks of Bristol
were home. They told me stories of savage chiefs
disciplined to trade, reading the Bible.
I took the shilling. Mother hid her grief.

Their fire came up at us under the palisade.
Right of me, then left, soldiers went down.
When we took the pa it was empty. Wounded, I bled.
Settlers blame us for defeats. Trapped in their town
they will bury me, somewhere inscribe my name
and soon forget. The medal I won will go home.

1861 The Boy

Storm Bird out in the roads. Must we wait
till morning for news and mail? My editor father
and the port health officer sail a dinghy out.
Just five years old, I crouch quiet in the stern.

I remember vastness of plains and air like a window
that let you see them. Nothing happened, it seemed,
nor ever would, except that into our harbour
ships brought stories of cities, wars and crimes.

The port-holes shine, mysterious caves of light.
A shout to us from the deck, solemn over water –
what does it mean? – '*Death of the Prince Consort.*'
'The Queen's husband has died,' my father whispers.

A year later with six hundred children I walked
through muddy streets of Christchurch. It was to honour
the Prince of Wales' wedding. Did anyone speak
of war in Taranaki? Not that I remember.

1864 The Warrior

Not the taste of peach but its hard wrinkled stone
to suck on, bite. It's so quiet in this grove,
the autumn air so still, peach leaves, apple leaves
falling. I think the dead come to me here –
the woman lost, her child, my uncle, cousins.

Three days they shelled us, stormed, sapped –
we drove them back. What was it made two hundred,
facing two thousand, so resolute for death?
Those Tuhoe, mad for battle, put us here.
Rewi kept us. 'Ka whawhai tonu ake!'

Chewing raw kumara, licking dew from grass,
counting bullets – and then, by daylight, the breakout!
Orakau seemed to hold its breath as we came,
not running, one body, women at the centre,
warriors at the front. My heart thumped in my throat.

Eyes shut among the peach trees I see them again,
their bayonets ready. Only Death could stop me.
He was busy with my friends – I got away.
The Pakeha cursed – and praised us. Was it worth it?
Is life worth it, e hoa? Ake! Ake!

1869 The War

12 April *The Raid*

From a low hill I saw the Ringatu pennon
black and white in the sun. Inside the stockade
were women, old men. Warriors? At most a dozen
and my father's friend, Mr Hill. They were fighting hard

244

but it couldn't last. I think I ran in fear.
Next day I met some soldiers dragging two guns
that stuck in sand. They'd spent the night drinking beer
in an abandoned house – Mr Finlayson's.
'Too late for guns,' I told them. 'Take your spades.'
That day we found poor Mr and Mrs Lavin
in front of their house, arms round each other, dead –
their two small boys dead also. I walked to the river
and washed my face and watched the water running.
My fear was gone. Now truly I wanted this war.

14 April *The Colonel*

The Press complain of defeats. They say his men
call him 'Gravedigger'. He answers that all such slanders
are only the other face of our settler fears,
and needless! – already Te Kooti's power is broken.
We praise him. Over dinner he talks of his acres.
His wife shoots like a trooper. He tells us she rode
dispatches for him when Panapa's rebels tried
to take the Coast. From Auckland he has sent her
live rabbits, pheasants and bees for their estate;
blackberry also, and gorse. Oak and elm
are growing well. They want it to look like Home.
He raises his glass. 'But luxuries must wait.
Gentlemen, I drink to a nation in the making.
This war must be won.' He rides south in the morning.

1875 **The Girl**

Here come the stores. Three days it takes the drover
from Timaru. With them he brings the *Cornhill*
and *Illustrated London News*. 'How could anyone'
(my mother asks) 'feel isolated here?
These pictures keep us abreast.' She lets me look.
I see the late Prime Minister Palmerston's whiskers,
Dizzy's curls, Gladstone, the Paris Commune.

Our neighbours have a bathroom lined with pictures –
the Queen, her Windsor castle, Piccadilly.
They have American plumbing – a big bath fixed

to the floor. The water runs out through a hole.
New Zealand's Premier is Mr Julius Vogel.
I saw him in Dunedin, sitting in a chair
in a strawberry garden. I thought him fat and greedy.

My father comes from England. Once, in Timaru,
I saw him waving his hat at a dot in the sky,
running, shouting 'Hurrah!'. It was the first skylark
he'd seen in New Zealand. He did a cartwheel.
This morning ice from the eves has glassed the veranda.
Sunlight rainbows through. I look at the pictures
waiting for the thaw that will let us see the hills.

24 January 1884 The Visit

Up early churning, I hope to sell my butter
tenpence per pound to campers on Waihi Beach.
A crowd, all Maori, gathers at our gate.
I'm told it is Te Kooti – a sort of royal tour.

I signal welcome and he steps from his buggy
flanked by armed protectors. My son Mervyn's
childish nightmares were all of this rebel prophet.
On the veranda Mervyn hongis with his dream.

My visitor asks for beer. All I can offer
is tea – a billyfull – and scones for his party.
The rest, I say, can pick flowers from my garden.
They do, decorating their hair and horses.

The hard old killer, pardoned but never safe,
sits in my drawing room holding a china cup.
My house, he tells me, is ka pai – and he smiles
at something in his head I cannot guess at.

This night I have dreamed of the children of Israel.
Woken, I listen to the river rushing over rocks
under pines in the gorge. Somewhere above the rapids
inhuman voices are raised in lamentation.

1889 The Gentleman

Was her face dirty – or bruised? Her heavy swag
had rolled into the gutter. The child was silent.
A crowd had gathered. Some thought she might be drunk.
'Not fit to be a mother,' a mother declared.
I bent over her. She whispered that she had fainted.
I helped them into a cab and got in with them.
She was pale and pretty – poor, but respectable.
She said her drunken husband, home from the gumfields,
had beaten them both. She'd gone in search of a friend
but failed to find her at her former address.
All day, without money or food, they'd carried the swag
until she'd fallen. With the cabby's help we soon
located the friend. I gave her a pound and my card.
Today, I wait in my office. I know she will call.

1889 The Empire

Khaki tunics, riding trousers, leggings,
tents and bugles: I lie up here on the ridge
over Newton Park. Cabbies offer their horses
and a vet. checks them. He looks into the mouth,
waves a handkerchief at one eye, then at the other,
puts a rider up. Mostly they fail at the jumps.

At yesterday's rally Mr King Dick Seddon made
a speech about the Empire. We all cheered madly.
The Otaki Band, St Patrick's College Band,
the Garrison Band, Wellington College cadets,
the Fire Brigade, the Police Outriders and Cyclists –
all marched. The crowd sang 'Soldiers of the Queen'.

In the book I'm reading the bugler is a boy,
but that was long ago. My brother's mount
is a chestnut mare. He lets me hold his revolver.
My sisters have joined the Company of Amazons.
On our map of South Africa mother moves red pins.
I play 'Bash the Boers' along Tinakori Road.

1908 **The Actress**

On the river it seemed it was always late afternoon,
summer, and quiet. Our oars clunked in their rowlocks,
willows trailed green streamers on a perfect surface
reflecting our drifting through suburban gardens
in lovely hats, as if all life were a poem
composed in Edward's England and enacted
dreamily here at the farthest reach of his Empire.

Oaks, playing fields, the spire of Christchurch cathedral,
and the Port Hills – I could see it all from a tree
behind our house. How thrillingly more-than-English
our visitor declared! But when I looked to the north
across forty miles of the Plains on a clear day
the Southern Alps stared back, white in the sun.
To see so far – it was frightening. This wasn't England.

It was then I decided everything was unreal –
everything but the theatre. It was all theatre,
and they in far places, the great executors
of the world's will – they didn't know they were players!
The Alps spoke to me, beautiful, hard and cold
against that blue which goes up and away for ever.
I answered as I could, in the language of Shakespeare.

August 1915 **The Commanding Officer**

Irish-English and Catholic, I hoped for glory
fighting in Europe for Britain against the Hun.
I found it leading a force of New Zealanders
against the stubborn Turk defending his homeland.

Twelve hundred yards of open ground we crossed
shelled and machine-gunned, keeping our intervals,
pace even, no shot fired until I gave the order.
The British watched. They called us the White Gurkhas.

I wanted a clean force, moral, disciplined, strong.
I thought my men should fear me – didn't foresee
that I would love them and war have no other purpose,
or none greater, than our brotherhood in death.

I had posted Ruskin: 'In war, waste never a moment' –
but how is a moment wasted? Beyond my trench
eight acres of corpses shimmered and droned in the heat.
I looked for wild-flowers, wrote of them in my journal.

Yes we took Chunuk Bair and, unsupported
(just seventy-six surviving of seven hundred),
lost it. A British gunner delivered my death.
A gateway in Taranaki remembers my name.

1917 The Mother

Widowed, I came north with three small girls.
A nail was all it took – a gash that swelled
and he with it, three days. He died in pain.
Despair was my bitter secret, married again
for need, not love, to a Gospel-harsh
and mortgaged farmer. I bore him a boy.

Owen Vincent Freeman – how his names glow
on the bronze plaque, as if we had foreseen
death and glory. 'He died for Freedom and Honour.'
I see his little legs running to school
over frosty paddocks. I can forgive so much
but never this. The blast took off his head.

These green hills of Kamo – see how the sun
shines on them after rain. Two of my girls
are buried in the churchyard, Owen in France.
I listen to the tui, smell cut grass,
read and remember. If I believe in God
there's no love lost. Here, we are out of touch.

Cornwall 1918 The Expatriates

The Painter

A great war, my country sending young men –
a nephew, a niece's husband, sons of friends –
and all my commerce still with canvas and paint.

To a woman committed as I, which matters most,
Art, or this conflict? Seagulls under my window
articulate the quarrel I have with myself.
Last week I watched a young New Zealand woman,
a writer, I'm told, whose brother died in France.
She was struggling into the wind. I wanted to say
'Go home! The cost is too high' – but who am I
to give advice I never would have taken?
We smiled vaguely as strollers used to do
on Lambton Quay – everyone someone's friend,
or friend of a friend. I know she was thinking of home.

The Writer

Strange, but I go on seeing this empty building
as my father's office. If I shut my eyes and sniff
I see the wooden goods-lift with its tarred ropes.
Out there the sea is unreal, like liquid metal;
the wind a 'Wellington' wind – everything flying –
yet not the same. Rudderless birds dash by
as I walk along the seafront. I shield my head.
But the voice of the sea at night is universal –
it takes me across the world. Not far from here
there's a woman making her name as a painter –
Anne says she's from New Zealand. We pass in the street.
It gives me courage to see her, but we don't speak.
Could I talk to her of my 'undiscovered country' –
or of my only brother, buried in France?

1925 The District Nurse

Chicken, pipi, puha, kumara, peaches,
all in flax kits piled up on my kitchen table –
this was my welcome back from a week up the coast.
But where was Turi? The family shack was empty.
Worried, I followed the track through manuka
up-hill to the tohunga house. They were all there –
Turi stretched out on a mat in front of the curtain,
a ha'penny tied to his arm in a dirty rag,
pulse weak, sweating, the breath rasping in his throat.

'Hospital,' I told them – there wasn't a moment to lose.
No one answered. No one would meet my eye.
From behind the curtain the tohunga spoke in Maori
with spells, and naming herbs – and then to me:
'The Maori goes to the Pakeha hospital
only to die. Turi's people will save him.'

I argued, cajoled, threatened – all no use.
They were sad, frightened, knew how I loved their boy,
but that tapu voice from behind the tatty curtain
had power. In useless rage I returned their gifts.

Today is the tangi. I hongi with Turi's mother.
We hug one another and weep. When they've buried him
they'll feast and sing all night. They've taken a cake
to the tohunga house and left it in front of the curtain.

1929 The Immigrant Artist

Last night I met the Capital's captains of Art –
old Nugent Welch with his blue, watercolour eyes,
Colonel Carbery, Mrs Tripe. But Isobel Field
I'm told controls the purse-strings. She was heard to say
she thought me handsome – 'A pity his work is not.'

This morning I climbed the streets. Paint peeled from boards,
iron rusted, concrete stairways cracked and slipped
and weeds pushed through. Part of me longed for home.
But scent of fennel and this hard unbroken light
on broken branches – they made me see fresh pictures.

From the cable Car I looked down on a tumbling town,
a deep harbour, mysterious glittering hills.
The Colonel, the Tripe and the Field – all were dissolved
in air and light. No it's not the Promised Land
but a land of promise. I am choked with foolish hope.

1932 The Student

Lights on water. Under-echo. Wharves.
What madness has us here, swimming at midnight
naked, waiting for a ferry? A red-tipped mast
wags at us like a finger. I see the hull
of a white cruise ship. I want to travel –
Covent Garden, La Scala. The vast stars approve.

Tonight has sung the soul of Marguerite
to heaven – one of the oppressed made whole.
Bourgeois Faust has damned himself. I saw
in Mephistopheles, not devil, but History!
He offers gifts at a price. The choice is ours.
Karl Marx, even in water I don't neglect you!

Six months ago I stood at John Courts corner
watching the silent, glum, suffering columns
go by up Queen Street. Tears seemed insufficient.
I gave myself to their Struggle. This was no opera.
Now music, stars, water, friendship seduce me.
Do revolutionaries laugh? We miss our ferry.

1939–45 The War

1940 *The Wife*

Girls croon outside the booth, 'Enlist today!'
They tap-dance, hand out pamphlets. A tinny speaker
plays Tiny's speech: 'The spirit of Anzac, I know
won't call in vain.' I'm proud of my volunteer,
but eight pounds a week exchanged for soldier's pay –
that's hard. It's almost five years since we met
and married for love. Will our little girl and boy
remember their father's face? Will I forget?
So far away these man-eating giant wars
that rob us – are they really New Zealand's concern?
On last home-leave he's been digging an air-raid shelter
and planting beans while I put up black-out curtains.
We cry when we kiss. Too late to say it, I know,
But I whisper in his sleeping ear, 'Don't go! Don't go!'

1941 *The Soldier*

So long since I slept so long! The slatted light
of Cairo wakes me at last. A smell like urine
mixed with exhaust comes up from the noisy street.
Under the fan, a woman's legs lock mine,
her fingers thread my hair, her Ionian eyes
open, dark as olives, surprised and smiling.
After the chaos of Crete – that sky full of paras,
our loss of the airfield, days in the rocks hiding
waiting for a boat – I think I must have forgotten
how well the body, well-treated, will treat the spirit.
Twice satisfied, I want to want her again.
I'm unsure of her name – she's a mistress, not a wife.
I love her in the way you might love the planet –
impersonally. She might be 'Beauty' – or 'Life'!

1942 *The Wife*

A quarter for Jean, a dime for little Barry,
gum-sticks for both: he was sitting looking unwanted
in Cornwall Park. We talked about the Maoris,
the olive trees that Logan Campbell planted,
the monument up on the hill. It began like that.
He was just another Marine on leave from the war
with Japan. I told him my husband had been in combat
in Greece and Crete, and now North Africa.
'It's a mad world,' he said. I must have known
what would follow – the phone-calls, flowers, scent,
kissing in taxis. If I could love two men
the same, it wouldn't have mattered. Today he sails,
and that's the end. He gave me farewell presents.
I gave him nothing. Already I'd given it all.

1943 *The Soldier*

The silence wakes me early. We're winning our war.
Under desert sky, blue-pink and pale as a shell,
tents and tanks seem welded to their shadows.
It's more like Genesis than the Gates of Hell.
Not a man in sight. I award myself a shower
in a box rigged for the General. I'm soaked and shiny

when he comes in a towel. This is a nightmare –
one ballocky soldier face to face with Tiny
in his own shower. The big man waits till I'm done,
nods and says nothing. They say when Monty complained
we didn't salute he replied we were fighting men.
'Just give them a wave,' he said, 'and they'll return it.'
As I dry myself I watch the tracks of water
down those hard white ridges of his battle scars.

1944 *The Boy*

I look at my Dad's picture. I think I remember
the day he left. His battle-dress tunic was rough
like sandpaper when he hugged me. In it somewhere
he had my goodbye present. It was a knife
with three blades and a corkscrew I used to throw
at tree-trunks so it stuck. One day I missed
and couldn't find it. I didn't let anyone know.
It seemed bad luck. If the knife he gave me was lost
it might mean he was dead. My sister says
how good it will be when our soldier-dad comes home,
but how does she know? Mum says, 'We're counting the days.'
He's in Italy now. He wrote on a card from Rome
'We'll all be glad to see an end to this war.'
I can't tell Mum, but I like things as they are.

1945 *The Soldier*

'If I should die think only this of me,
that there's some corner of a foreign field
that is for ever . . .' what? Do I say Kiwi?
The way we like to tell it, and to be told,
New Zealand's best, most prosperous, beautiful;
but something has turned my telescope about –
I see it small and mean. 'This Europe's rubble,
destroyed, *finito*' – even the Italians say it.
It isn't true. There's something here that soothes me.
I've buried mates, and killed a man so near
I could smell his breath. I don't want scenery
and a prosperous suburb. On the Via Flaminia
the whores are tough, unsentimental, funny.
They live without hope. That means they live without fear.

1945 *The Explanation*

I try to give them the scene: Crete under starlight,
our troops moving to attack, the flash and thud of a mine
and their son horribly wounded. 'Finish it, Major,'
he says in pain – the worst moment of my life.

Those mines were ours and laid without my orders.
The stone scarps and caverns echoed his moaning.
At any moment an enemy unit might come
and abort our mission. I drew my revolver . . .

The Tribe's elders treat me with grave respect
but the makutu stands. I am to suffer their curse,
I and my children's children, not for his death
but because I fired at the head. The head is sacred.

Down the long road that's fringed with toetoe and flax
a big surf booms like guns. These sad bronze Popes
have delivered their kind of excommunication
on a Pakeha soldier. Absurdly, I salute them.

The parents say goodbye. Do they weep for their son,
or for the one who answered to his last request?
Why should I fear? I was cursed before I came here.
We are all cursed. I merely pulled the trigger.

1945 *The Anniversary*

Here's the *Star* photograph – my parents heading the group
to the tomb on Bastion Point. Holding her hat,
her head dipping in the wind, my mother smiles.
She carries flowers. My father is Chairman of the Party.

Five years ago he hoisted me high on his shoulders
to see the coffin of our late exalted leader
covered with a flag and flowers borne on a gun-carriage
to the beat of a drum to its burial on this headland.

255

My mother lays her wreath, Dad makes his speech.
I peer through dusty windows. In the cold tomb
you can see the concrete casing shaping the coffin.
He's in there alone in the horrible silence of his fame.

He never framed a sentence anyone remembers.
He kept Death waiting until the news was whispered –
his rival, a writer of power, expelled from the Party.
His legend lives on, but so does the scallywag writer.

1947 *The Orchestra*

So thin, my school-friend's mother, I had her confused
with Olive Oyl. His father had muscles like Popeye.
Each evening, heading home, he passed our house.
A cabinet-maker, his shirt was always open,
his chest hairy. In a room where three brass balls
swung in the globe of a clock, he played the flute.
My cousin played the oboe. It made our spaniel
lift snout and howl. She practised the Dvorak solo
from the 'New World'. Mum accompanied on the Grand.
All that was during the War. Years later I heard
for the first time our National Orchestra.
There was my cousin at the oboe, and at the flute
starch-fronted and bow-tied, the cabinet maker!
Defeated Germany lived again in the woodwinds.

1951 *The Wharfie*

'Good morning, good morning, good morning everyone!' –
out of the mouths of new State houses spread over
the green and gorse of my youth, the voice of 'Aunt Daisy'.
Housewives are pegging their washing to the wind
and vacuuming their halls. From school sash windows
comes the chant of times tables. A man not working
feels awkward here. I put my felt hat on
and walk to the shops and take a tram to town.

Is it ten years since the gun we called Mickey Savage
died at Sidi Rezegh? What a team we were! –
that rhythm of loading and sighting, sighting and firing –
six of us, then five, four – their tanks closing,
machine guns . . . Something like a white hot shovel
bashed me into a ditch. My war was over.

We make tea in the wharf-shed and play chess.
One hundred days we've been out, no end in sight,
the public howling for blood, the Press muzzled,
Syd Holland riding the airwaves. My kids need shoes,
bills are unpaid, food short. I feel it again –
that dark taste of defeat. Poor Mickey Savage
you must die again. Poor mates. Poor wounded self.
I win at chess. When will I win at life?

Christmas 1953 **The Queen**

Strange flowers and shrubs, nice lawns, a big flame-tree
planted by Governor Grey; a Georgian façade
all wood, but well-designed in the eighteen-fifties
to look like stone; French windows opening on a terrace –
this is Government House, Auckland. Daylight brings word
of a frightful event: the lake in a mountain crater
broke out and flooded a river which in turn destroyed
a viaduct just as the night express passed over.

One hundred and fifty dead. My Christmas broadcast
is being redrafted. This morning a children's choir
sang in the garden. My standard is flying half-mast.
A Father Christmas is waiting down below
sweating in his flannel and fur. I talk to Mother
long-distance. She says it's cold, but no sign of snow.

Rome 1960 The Athlete

Two years ago on a visit I prayed to the gods
of Olympus. They listened. They promised victory.
After that it was home to Auckland's steepest roads –
Mt Roskill, Waiatarua, Waitakere.
You learn to push through pain as through a mirage
and keep on pushing. Specs ran with me, and Peter.
Arthur kept at us – always for greater mileage.
A three-lap sprint to finish five thousand metres
is the greatest distance the human mind can travel.
They let me go. Only a man who'd been told
by the gods to do it would break so soon in a final.
The crowd was my rainbow. There at its end lay gold
and my own body, discarded, sprawled on the track,
watched, so it seemed, from above, and wearing black.

1971 The Revolution

Sexy with grass, groggy with sex, and happy
I sit on the floor among cushions picking out a song:
'Vietnam is a War. Two men have walked on the moon.'
He loves my playing, loves my singing, loves me.
Out there old birch trees blaze; we have a garden
of weeds and wildflowers; a gully of ginger and fennel.
This house, once white, grows out of green like a mushroom.

I want him again. He rolls on his back, playing dead.
He's thirty-eight, my professor – 'middle-aged'
I tell him. He says it's true, and he'll be middle-aged
still when I'm old. I tell him that will be never.
Cat-like I lick him, I croon in corners of his body
'Vietnam is a war. Two men have walked on the moon.'
You can't love more than this. The world will have to change.

Down the gully, he tells me, one day a motorway will come
and sweep us aside – old houses, derelict gardens,
our hair and beads and beards, our protest banners.
Only our songs will survive up there where today
tree-branches print themselves on a page so blue

it swims with my tears, it smiles because I'm singing
'Vietnam is a War. Two men have walked on the moon.'

31 August 1974 The Private Secretary

These months always one question: was he really dying
or were my fears groundless? In India last year
he collapsed in his room. He shook, could scarcely speak,
saw a vision of his mother, refused a doctor.
I stayed awake all night, thinking him dead.
Next day he made the most moving speech of the tour.

So it went on. Last April when he needed rest
why did he think of travelling up the Wanganui
to Baxter's grave? Then it was the Bay of Islands.
He phoned me nightly in pain. No one was to know.
Coming home he lay on the back seat of his car
coughing blood-balls while they drove it into a transport.
His doctor, a Nat, described him as 'uncomplaining'.

The specialist wouldn't make house-calls. 'You're the P.M.'
I reminded him. He smiled. 'And this is New Zealand.'

Driving home in May he hit the curb four times.
When he sneezed, his nose bled; when he urinated
the bowl was scarlet. 'Four P.M.s have died in office,'
Truth crowed. He quoted that in a Conference speech
and added, 'Some who didn't had to be prodded
to check they were really alive.' Sixty-nine words
in a shaky hand his speech-notes. It rallied the Party.

Tonight we have it – the answer to my question.
In his last phone-call he told me he was happy.
I drove away up the coast and watched hang-gliders
soar up and out over water in the winter sun.

25 July 1981 **The Clergyman**

What stays in mind is the scrape of boots charging
the perimeter fence, and staples flying like chaff.
Like the parting of the Red Sea, the shocked crowd opens
a path to the centre. They take it. They take the field!
Now thirty thousand are howling for their blood.
Nothing to be done but lock their arms and hold
while police in visored helmets with new long batons
close and threaten. Watching, I am weak with fear.
It's not recorded what Daniel does in the den.
The stone closes, the king seals it with his ring,
and a night passes. Does Daniel sing, pray,
talk to the lions? Does he remember his brothers
who walked through fire with the Lord? The game is cancelled.
On my knees in mud I give thanks for this victory.

10 July 1985 **The Secret Agent**

Ten *bon points* were rewarded with a *belle image*.
I earned them for my project on the Pacific.
I was nine. I called it 'Our region of Romance'.
The people, brown and gentle, skilled at fishing,
sang at night under palm-trees beside lagoons.
Gauguin painted them – I should have looked more closely.

Out there's the Pacific and I hate it. Blustery squalls
blow in across the harbour. I long for Paris –
cafés, good bread, good wine, good conversation.
I didn't seek this mission. I wanted a child.
When I say I think there's a watcher in the yacht-house
Alain's shrug is angry. Nothing to be done but wait.

Here's the Zodiac back, but now the tide's so low
we can't get it up. *Désastre*! – we leave it moored
in Hobson Bay and scatter. Just before midnight
the first bomb shakes the city. The second is louder.
Was I born to fester here in a Third World prison
poisoned by English food? I pray no one has died.

1990 At the Grave of Governor Hobson

You started it all. Here for you it ended.
Here it goes on. A bridge over Grafton Gully
casts morning shadow. A motorway shaves the graveyard
and crops it back. Through oaks and undergrowth
the interrupted light on broken gravestones
writes and erases itself. Further down
was once a stream. Sometimes a former someone,
drunk, derelict, or dead by misadventure,
was found there. It was our forest in the city
with paths and dangers – most of it now cut down.

Immemorial aunts, great uncles, cousins
I'm told are here. A still decipherable headstone
remembers my forebear who walked behind your coffin
and five years later joined you under the oaks.
Your children went back to England. We remained
to inherit your city and that distrusted Treaty
you made as instructed by those who would later call it
'little more than a legal fiction'. Your dearest Liz
took home her title to two hundred Auckland acres,
prospered, a widow in Plymouth, and didn't remarry.

Shadow pickets fall on the raised white slab
that marks your grave. A Caribbean pirate
once put a noose to your neck, then changed his mind
and set you adrift without sail. You lived to die
at a desk in a dream of Auckland, clouded by
headaches that came from the south. A riderless horse
was led behind the coffin eight sailors carried.
All day the tribes lamented. 'Send us no boy,'
a Chief wrote to the Queen, 'nor one puffed up,
but a good man as this Governor who has died.'

'Remote,' they called it; 'lacking natural advantage.'
That you chose the Waitemata, that your choice attracted
artisans from the south, that from this site
you asserted your right to govern – these were facts
the Wakefields wouldn't forgive. 'It is not my purpose,'
you wrote, 'that I should disparage Port Nicholson,
but only, against deceptions, to say that I find
here a more genial climate, more fertile soil.'

No people chooses its history. Doubting our own,
we can say at least in this we know you were right.

Our chopper-cops go over eyeing Auckland.
From a car radio a voice I'm sure belongs
to Kiri te Kanawa skies itself through branches
with 'Let the Bright Seraphim . . .' Under the bridge
Maori street kids have tuned their ghetto-blaster
to Bobby Brown. A boy sniffs glue from a bag
beneath his jacket. Messages on the arch
in well-schooled spray-can read 'King Cobras Rule'
and 'The Treaty is a Fraud'. Governor, all about you
for better and worse, your memorial goes on growing.

Last night, yellow as butter, an outsize moon
sailed over the ridge of Parnell. In Emily Place
it picked the obelisk out that marks the place
where you laid the first stone for the first St Paul's;
it gilded the six-lane highway, once a track,
where you used to lead your Lila and her schoolfriend
Harriet Preece, and lift them over the ditch;
it laid a lily of light on 'this beautiful spot
on the slope of a wooded valley looking to the sea,'
once yours and, given to the city, yours again.

Let today be all the days we've lived in New Zealand:
stench of whale meat, a rat cooked on a spit,
morning boots frozen hard, the southern Maori
ravaged by measles, rum, Te Rauparaha;
wars in the north, gumfields, forests falling
to ruminant grassland, cities climbing like trees;
and everywhere this language both supple and strong.
You didn't start it, Governor. As we do, you fashioned
what time, and the times that live in us, required.
It doesn't finish. These verses have no end.

from *Straw into Gold: Poems New and Selected*

1997

America

1 *Angel, L.A.*

She used to sit on that springy turf
among sprinklers behind the house
                          under one tall
                                palm
                              waiting
for sundown
                for a breeze from the sea
                      for a studio call.

'Scratch these gardens'
                      Bertholdt told her
'you discover the desert.'

                  He loved its ugliness –
'A city that has no heart
                  and so many angels.'

The day the spies were to die
                    in the electric chair
Mrs Rosenberg in her black hat
Mr Rosenberg with his little
                              moustache
            she sat on a seawall
      watching the sun quench itself
                  like a fat orange
                  like a dying swan.

She could neither think of them
      nor shut them from her thoughts.

'Look homeward, Angel' –
            she said it over and over
              looking south and west
west and south
to what she thought
                was New Zealand.

2 *The Traveller*

I fucked her
                    (the traveller said)
while the hotel next door
was burning.

We could see people
                    across the gap
              blocked on the ninth –

down below
         fire-trucks   cops a crowd
long ladders
flashing lights.

              Soon came the guys
in silver space suits
            and the smash of glass.

Half-woken
                 half-asleep
she stood
on the Bay Area directories
            so we could make it
at the window.

It might have been
             death out there.
Nothing we could do.
            In here it was us
fucking.

             It was great
(the traveller said)
            she was small
lovely
an angel –

        never told me her name.

3 *Phoenix, Arizona*

Waking to the desert stillness
                    is how it might be
if this were Paradise
its green and glowing gardens
                        its air containing
nothing but air
                             its sky
nothing but sky
                    a light like only
light can be
                    when it's only
everywhere
itself
                    and coming up east
                    the fiery wrath-cart
eternal unforgiving
                    forger and spoiler
Lord of all.

4 *Moving East*

It was the white stretch
                            took you
            from the town of the Hassidim
shovelling snow in their big hats
through Princeton, Brick
                    and Lakewood
by the Turnpike to Staten Island.

Across water
                  against a grey page of sky
Manhattan was the ghostly
                      graph of itself.

Now
                  among the yellow cabs
black hustlers
pastrami-and-gherkin delis
                  in freezing rain
that hangs white fingers on street-signs
you look for a bookshop that knows you.

You have lived here most of your life
dream-man
                              best boy at the movies.

It's New York, yes –
it's the world.

5 *Lullaby*

It's called the Memory Station
                                        and it plays
'the greatest music of all time'
                            meaning 'top of the charts
                                    '40s through '60s.'

My memories too –
                                not 'the greatest'
but the half-life an ear had
                              while we were making
love
breakfast
                              worrying about work
                                          the kids
the missile crisis –

Sinatra for example
                              who could only ever
get worse

                        the King who could sing
really –
and Bing.

Strange to have come
                          half a world to recover
                                    the Inkspots
                                    Mills Brothers
Platters
                          Simon and Garfunkel
                          and that cruisy-dreamy
laid-back tremolo blow-job
Dean Martin singing

'Everybody
loves somebody
somehow . . .'

At night here
in my nun-narrow bed
while snow falls
                all down the Jersey Shore
I give it twenty minutes
                            pre-set
'the Memory Station' –
                my white noise
my time machine.

6 *'It is only at the hour of darkness that the owl of Minerva descends.'*

One of the Hassadim
walks ahead of me
down the centre
of a snowbound road
muttering prayers
under his big hat.

There's no traffic
and no sky –
only a grey lid
and this tumbling
drifting
brightness of snow.

On the lake shore
waterbirds
huddle in the lee
where a stony Virgin
outstares
a marble boy.

In converted stables
where scions once
played indoor polo
students will serve me
hot soup
and good cheer.

Is it Wisdom says to me
'Don't whine in the cold
because the party's
almost over.
Come in!
Have one for the road.'

7 *I've seen the future and it's OK*

Cal in Santa Monica
Gail in Lakewood, New Jersey
Helen in Boston
I e-mail you greetings from Auckland
knowing they will reach you
the day before they were sent.

This is the kind of conundrum
I used to discuss with Albert
before dementia sent him
into the Seventh Dimension.

Albert, you remember,
was the one with the Theory
that if you sent a Relative
(your Granny, for example)
deep enough into Space
she would come back
looking like Marilyn
Monroe.

We all wanted to believe him.

Happy Christmas, friends –
it's a good one
and on its way to you
right now!

Catullus Again

1 *Clodia*

             I used to call her
my Pillar of Salt.

               I told her
she was like a dog
        a hell-hound
fed on dry bones.

I put it about that she shat
just ten times a year
        so dry and so small
she could crumble a turd
        in her fingers
    without needing to wash.

I said there was no smell
           but soap
and an odour of sanctity.

      I said when she died
she would go straight to
heaven
wafted on blasts
      from a Lowry Organ
tuned to exalt.

        It was all true
more or less.

        What a bitch!
        How I loved her!

2 *Ode to Emptiness*

With its blue crackling paper
two cameras
        monitor and lights

                              the crew arrives
at the house of Catullus.

Vacuous will follow
in his own good time.

                    A makeup girl
who says she once cut
Caesar's hair
                              lays out her gear
on the kitchen table
                              and goes to work.

                    The cat decamps.
A neighbour stares from his window.
            He can see an unknown girl
touching the face
of his neighbour the poet.

Made up to look like himself
    Catullus escapes to the bathroom
while they set up shot.

                    In preparation
for the emptiness of the medium
he empties himself.

                    Across the street
meeting demands for silence
tree-cutters have cut
            their chainsaws and shredder
for the any-moment-now
            when Vacuous will begin
'Since we last spoke
                    on this programme
Catullus . . .'

3 *The Invitation*

                    Brother in poetry
25 years ago
        my scribbled note was meant

                    to entice you away
from her whose sense of form
was such (they said)
she paid you

                              caresses
                         for sonnets
sex for sestinas.

            She was right of course –
half right.
            The gods had given you
a silver tongue
but a damaged heart.

You should have answered my call
Hemi.
                  Talking to Catullus
would not have launched you
so early into the dark.

4 *Honoris Causa*

                        Cornificius
            whose 'mighty pohutukawa'
tower over the suburb
        earns praise for his stout defence
of the native flora.

                  This is one honour
he might have had to forego
if their shadow condemned his house
to damp and darkness in winter.

                  Since it falls however
exclusively on his neighbours
                        he is able to enjoy
                        the acclamation
with a clear conscience.

5 *Dogs I* (*Society of Authors*)

Calvus of miniscule talent
makes friends with all
        the neighbourhood dogs
           – it's his policy
to become one of them –
one of the boys.

           Some are easy
they wag and roll over.
           Others snarl
       and bare their teeth –
he has to work on them
crouching
        not meeting the eye
pushing forward a vulnerable hand
        as if it were a snout.

Does he offer his arse for sniffing
when there's no one about –
his balls for licking?

      Why do you want so much
Calvus
       to be loved by the whole
canine community?

6 *Dogs II* (*Calvus replies*)

Jealous Catullus
      with his two mangy cats
and his thwarted love
       for a famous bitch
sees me two days in succession
     on my haunches in the street
      talking to a nervous dog
and down it goes in his notebook –
   image of a man hungry for love!

      No Catullus
it has to do with childhood

                    the feel of fur
                    smell of it wet
sound of bones
                    crunched in the yard
and yes OK
those big doggy eyes
sad and loving.

No I don't think they're human
                    or that I'm a dog
                    but isn't there a kind
of planetary kinship –
          all of us in the same lovely boat
          under the same harsh sentence?

                    Give over Catullus
               stop playing the lone wolf.
Living's our only offence.
We do it together.

7 Soror, Aue atque Uale

In the refectory
Quintilia
                    in squares and gardens
once in the London Library
                    often in Soho
over dim sims
and duckling in ginger
                    Catullus heard it all –
your griefs, your dislikes
even sometimes your envies –
                    listened moreover
(and with what pleasure!)
                    as you recounted
twist upon turn of invention
to the unfolding
of your latest fable.

But since the Wheel of Fortune
                    hoisted you high
                    he sees you no more.
His unanswered letters

his recorded messages
           that receive no replies
remind him of a bitter truth –
she who has Fame for companion
           will feel less need of a friend.

           Best of luck then
                   Quintilia
enjoy your hour and your day.
                   Catullus
           wishing you well
           grants you for ever
this small corner
in a sacred place.

8 *Like*

Young poets before us
Licinius
                   had done as we did
all those years ago
                   working together
finding words in wine
           wit in one another
                   a clever rhyme
a metaphor
the mot juste.

I remember walking home
too late for the trams
                   too poor for a taxi
           holes in my shoes
letting in water
thinking what a marvellous
meal
           words made of the world
of the real.

           It was like love
                   like war
like nothing else –

like poetry.

9 *Si quicquam cupido optantique . . .*

Longed for so long
no longer expected
look! – you're back
rarer than gold
than hen's teeth
whom I in my need
denied
derided.

More mysterious
Muse
in your return
than ever in your absence
see what you've done –
a notebook almost full
poem after draft of poem!

Here to stay
or gone tomorrow
Clodia
what can I do
but bow the knee
what can I say
but welcome!

Dreaming Real

1 *Remember?*

Hotel Récamier
Place St Sulpice
a dream ago
when Scorpia held a hand-gun
to your head
and asked
would you die for love.

You called it a loaded question.

You were afraid
not so much of a bullet
                as of a woman
        like the throw of a dice
that could bring you luck
or disaster.

It might have been a scene
                from an old movie –
real people pretending
to be real –
or just one poet's
                idle imagining.

                'Tread carefully
for you tread on my dreams.'

2 Words

        He saw them as leaves
filling the window in summer

in autumn
as golden
abundant showers.

        I saw them as the glass
                (a shadow of itself)
        through which the leaves

appeared.

3 The real thing

This was the dream –
                the moon a big
                        complete
circle
yellow as
                no not butter
but as the moon is

except there was one
small
perfect
triangle
clipped out of it
through which could be seen
the darkness of forever.

Not a ball then
not at all
but as we'd known it
in childhood
a flat disk
a coin of gold paper
local
ours
in our own sky
and rising
over the Bay.

4 *Angel, 1959*
Fellini's La Dolce Vita

Marcello in the wind
sees her across the inlet
calling something.

'Non capisco' he mouths
and she smiles
her angel smile
pointing to her brows.

Is she telling him
he has horns?
that he's becoming
a devil?

Across the agitation of waters
his eyes
rest on her.

'Non capisco' –
he says it again

                  shrugs
waves
and turns away to where
            his wild friends
from the all-night riot
are drifting back to the woods.

          Dead on the sand
God outstares the light
with a blind
            glaucous eye.

          It doesn't matter –
nor should Marcello grieve
that innocence once lost
           is gone for ever.

         She has shown him
that beauty is particular
             unqualified
             absolute
             eternal –

that it is real.

5 *Lit Crit*

He dreamed he was the world's
          best-dressed Bedouin
with girls for guards –

or the Wizard of Ozymandius
         in a Disneyland desert
              crying

'Look on my works ye Mighty
and despair!'

Personae

1 *Ludwig*

'What we can't speak about'
Wittgenstein told us
'we must pass over
in silence.'

I asked him
how absolute was the silence
of passing over.
Could we not speak about

being unable to speak?
When I suggested
we discuss this further
over lunch

he said he didn't lunch.
He preferred to nibble
dry toast alone
on the banks of the Cam.

2 *Adolf*

Germany, the 1920s –
                   Hugh Walpole
English novelist
            (born in Auckland)
planning a walk down the Rhine
                is prevailed upon
by German friends to take
a 'returned soldier'
                they say is in need
of R & R.

Later Walpole reports
            that his friends' friend
was mainly silent –
but in the evenings

                    at supper on the terrace
                            above the river
or drinking beer in a cellar
he might do surprising
imitations
                    especially of Jews.

'A bit mysterious'
                Walpole remarks.
                'Sometimes brooding –
but as a companion?
                            No,
I had no cause for complaint.'

3 Kendrick Smithyman (1922–95)

What a poet you are
                        Death
even our loquacious smithy
falls dumb before you.

What puissance
                        finesse
                    closure!

            Hail to you
Master of our craft
                Majesty of silence!

Invention
ends here.

        For completion's sake
the story ends.

4 Jealousy
Katherine Mansfield, April 1920

Tonight the T. S. Eliots
                            to dine –
            John has just gone down
to see them off.

Tom's an angel
                    but Vivienne –
how I detest her!

                    'My husband,'
she brays –
          'Oh don't be sorry for *him*!'

And when John dropped the spoon:
'You are noisy tonight
                    my dear.
What's wrong?'

                         (Tom
leaning towards her
                    attentive
admiring.)

Later in my room
                    sprawled on a sofa
she drawled
          'The furniture's *changed*
since you came back.'

                    I shivered.
When had she been here before?

When John returns
                    and defends her
I feel I've been stabbed.

                    How could it be?
And with
          that *teashop* creature!

5 *Jealousy*
Virginia Woolf, January 1923

Katherine believed I despised her
                    as a colonial
or so she told Ottoline –
                    and it's true I wrote

after our first supper
       'She stank like a civet cat
that had taken to street walking.'

It wasn't just the perfume –
      there was something hard
               clever
inscrutable.

     Later I was in love with her
but she would have none of that.

         Now she's dead
and I can confess in my journal
      'Hers was the only writing
I was ever jealous of.'

       Oh yes but there's more
and I won't write it.
        She was the one
who could make Leonard laugh.
I caught us once in a mirror –

    Katherine with her mask-face
dark eyes
quick wit

         Leonard on fire
admiring

            and I
long-faced
lugubrious
superfluous.

        No
that I couldn't forgive –
not ever.

6 *Rupert Brooke (1887–1915)*

Just think if he'd died
            in Aotearoa
rather than Greece –
his 'corner of a foreign field
        that is forever England'
would have been right here –
  in the Waikato for example,
or Taranaki –
a clear breach of the Treaty!

He passed through in 1913
        on his way to Samoa –
            it was *that* close!

7 *Robert Graves (1895–1985)*

When his mistress jumped
from a third-floor window
he ran downstairs
and jumped from the second.

Thus he proved
his right to the title
'Great love-poet of the age'
and lived to enjoy it.

8 *Old 'G'*

When it came time for old 'G' to go
            he dug in his heels
wouldn't meet the new Head
or speak to the Board
            and left no records.

Did he not remember
        his own classroom story
                how Petronius
arbiter of taste and manners
having given offence to Nero

and knowing he must die
opened his wrists at home
closed them with plasters
and entertained his friends
telling stories
singing the old songs
letting a little more and a little more
of life leak out?

Goodbyes are hard
self-discipline harder
style hardest of all.

Poor ghost of 'G'
had you forgotten
how you thundered in Assembly
'Lessons must be learned
Gentlemen.
Go well –
learn them!'

A Discursive Poem about Poetry & Thought

'*Opinion is not worth a rush.*'
    – W. B. Yeats

Who cares what the poets think?
Shelley said they were 'unacknowledged
legislators'.
He made paper boats of his thoughts
and set them sailing
on the Thames at Marlow –
much like writing a column for *Metro*.

Today a blast from the Pole is keeping
Dunedin city indoors.
It makes the Southern Alps
put on that postcard look.
It drives the *Aratika*
back into port

285

demands chains on the Rimutakas
closes the Desert Road
and puts a dusting of snow even on the Kaimais.
It climbs the Bombay Hills and unloads
cold rain on the centre-point of the world
where my Montana Book Awards Prize Pen
touches this sheet of paper.

None of this calls for thought –
it expels it
like used air from a lung.

When I was young
I needed allegiances
which needed thought.
There was my country
my political party
the community of writers.
I was weak then, I had no self.
Now I have one and shouldn't be approached.

One day when the ache in my gut
or the pain in my head
has turned into a slavering lion
and eaten me up
someone will say, 'This is what he thought.
He was right of course
but it's no longer an issue.'

Then the poems will come into their own.
'Listen to us,' they'll say. 'The Odes of Keats
the cantos of Ezra Pound
Jim Baxter's sonnets
were our brothers and sisters.'

I still have strong opinions
like to hold forth
but it must be the poet in me says
'Thinking is what creeps up on me
when I'm not thinking.
It's the living that matters.'

Tübingen

    The leaves on the tower
that was Hölderlin's prison
        are turning red
          and gold.

Down there
    on an island in the river
huge trees are giving up
their ghosts.
In a small tavern
of crooked beams and stairs
        I eat one slice
          of onion pie
and drink one glass
of frothy
Swabian wine.

      Through the trees
dismantling themselves
looms the sculpted figure
      of a folk composer
    honoured by the Reich.

Out of his bronze pockets
from under his bronze coat
      climb men-at arms –
    the spirits or sprites
of Germany at war.

Mad Hölderlin's ghost
      35 years in his tower
        looks down
          celebrating
the lengthening shadows
and
longing for death.

Faber & Faber

There was only one Faber
but a second was added
for ballast. I am proposing
the firm should add another –
Faber Faber and Bleistein.
It would counter that cruel canard
about Tom and anti-semitism.
Faber Bleistein and Kwagongkwa
would be culturally sensitive
but perhaps excessive.

I remember back in the '50s
Tom worked at home in the mornings
writing starchy plays about clerks
and martyrdom in Africa.
Afternoons he came to the office
in Russell Square. Young Valerie
was his secretary. He married her
and the Evening Standard headline
read 'T. S. Eliot and how the Love
grew Younger than Springtime'.

It was Tom established
the Faber Poetry Principle:
'Poets are not published by us
because their work is superior.
Rather, the work is superior
because it is published by us.'
Around in Queen's Square
little Craig has maintained it,
and more recently, little Christopher.
'Life is very long,' Tom wrote
and so is the Faber list.

In the Trattoria Verdi
I sat once back-to-back
with Valerie. One of us bulged
a little, and our flesh touched.
I thought to serenade her
and hummed a tune from *Cats*
but she didn't respond.

Treasure Island

The Treaty of Waitangi
           or Treedee
as our Orange calls it –
What is it?
           the visitor asks
who hears it at midnight
in the next room
           outside the window
under the bed
           'The Treedee!'
        as in ghost-speak
'*Whooooaah. The Treedee!*'

It's a shibboleth
           I tell him
a jackup that went wrong
           a royal present
           an exploding cigar.

           It's a mantra
       a midden
     a mistake
a line from an old song
come back to haunt us.

It's a heaviness in the limbs
           a very private
             very secret
boredom.

When I call her at the library
'Kia ora Kay'
I say
           'Kia ora Karl'
             she replies
then we go out
           to an Italian
        meal or a movie.

           It's words really
I tell the visitor

or you could say
                    (taonga in cheek)
a *treasure*!

Auckland

Lovely for the long ago
child in the night
to hear the huge rain
beating on iron.

No fibre-glass muffle –
only that raw rough
sleep-inducing
din.

We've eaten the 12
jars of plums
I stewed and froze
at Christmas.

Now it's the season
for early apples
autumn dowsings
and olives.

A good crop
they drum down
into the bucket
like ancient rains.

Last Poem

'What have I to use?'
      grumbled the poet
      ugly and old.

'What have you to lose?'
      responded
      the bodiless Muse.

'Straw into gold'
      she urged him –
      'straw into gold.'

The Right Thing

2000

The Right Thing

'Have you cracked
the snowfall's code
or the language of light?

'How much honey
do the Pleiades hold?
Where is Orion unclasped?

'What is the weight
of shadow
on a hardened heart?

'How do the ten
standing orders of heaven
differ from sleep?'

'I am a sod, Lord'
Job answered correctly.
'I can answer nothing.'

Sheep were his reward,
good pasture and camels,
also daughters

and the defeat of foes –
Eliphaz the Temanite
and Bildad and Zophar.

Janet Frame's House

There's a pool table
she plans to exchange
for a desk
of the same size.

At the back are pines
and a tidal creek
with mangroves
and crabs.

Downstream
from the racecourse
a traffic bridge
rushes and whispers.

Needled grass
under the pines
remembers
summer picnics.

At full tide she says
if she had a dinghy
she could row across
for the shopping.

Indoors again
I take down a cue
from its wall-clip
and pot the black.

I too would like
such a vast desk
but secretly wish
she would keep the table.

Good Morning

To greet
after a night of frost
the oldest of the gods
alight in the mangroves
walking on water
clearing the air
all the way to the blue hills
best to behave as if
several inquisitive centuries
with their books and banks of knowledge
had passed you by.

Time is now
now is for ever
and the god is risen.

Innocent
ignorant
enjoy his hands on your face.

Ars Poetica

i

Barefoot in shallows
                        his sleeves
trousers
sodden
                        the small boy
talks to the tide
                to the water-birds
to the tall sky
                        and the Bay's
furthest reaches

                        If your words
                        could speak
his world . . .

ii

would it be enough?

                Was it Yeats who said
poems must be packed in salt?

iii

                        The birds are
migrating somewhere

They pause here
to feed and to quarrel
and the nights
        are full of their noise

iv

        Recipe for poetry
(or Spanish omelette) –

          potatoes
      green peppers
        deep oil
in a heavy pan

eggs beaten lightly
        cooked slowly

eaten cold
with white wine

v

Centre-table
the potted cyclamen
        responds to
'Reach for the skies . . .'
        or
'All in favour please raise . . .'

Its five eager hands
        in white gloves
on thin stems
    catch light from the window

vi

        The birds stand
each on one leg
        in a wind
that ruffles and nudges

>   They don't topple
>   but hop
> the favoured leg
> asleep in its feathers

vii

Vice-verse
arse-verse

>   the poem as
>   scatological
>   or obscene
> artefact

is more than
>   cocks and cunts
>   twats and dicks
> or the rhyming of bum
> with come

>   It is Martial
> Catullus
>   the Roman realists

testing
testing

viii

>   The four-year-old
> lost in a crowd
> fists in eyes
>   and wracked
> with sobs –

>   this is apocalypse
> the poem at the end of the
> world

ix

The wind has died
               and the moon
      will not settle the question

          It lies on the water
              mimicking itself
in a French accent

         'Alfred de Musset'
           it reminds me
'died young'

              and

'Where is your blue guitar?'

x

Persistence
               of the child's
rainbow and rose
             but a glory
(Wordsworth)
gone from the earth

Les Enfants du Paradis

Garance! Garance!
Come back!
She rides on in her coach.

This is the final scene.
The mime-artist
jostled by the Mardi-gras crowd
is losing her for ever.

The villain
with his villainous moustache

the contemptuous Count
the brave thespian –
each has loved her
after his fashion.

It's the mime-artist she loves
and he loves her
but Fate has determined . . .
(and so on).

Garance
with your round eyes
and your beautiful smile . . .

Garance!

Ode to a Nightingale

When one joked
she laughed
when the other
danced with her
she crooned in his ear
songs about booze
and forest murmurs
and flowers-in-the-nose
unseen in the dark.

At her door
she kissed them both
first one
who laughed again
then the other
who experienced
a moment of blackout
kiss kiss
goodbye
to comrades in arms
veterans
of magic casements.

Mercredi-Gras

What stays with me most
of that Edmonton winter
is the bitterness of wind
on the High-Level Bridge
and the whiteness of snow
on the ice of the river.

The bus drivers struck
and I walked to my office
over the bridge
wearing ear-muffs under my hat
pyjamas under my clothes
thinking about Wittgenstein
as I checked off the days.

Far below
lithe skiers threaded among trees
down to frozen water
while an orange sun-ball
too sluggish to lift itself far
hugged its pillows.

Wittgenstein was troubled
because it seemed to him
Wednesday was fat
and Tuesday lean –
not as we say that meat
is fat or lean
nor as he and his landlady
were respectively
lean and fat –
it was more (he reasoned)
a question of usage.

But the particularity
of his sense of it
the sleekness of Tuesday
and especially
the grossness of Wednesday
troubled him in the night.

Indifferent in Edmonton
Tuesdays and Wednesdays
came and went.
The bus strike ended
but even at twenty below
I went on walking
inside my pyjamas
Wittgenstein beside me
in that ear-biting wind.

John Cage at Harvard, 1988

Sonorous
he reads into a mike
a text he means should be
devoid of meaning.

In the semi-circle
of the wooden theatre
we're respectful
of his fame.

A handout explains
the trouble he has taken
to achieve
a random text.

'To have so tinged'
he intones
'my Soviet sudden change . . .'
He gives it light and shade.

Feeling floors and walls
begin to melt and slide
I cling to grammar
and to fact.

A student
scrabbles in her bag
to silence a radio
turned on by his talk.

Under a young man's legs
in the front row
an unscheduled dog
shakes itself.

Xanadu
to Helen Vendler

Drying dishes with
the teatowel
you bought me at the

Kennedy Centre
depicting (faded now)
Boston's

first church and
the ride of Paul Revere,
I remembered

a Harvard dinner
when jointly we
offended a

Catholic and a
Jew by insisting
there was no God;

recalled our
obstructing traffic
on the steps of the

Casino at Monte
Carlo while we
teased out the

'pastoral
eglantine' of the Keats
ode, and Shakespeare's

'vagabond flag upon
a stream'; and a
year later

together at Sligo's
White Swan Hotel
watching the

rush of waters
seaward from the Lake
of Innisfree.

How make a locked
box for the lady
famous for keys?

How cook for one
whose sure taste will
locate the secret

ingredient?
Rationalists, yet for whom
poems bespeak

a First World, what's
common between
us is open to

public view. No
secrets – only perhaps
a hint that

once, in a parallel
life, lissom
in Xanadu,

we may have danced
away our innocence
and the night.

Reservation

I hope you got that stuff
              about the Navaho
did you Gretchen
like your own Maori
              a highly spiritual people

                    those pottery beads
for example
and that leather thing
                    they meant something
also the way they stepped here
and stepped there
and stepped here again
                            did you notice
to the drum-beat
                    woggle woggle
                            jim jim
tittle tattle
whatever.

            My goddamn camera's
jammed Calvin
                    how about you
                    Mary-Anne
for Christssake
            what are we here for
didn't anyone get a shot?

Cartoons

8.8.96

Scientists discover
there's been life on Mars
though dead for aeons,
that's to say yonks.

President Bill says
if there's life in space
he wants the United States
to have an input.

Somewhere in Siberia
a bronze statue of Lenin
falls over
and kills a man.

Watch out for the dead!
They leave their traces –
ideas for example
and heavy statues.

12.8.96

A lost tribe is found
in the Manokwari
jungle region
of Irian Jaya.

Pale-skinned and timid
when spoken to
they hide
behind trees.

Mornings they gather
food in the forest
afternoons
they fish their lake.

Maybe they sing
at evening
omba omba
the reports don't say.

Their sentinels
are green parrots
taught to screech
when strangers approach.

13.8.96

Today it's revealed
that ex-Prime Minister
Paul Keating
kept a trampoline

in his back garden
and bounced on it
daily
to ward off cancer.

At the weightless
apogee
of each bounce
he believed

was the nanosecond
when bang!
the malignant cells
were expelled.

26.8.96

Alzheimered
Ronald Reagan
no longer remembers
he was the world's

most powerful man
carrying in a flat case
the codes
to corpse a planet.

All forgetful
he knows however
that Nancy
is his mother.

So why
after his haircut
does she lock him
in his room?

When the big light
goes down
he sits at his window
in pyjamas

hearing the moon
mumble to the hills
its threats
and rumours.

21.9.96

A Catholic Bishop
runs off with
a Mrs MacPhee
and sells his story

to the popular press
but the cash is to go
to his teenage son
by a former mistress.

His housekeeper
who used to browse
his wastepaper basket
says there were others.

Everyone's distressed.
The ailing Pope,
the nervous clergy,
the sad parishioners

of Argyll and the Isles –
even (I think)
I am distressed.
How could it be?

we ask one another.
Isn't a handjob
good enough
for the modern priest?

29.9.96

In this state
the dead man rules.
All bow at morning
to the figure in bronze,

all sing at evening
the late leader's song.
Here is the Future
as the Past saw it

and it doesn't work.
In the countryside
peasants and workers
inherit the earth

which is barren.
Evening television
offers 'ten tasty tips
for cooking grass'.

30.9.96

Faber and Faber
the beautiful woman
among publishers
has a stalker.

A disgruntled author
he threatens
by phone and fax
to slash her tyres

and smash her face
if she won't oblige.
It's rumoured
her biggest boyfriends

Hughes, Heaney, Harold
Pinter, and the like
are taking turns
to see her safely home.

1.11.96

After two centuries
of displeasure
Horsham will acknowledge
its famous son.

A sculpture
honouring Shelley,

poet, atheist
and adroit eloper

will be unveiled
in the town square.
Three thousand
gingerbread men

each with a fact-sheet
about his life
have been distributed
to local schools.

25.3.97

Thirty-nine men
in black trousers
and new Nikes
have packed their bags

taken drink and drugs
put their heads in plastic
and stretched out
under purple sheets.

They're off to join
a space-ship travelling
behind the comet
Hale-Bopp.

'Goodbye
hard world
so much less than
the heart desired

'we've had enough
of your impure
inequitable
website ways.'

Everyone's dead
but look –

the packed bags
all left behind!

Who can be held
responsible?
Such an oversight
at the moment of glory!

Up there
trekking behind Hale-Bopp
they're quarrelling
over a change of clothes.

September, Périgord

Walking to the village
to buy our breakfast baguette
she grazes on the small black
vineyard grapes.

Returning
she picks six apples
from trees that skirt
the millhouse drive.

She will stew them
with peaches and plums
and the bowl of blackberries
from roadside ditches.

After pasta and salad
to eat them out of doors
with fromage blanc
and the local wine

under the silent wing
of bat and owl
is a kind of grace –
thank you to the gods

or our lucky stars.
A grandchild
cries in the night
and she lies awake

listening to the stream
discourse to the millrace
on gallic themes –
how enjoyment

can be gratitude
made manifest;
how luck and good order
are the twins of fortune.

Likenesses
for Craig Raine

King of Comparison, clever as the Reverend Moon
you marry a dozen thises to a dozen thats

in a flash of light, while I admire and demur.
Nothing, for example, is so like a swallow

as these swallows are, describing their twittering arcs
without analogy, in and out of an archway

that opens on a village square. Under umbrellas
we sit out on the cobbles with cool drinks, eating

a sandwich of crudités made for us in the bar.
Under the arch roof we can see the mud-fixed nests

like inverted igloos, or those domed African huts
on a stone landscape yellow and pitted like the moon.

Siesta time. The swallows have a silence to fill
and the stones for echo. They are the bats of the day

as bats are the swallows of darkness. There's no end
to likeness it seems, only because nothing is the same.

Running in Oxford

You might have done this
forty years ago
loose limbed
and two stone lighter.

To wrench
from its fabled lodges
ordinary 'Oxford'
and make it real –

would that have been
a life's work
worthy
as any other?

No answer!
A snaking spray
practises
its signature

on the greens,
the famous spires
make their points
over the heads

of autumn trees,
and look –
an elderly visitor
is running in Oxford.

The Keys of the Kingdom
for John Kelly

'This is the Late Key – use it only
when the porter's lodge is shut.
It opens the small wooden gate in the wall
on the St Giles side.
This mortice lets you into the College Library.

(At night, remember, you may see the ghost of Laud.)
This other opens the carpark gates,
and also the iron gate to the gardens
from Canterbury Quad (the one
Wilde remarks on, though he wasn't
of course a St John's man).
And this – this is the V2.
It lets you into the Senior Common Room,
the Xerox room, the Japanese garden,
the North Quadrangle by the door from the carpark,
and also the gardens by the back gate
through the wall from Parks Road.
If all else fails, remember
try the V2 –
it will seldom let you down.'

Loyalty and Booze

Over dessert he sank low beside me
seeming in his cups to slip under the board
so that he eyed his glass directly
and it stared back at him, a woman
perhaps, dangerous and much desired.

Around they went and around –
the port wearing about its neck
on a chain a medal declaring it was PORT,
followed closely by the florid claret,
the sweet wine, urine yellow,
and a silver snuff-box.

We'd come from High Table to this panelled room
a dozen gathered over dinner
to celebrate his birthday.

'Your friend,' he murmured of one recently dead
'was an officer. By that I mean he was loyal.'
Loyal to what? I wondered
since all the talk had turned
on his manifest failings.

'Drink was what did for him,' my companion declared
  allowing the port to pass.

Exit

At sixty Cicero
you'd resolved your silence
would sound a lament
for the lost dignity
of better times
but the ravens came
that day we brought you ashore
roosted in your rigging
beat on your windows
followed when your servants
(fearing such omens)
carried you to a wood
where your death was waiting.

It's said you pushed
your head out of the litter
to afford your assassins
a cleaner strike.

Death, Velleius declares
in his farewell oration,
has taken from you
only pains and griefs
and made your glory greater.
Against the tyrant, he says
your name stands for ever.

We nod and murmur
graveside concurrence
but truthfully, friend
if the choice had been yours
old age in the shadows
or this glorious death
which would it have been?

Suffenia the Poet

Cleopatra, Helen and the Mother of God
are some of her roles, but also I think Cassandra
truth-teller, deeply regretful, painfully honest
as she reads her lying verses in a lying-down voice
a neck-scarf hiding her wattles, and that painted-on face
the one, she thinks, that launched a thousand ships
but more likely sank them, smiling in the lectern light
saying over and above the words, 'Believe me! Believe!'

Ravidus the Bookman

Don't forget, Catullus
how that porker Ravidus
after his crisis
of lung and liver
(brought on he said
by the stress of a merger)
bounced right back,
left his job
as prince of publishers
to be literary editor
of a quality broadsheet
where he behaved
much as before
seldom reading books
(others did that) –
it was more a matter
of sniffing the wind
giving ear to gossip
having an eye for fashion
a feel for the market
and only now and then
hacking out a column
of consensus bookchat
in his execrable prose.

A hack is a hack is a
hack, says Cornelius
and I suppose he's right
but whenever did a Grub Street
penny-a-liner
sit above the clouds
in a comfortable chair
with a drink and headphones
doing the *Times* crossword
wondering where the hostess
with the lovely legs
spent her nights in New York –
and all on the profits
of other men's sweat?

Believe me, Cornelius
when lungs and liver
at last send Ravidus wailing
through streets of the city
down to where the dead men
write forever unpublished,
those who bought him drinks
will piss on his name,
those who were indifferent
will forget it,
and another and another
and another Ravidus
will press and elbow forward
to fill his chair.

Easter 1916

for Seamus Heaney to whom I gave the book

Irish Thomas MacDonagh
thirty years ago
in this dusty Oxford bookshop
I found your poems
published by Hodges Figgis
Dublin, 1910.

Songs of myself you called them
how lovingly
you must have turned
these long-ago pages
dreaming of fame
and your country free.

Alas Thomas MacDonagh
shot by the British
it's not your poems live on
in the mind of your country.
It's your dying, yes
your death.

Shelley

1 *Viareggio, 1822*

So long in the water
the face half-gone
but in the pocket
the identifying book –
Hunt's copy of Keats

and on a finger
the ring he'd ordered
to be inscribed
'*il buon tempo arriva*' –
the good times will come.

So now, on an iron frame
over a driftwood fire
with salt and incense and wine
the brain of a poet
boils in its skull.

Unable to watch
Byron swims to his yacht
a mile offshore.
Hunt waits in their carriage
parked in shade.

When the rib-cage
bursts open
Trelawney tears out
what he thinks is the heart
burning his hand.

Afterwards
Hunt dines with Byron
and they drive like madmen
through the Pisan woods
singing and shouting.

2 *Oxford, 1996*

Left of the porter's lodge
past the music room
on staircase three
of the College that expelled him
he lies now on his side

naked in white marble
under a domed sky
painted with stars,
his poet's head pillowed
on a poet's hair,

his penis pointing
earthward,
his blind eyes turned
towards the white
radiance of eternity.

The Other Place

We were talking about gender.
Not gender as it occurs in the popular mouth
meaning sex. This was grammatical gender
and how, even in the Germanic languages
where you'd expect concurrence

nothing is dependable.
A feminine noun in German
may be masculine in Danish,
and so on. Then there was the question
of the sounds of Dutch
so unfamiliar to the Anglophone ear
when the written forms are so close.
An ordinary chat over lunch, you see,
into which I threw, at a pertinent moment,
a forty-five-year-old memory from a textbook,
Jesperson's *History of the Language*,
scoring a small point.
It was then the blow-fly, very large, very black,
and very loud, began to buzz
my chicken salad. I waved at it
gently at first, then vigorously,
but with little effect. It persisted,
unfairly I thought, because to my left
was another chicken salad,
opposite were kidneys – there were, in fact,
no end of lunches appetising to a fly,
but it would have none of them.
And nobody spoke of it.
While I went on waving, the talk,
tenacious as my winged tormentor,
moved on to the politics
of calling the sagas Old Norse
or simply Icelandic.
I should, I suppose, have swatted it
and asked the butler to remove the corpse
but I lack the style,
or call it the habit of command –
and that, I believe, was its point.
Even the flies here
can recognise a stranger.

Horace III, 30

Drunk with pleasure
at what had flowed from his pen
the poet dashed off a letter
to Melpomene.

Greater than the pyramids,
proof against the worst
the south wind could throw,
his thirty odes, he told her
would outlast bronze.

He would die, yes
but what she'd given him
would defeat the goddess of Death.
Accordingly he demanded
Apollo's laurel.

Was the Muse offended?
Not for a moment!
He was the vehicle only.
The honour he was claiming
she saw at once
was meant for her.

Felicitations, Horace!
There's no euphoria
and no frankness
like those of a mind unchained
finding wings in words.

Revisiting Bristol
for Kay

Here's the street lamp
our first car
a grey Ford Popular

was parked under,
and windows we
looked out from afraid

to drive, wishing
it would vanish in the
pea soup. Back

after ten cars and
four decades
it's as if our black-

and-white snapshots
didn't lie. The colours
must have been

our supplement of
youth. The Senacas,
father and

sons, and grandson
Lucan, were Cordobans
addicted

to Rome. One came
and went; one stayed
and triumphed; one fell

foul of mad Nero
and bled in his bath.
Would they have

bridled to be called
colonials? Like birds
on some

needless but
habitual migration
we've crossed skies

and crossed them
as our 'opposite isles'
chased each other

never to meet.
So what's belonging
unless it's to

one another
and to our own
history, the books which

made us what we are,
and those that will
tell our story?

Fame and Companion

The young man on the door, reading her novel,
asks her to inscribe it. Around the pool table

in a smoky bar, the artists, stringy-grey haired,
are caricatures. We wait in a smokeless parlour

till her table's ready in the dining room.
Curtains are drawn on the garden. Eyes are on her

as we settle to talk. She wants to begin a novel
but the year's been wasted, she says, on promotion tours

that drove her close to breakdown. Ah that such
deserved good fortune should fall on such frail shoulders,

I want to mock, but it seems her distress is real.
Her work today was a review – nine hundred words

for nine hundred pounds. Mine was ten lines for nix.
It felt (I tell her bravely) like a state of grace.

The Sparrow

Hymenaeus
when Catullus called you forth
from Helicon Hill
promising to praise you
above all the gods
you were to wear (he instructed)
a scarlet cloak
and yellow shoes
and with flowers in your hair
carrying a torch of pinewood
you were to dance like a demon.

Son of Urania
all this no doubt you deserved
but was it wise
to give to powerful Venus
such cause for envy?

I saw you this morning
busy among leaves
under the apple tree
your eye bright
your movements quick
your commonplace plumage
unruffled in the autumn sun.

Like Catullus
you'd dispensed with
the scarlet gown
the shoes and the garland.
The whiff of woodsmoke
was not of your making.
Like Catullus
you were hard at work.
Like him
you'd survived.

The Universe

i Cogito ergo sum

He moves
not like winged Mercury
nor Venus rising from the sea
but on wheels.

He speaks
not with the tongues
of men and of angels
nor a zephyr among poplars
but with the voice of a robot.

He thinks
not as you and I think
interrupted by lusts and compassion
but like a computer.

Ordinary mortals
oil his wheels
feed him
and replace the batteries
in his voice box.

'There may be a God,' he quacks
imagining a brain like his own
but as large as a planet.

ii Poetics

Wild as
water on a hot-plate
as a summer ant
flicked off its trail
or an antigen
confronted by T-cells
here is a single atom
aurum
dropped on glass.

Things fly apart
that want to be together
things are forced together
that want to be apart.

'Conductivity'? Yes.
'Lymphocytes'? For sure!

But where are there words for
the pain and the panic
the escape and the joy
the I and the thou?

iii Lost in space

'How will I find it?'
asked Gabriel
sent Earthward
to bespeak a Virgin.

God told him, 'Go past
the Park of Cubes.
Just short of Chaos
find the region of
the Self-Igniting
Spheres-in-Flight.

'Ignore the fires
and blinding light.

'Find the Blue One.
Strike there.'

Lessons in Modern History (i)

1 *1956 West*

Anagram
ants

even in Eden
            need
honey so
spooner-like
                        he
hied to the louse
and she
(his Eve) said
it was as if
sewers
            were flowing
                        frew
'er sitteen room
            at numbah
ten.

2 *1956 East*

Mr B and
            Mr K
is there a tiger
in your well-hung-
arian tank?

            No
but there's a
            buda-
pesky student
            under it.

Lessons in Modern History (ii)

1 *C.K.*

Castro and Cuba
Kennedy and Krushchev
the Cs and the Ks
were strong that year
and so was fear.

That was 1962
when only the C and the K
preceded by an L and a U
got us through.

2 *1963 – HiJKL*

Oh but leave out the Ks
we should have known
it was the Js and the Ls
that mattered –

Jack and Jackie
and what Lee
did for Lyndon
and what the other Jack
did to Lee
also (you could say)
for Lyndon.

There's symmetry for you –
History on first-name
terms with itself!

3 *1965*

was when
                        (for Death)
a line on a map
became
                        (for Death)
an international
boundary
and a zone
                        (for Death)
a sovereign
state.

4 *1968 made*

a bullet for Bobby
a martyr of Martin
of Tet an Offensive
of Lyndon a loser.

5 *1974*

Broken by a break-in
tangled in his own tapes
it's goodbye again
to Tricky Dicky
Cold Warrior
and Comeback Kid
who was going to end the war
with more bombs
and fewer boys.

6 *1975 – Saigon*

It ends in panic.
It ends in helicopters
shuttling to ships offshore.
It ends when a single tank
laden with flags and flowers
and peasant soldiers
bursts through the gates
of the President's palace.
It ends (don't say it)
in defeat.
It ends in the timely divorce
of Mars and America.

Absence

Have you left at last, my Clodia?
Catullus hunts for you upstairs and down

from room to room through the empty house;
looks for you in the leaf-strewn garden

where the squirrel wars with the magpie.
In books, in memory, in the mysterious rattle

of language where he so often found you,
he searches without success. This winter morning

is windless, cloudless, and a low-angled sun
drives its shafts blindly up the Woodstock Road.

But you on whom he waited, on whom he depended –
you're gone, leaving him nothing but a silence.

O.K., but you know he'll wait by the broken gate
under the beech tree at evening, and in the night

when the house creaks, he'll listen for your return
never expecting it, never giving up hope.

Zagreb

There were four in the café,
the poet
and three women
(a perfect world!)

Jadranka
who asked the questions
Ljiljana
who translated them
and Kay
his second self.

So much intelligence
and so much beauty
trained on the one who must answer –
how could he do other
than shine like a star?

Out in the countryside
even the terrible war
held its breath.

Hollywood
for Roger Donaldson

In winter sun
we lunch by the pool
in a garden

of oranges and lemons
palms and olives
where the

chill of desert shadow
signals
snow in the mountains.

Spring, you tell me
will flower purple
in the courtyard

and in high summer
only the drift
of mists up from

the Pacific
will temper hot winds
down from the hills.

All day with our script
we play the game of
put and take

each 'Say we do
this' sending me back
to the keyboard

to the mysteries
of 'slug line', 'cut to'
'action', 'fade'.

Evenings
we watch classic movies
suggesting 'Say we dos'

for tomorrow.
My novel's shrinking
under our hands

into scene-and-speak
the rest dropping away
like ripe

olives on the path
to your front door.
Last night I dreamed

those giant letters
high in hills
spelled GOLLYWOG

and the tall palms
running seaward on Sunset
were fountains.

'Will our movie be made?'
I asked the ocean
and heard

clear beyond wave-break
the budget
whistle in its cage.

Even Newer English Bible

The Lord is my caregiver so I'm OK
He suggests I put my feet up
or take a stroll down at the Bay.

That way, He says,
you keep out of trouble.

I have one fractured rib
and three more cracked or bruised
from a dive off the stairs –
but the ambulance came
and the hospital staff
they comforted me.

I eat out
where my reviewers can see me.
Someone puts pasta on the table
with basil and cheese
and a bottle of red.
Someone promises me a massage.

This could go on for ever!
Who needs to win Lotto?
God, I'm so lucky!

Play it Again
for Les Murray on his 60th birthday, 17.10.98

Corporate raider
in the larder
of language

with more than a tyre
to spare
and girth to go

he lacks the classic
pose of restraint
his motto

'Never say When'
his poems pack-horses
unloaded

line by line
under a blazing sky
or in the

downpour that speaks
in gutters and spouts
of Excess.

Here the Golden
Disobedience
is practised.

Here the Dark Celt
meets Anglo-Oz. Here
the Fat Boy

cries in a cave
for his Mother
and tries to grow

into the shape
of a woman.
Here the Poor Cow

finds words to match
its beautiful eyes
and takes heart.

Here the Coolongolook
stops
to reflect and the

Jindyworobak
finds itself
sophisticate.

None-the-Les Murray
now that the Black Dog
is gone

this day brings you to
a number
cheerfully round.

Nouns will be busy
at being
verbs at doing

down the long road
where gums flap
their bark bandages

at a rush of galahs
and the world
(your reader)

urges you
in the glint of webs
and the scents of

morning
to go to your desk
and play it again.

Nine Nines

1 *America*

Not its railtracks and freeways – they go through it.
Not its great cities – they hide it behind their eyes.
Not its small towns – they tell us only stories
of what it once was. Not Rocky Mountains, and not
the red rock canyons where John Wayne whacked the Apache.
Oval Office, Pentagon, cookies, cute freckled children,
Blacks singing Blues – these are not America.
America is a continent hidden in a broken promise.
It lives in a word. Think of it. *America!*

2 *Moon*

One daughter had borrowed the other daughter's shirt.
There was a stain wouldn't come out. After the row
he sat outside in the dark and smoked just one
forbidden fag that made his heart thump harder.
Ti-tree and toetoe pushed their spikes and feathers
into a scudding sky. Briefly the moon sailed out –
now a veiled disk, now a pale and furrowed brow.
It didn't say 'Don't take these matters to heart,'
or 'Life is conflict.' The moon's great virtue is silence.

3 *Sylvia*

Ten days after he was, you were born.
Heading out past sixty he's still hanging on
but you baled out at thirty telling the world
'Dying is an art. I do it exceptionally well.'
Now you're a young poet of deserved fame,
he an aging one, forgetting reputation.
From where he sits cool Daddy looks at you.
He sees the pain, and the brat, and the brat in pain.
Living is an art. He does it as well as he can.

4 *Zen*

Must poems have always the extravagance
of Death or Love? Nine lives might not be enough
even for the cat sleeping in the almost silence
of a distant handsaw's panting. Blue sky, green trees,
white weatherboards, a garden full of washing
all arms and legs, cram full the breathless moment.
Nothing to be gained by running at it headlong.
Answer the Master. Tell him what the World saw
when the thrush flew down from the pear tree.

5 *Miroslav Holub in Toronto, 1981*

His passport feared the man from the Embassy
in the back of the hall. One word out of place

could cost it a life. Scientist Holub professed
to no opinions. As poet he was openly opaque.
On his last day we bought umbrellas together
and stood in a glass cage with a girl with red hair
pelted by flowers of rain. How could he know
the trump had already sounded for Jericho?
His passport-faced goodbyes implied for ever.

6 Oxford, 1997

That was no ordinary season – both rivers iced,
also the canal, and the fountain outside the Radcliffe
forming a curtain around its man of bronze
who held a platelike shell which day by day
the god of winter heaped higher with frozen snow.
Ducks went walking on water; swans caught napping
were closed upon. The world had become its own
white wedding cake, or a virgin, holding her breath,
conjuring behind her veil the turbulence of green.

7 Night Sequiturs

At 4 a.m. remembering reading Frost at midnight
and thinking of 'Frost at Midnight' by S.T.C.
put me in mind of that shark with its fin de siècle
languidly cutting warm shadow in Hobson Bay
south of the pipe in bright blue autumn weather
promising cool nights. It was Paavo Nurmi of Finland
and later Murray Halberg used to run round and around
the track at the same pace steady as the second hand
of my second-hand stop-watch going, not counting the sheep.

8 Isambard Kingdom Brunel – Bristol, 1830

First build four stone ramparts, then fire an arrow
dragging a fine thread, the thread to draw a cord,
the cord a light rope, the light rope a heavier,
and so on until the heaviest, aided by a winch,
will drag across the valley the weight of one chain.
This action repeated twice times thirty-three

puts something where nothing was – sixty-six chains
on which to suspend your bridge. It's there still.
The weight of modern traffic hangs by a thread.

9 St John's College Library, Oxford

Fading, sensitive to light, the pencilled head
of the king who lost it hangs under ruffs of curtain.
His son, a king restored, once asked the College
if he might have it. In return, he assured them,
he would give whatever in reason was asked of him.
Can a Sovereign's wish be refused? Gravely the dons
present him with his father's depicted head.
And what in return, he asks, do they ask of him?
'Sire,' they answer, 'our wish is to have it back.'

Encounters
for Peter Porter on his 70th birthday, 16.2.99

i Sydney

I had the chair but
he was the one
who professed.

Small talk
was never less
than interrogation.

His big flinty specs
strip-searched my mind
for reasons.

I was arrested
for a coolness
re Schubert

and the heroic couplet
of Alexander
Pope.

No bleating about
the bush,
this was Les Murray's

Athenian copper
back home where
the heart was not.

ii London

Dick Whittington
at home in his head
up the long

Paddington stair
from fabled streets
paved with paper

he's listening for
the dinkum oil
the ring of gold –

Peter the rock,
Porter the carrier,
the burden

no more than knowledge,
the object
no less than art.

Crete

i Hania

I wrote that swallows
are the bats of the day
as bats are
the swallows of darkness

but here they are at dusk
the bats up early
swallows working late
over and through a roofless ruin
made by German bombs –
as you might watch
in the undersea half-light
of Suda Bay
fish cruising or stalled
in the split and sunken tonnage.

2 *May 1941*

Poland France Belgium Holland
Yugoslavia mainland Greece
all these have fallen
and with fewer German deaths
than in the first three days
of the battle for Crete.

Something has begun to go wrong.

3 *The Memory in Stones*

Three small and perfect
sea-crafted pebbles
I took from Maleme Beach
one mottled grey
one bauxite red
and one a dazzle
of white and whiter –
but the red
bled on my hand
stained what it touched
and I left it behind.

4 *Hill 107*

Who commanded the hill
commanded the airfield –

who commanded the airfield
commanded the island.

It's a graveyard now
(Soldatenfriedhof) –
four thousand-something
dead young Germans
claim each his piece
of Crete for ever
in the name of the Reich.

5 Zen

Rough clad
facing forward
he stands in his skiff
and with quick light stabs
of blades in water
guides it slowly over
the almost glass
of the morning harbour
looking ahead and down
left, then right
then left again.

From my balcony
on the second floor
of the Hotel Lucia
with a matching patience
I watch and wait.

6 E.C.

Venice built the sea wall
Turkey the mosque
modern Greece the hotels.

Time made the ruins
with German assistance.

7 *He learned . . .*

That the entrance
of the bearers of death
can be beautiful
as a season of flowers
opening all at once
across a field of sky.

That the underworld
of the olives
is its own place
of red earth
and green lizards.

That wild daisies
can be midnight blue
and that the Anzac poppy
blooms also in Crete.

That birds will sing
between bomb blasts.

8 *In the Clearing*

'Face to face
at fifteen paces
both surprised –
he in grey with his rifle
I in khaki with mine.

'Hit the deck?
Fire from the hip?

'I waved him away.
It was an impulse
as if to say
"There's no need . . ."

'He grinned
waved back and was gone
among the olives.'

9 Headstones, Suda Bay

Last parade is for ever
and the drill perfect.
Pale-faced in the sun
rank on rank unflinching
they out-stare
the Aegean blue
and a white ship at anchor.

British
                Australians
New Zealanders
each with name and rank
or the inscription
  'A soldier of
    the 1939–45
        War
Known unto God.'

10 Veterans, 1998

Climbing the hill
into Galatas village
for the commemoration
I trudge behind them
the tall RAF man
and the little brown Kiwi
Mr Edwards from Thames.

'Your lot pulled out
before it really got started'
says Mr Edwards.

'Ay,' says the other.
'But by that time
we'd only one plane left
and a third of us were dead.'

11 *Minoan*

These stones you see
of an irregular wall
yellow-orange
below the level of the street
where the church was bombed –
they're Minoan.

What does it mean
Minoan?
It means old.
No. Older than that.
Before they started the clocks.
Ancient. Oldest.
Minoan.

12 *Blitzkrieg*

It must be their speed
gets these giant ants over
the hot sand and stones
on Maleme Beach –
each ant-foot touch
a microsecond.

Shelled with heavy pebbles
they survive even
what appear to be
direct hits.

13 *Fear?*

'I'd lived with it
– or call it anxiety –
all my twenty-one years.

'It was a relief, really
having something
to be afraid of.'

14 *At the Villa Andromeda*

These are career soldiers.
Their weapons are formidable
but they'll never use them.

Brass and bellows.

These are the diplomats.
Here's a famous hostess
and an admiral of the fleet.

Wind and water.

These moustaches belong
to local politicos
eager for advantage.

Subtitles superfluous.

Here are the plates and glasses
on tables pool-side
under tragic stars.

Food for reflection.

The dirge is for lost lives –
or is it for a glory gone
beyond reach for ever?

Anthems and flags.

15 *Hotel Lucia*

Morning light
strikes up off water
and the shutters
make lines of it –
a glittering
                 flickering
handwritten message

from HQ –
untranslatable

the writing on the wall.

16 Bayonet

'. . . hiding in a well
or behind it.
He fired at our backs.

'"Get him," the Major shouted.
"Get the bastard."

'If I'd shot him
there would have been a bang
and silence.

'Half a century
he's been quiet on the hill.
Half a century
I've lived with the scream.'

17 Last Post, Suda Bay

Should we disturb you
my dead compatriots
so well-placed here?

Should we disturb ourselves?

Your silence is absolute
unless we pretend
it's you who speak in the wind.

Not forgotten
but unfathomable.

More vivid than yesterday
and like yesterday
gone beyond call.

Stories

to A. S. Byatt

Bright children
alert to the Dark
and what it might mean

like to be told
a story, and some
grow up to be

themselves tellers of
tales. Today
driving from Uzès

I found the gorge road
closed by slips
and was forced upward

into the mountains.
Now we've swum
in your pool and walked

to the local *auberge*
and you tell,
as dark comes down

your tale of one
who wished to write
a Biographer's

biography,
and how you made up
all the names of

your characters
from the elm tree
and its predators –

Sir Elmer Bole,
Phineas G. Nanson,
Scholes Destry-Scholes

who join us
at our table outdoors
while the near hills

listening
loom nearer, and the spirit
of ancient

France, wary as always
but attentive to
la langue

anglaise,
holds its vast breath
or sighs along the roadway

and in the branches
over our heads.
Twenty-one years

since we began
this game of giving
and receiving

and still we play it,
as by the firelight
in caves and

flame-lit farms
invention must once have run
stride for stride

with probability its
partner
holding at bay,

but only while the breath
lasts and the last
word remains

unsaid,
the bat-winged person
who must come to the door.

H/oration

The days they run, they run
keeping the score on our faces
Licinius, and Death
with his fluoride teeth
and famous, boring torso
must always win.

We who've lived
paying our dues to the sun
on a fruitful isthmus
between two harbours –
what can we offer as bribe
to that dry-eyed skuller
on the darkest river?

What use that we escaped
war, and the worst of weathers?
Soon his sporty Lordship
will beat us to our knees.
The last lips
will have been kissed,
the last race run,
and in our cellars
the best bottles
will belong to another.

Together then
Licinius
let's practise it bravely –
saying goodbye
and meaning for ever.

Dog

2002

King's Lynn and the Pacific

The Music Master
Dr Charles Burney, 1759

Heaven's infinity
here in the Fens
is horizontal

a low roof going on
for ever
in all directions

through which the
colourless light
of Jehovah's 'radiant feet'

colourlessly lights
Charles Burney's page.
Astride dependable

Peggy he's reading
Don Quixote
in sight of windmills.

Tilney-St Lawrence,
Wiggenhall-St Mary,
Wormegay and

Wattlingham . . . 'There goes
the music master,'
they call, 'reading

as he rides,'
while at home in Lynn
his Esther with her true

blue-stocking friends,
Mrs Allen and Miss
Dorothy Young,

is reading too.
'Books and music,
the Italian language,

Sir, your own *Rambler* –'
he writes his friend
Johnson in London:

'A richer tide
is flooding our lowlands.'
He hopes it's true.

The Captain's Servant
Master James Burney, 1760

Mud knows how water slides
    and Jem knew mud but longed

for the bigger picture –
    the rigging forest, waves

that bucked and tossed, and then
    mysterious shores. Danger?

(Jem was ten.) Hadn't he spent
    two years at Lynn Grammar

hearing his usher tell
    murderers' tales, who proved

himself to *be* one, with
    a corpse hidden in a cave?

Let his father compose,
    his sister scribble, his

mother suckle her pups.
    Jem was for the Navy.

In Principio . . .

George Vancouver, 1772

That seal pup George had spotted
on his fourteenth birthday –

he'd known it was an omen.
Lynn's ropes and spars chalked letters

on a slate of Norfolk sky
signing him off. Signing him *on*.

No more Latin, he was free!
Now let God's southernmost

ocean open its arms
where islands asked for their names.

Underfoot, Ferry Lane lurched.
His guts went too – down in the storm

before the storms. Oh he was happy
and full of fear. He was to sail

with Cook's ship *Resolution*
where October would be spring,

Christmas mid-summer, and the sun
would go round to the north –

a front-to-back, downside-up
world, he imagined it, as if

the Beginning hadn't begun
and the Word was Dog.

Otaheiti

Lieutenant James Burney, 17.8.1773

Out they came in their double canoes with prows turned up
like Arab slippers, the paddlers' strong shoulders shining

with sweat and flying spray. But reaching us first, the scents –
leaf-mould and loam, frangipani and over-ripe fruit.

Generous thieves, beautiful killers, dangerous friends –
the usual puzzle – with whom Cook has ruled there should be

no unsupervised trade, trade only for provisions.
How we longed for pork and greens and their women's bodies.

Both ships inside the reef? We thought it could be managed
and soon were in trouble – the opening too shallow,

the current and an onshore breeze pushing us landward,
our cutter and boats acting tugs for *Resolution*

and we on *Adventure* kedging ourselves out against
our heaviest anchor, losing the kedge and three hawsers.

Only a shift of the breeze that came at five-thirty
saved us from double disaster. Now, close to midnight,

moonlight in the rigging like a white translucent mist,
music and drums still throb at us over the shallows

from that beaten ground where tonight our men did their turn –
country dances with bagpipes and singing of shanties

to amazement and laughter. Yes, this is Paradise –
the day just gone forgotten, no thought of tomorrow.

Bread etc.

James Burney, two days out from Otaheiti, 19.9.1773

When we gathered on the foredeck
for Sunday worship, our Native,
Omai from Otaheiti, thought
we were planning his murder.

Had he picked up a word or two
about the Body and the Blood?
I remembered at St Margaret's
in the loft with my sister
hearing the Reverend Dr Pyle
thunder about Jesus *Crust*
making me think of the wafer,
'setting me off', as Fanny complained.

Poor Omai! Having so little
of your language, how could I explain
my blasphemous laughter at
a joke about our *risen* God?

Tonga

The words of a song as James Burney heard and wrote them down, 5.10.1773

O chicheto   O chicheto mattala
O chicheto   Vette vala vala
Keonemar   Keonemar
Koar   koar   koar
Kohey   kohey   kohey
To allellerlay
Ki allubey.

What the words probably meant – a loose translation.

Throw off the mat
the beaten cloth
you have cane leaves and flowers
about your throat –
that is enough.

Taste the sweetness of the cane
the fat of the pigeon
plucked of its feathers.

The drum is silent.
Our bodies hear it.
They buck and dance to its beating.

New Zealand
George Vancouver, Ship's Cove, 15.11.1773

Far and wide
the sea's the surface
Adventure at anchor
sits on.

There's height and distance here
but no depth.

The sky has placed
its white extravagant confections
discreetly.

Beyond the beach
the bush glitters
darkly green
and doesn't speak.

Half way between
ship and shore, between
a word and a world,
alone,
he leans on his oars.

The Hand

James Burney, Queen Charlotte's Sound, New Zealand, 18.12.1773

We knew it was Tom's hand –
Thos. Hill, forecastleman.
He'd tattooed it in Otaheiti,
just his inititals, T.H.

There was another hand –
an officer's we thought,
Mr Rowe's; and the skinned head
of our Captain's servant.

The rest had been baked
and packed in baskets
or lay about in the recognisable
remnants of a feast.

None of these details
I entered in a private journal
kept for Fanny and my father.
The journal was discontinued.

I wrote my official report:
ten of our stoutest men –
four from the forecastle,
two from the afterguard,

two officers, one servant,
and our quartermaster – all
murdered and earth-ovened
to fill these savage stomachs.

From the bay we fired a volley
sinking three canoes
in futile revenge – and left.
I could never speak of it –

the blood-stained shirts and shoes,
a trouser full of entrails,
picked bones, and that T.H.
standing for Tom's Hand.

Ice

30.1.1774, 71°10's, 106°54'w

Ice islands, taller sometimes
than St Paul's, we distinguish
from ice fields leagues long
that could be our Norfolk
lowlands under snow.
Before we've seen it, a glow
cast skyward tells us it's there,
its glass palaces showing
pale blue in sunlight, turning
black as the sky darkens.
Today because it threatened
to close on us, Cook ruled
we take our search no further
for the Great Southern Land.
It was then while still we
pointed poleward, young George
climbed out on the bowsprit
shouting, '*Ne plus ultra!*'
meaning to claim that no man
had travelled so far south.
Cook told him, 'Had you fallen
none neither would have froze
so quick and far from home.'

Dog

25.2.1774, and the days that followed – heading once again for Otaheiti

On the 25th, Captain Cook was taken ill of the bilious cholic, which was
so violent as to confine him to his bed; so that the management of the ship
was left to Mr Cooper, the first officer, who conducted her much to his sat-
isfaction. It was several days before the most dangerous symptoms of his
disorder were removed; during which time Mr Patten, the surgeon, was to
him not only a skilful physician, but an affectionate nurse. When he began
to recover, a favourite dog, belonging to Mr Forster, fell a sacrifice to his
tender stomach. They had no other fresh meat whatever on board; and
the Captain could eat of this flesh, as well as broth made of it, when he
could taste nothing else. Thus he received nourishment and strength from

food which would have made most people in Europe sick; so true it is that
necessity is governed by no law.

Captain Cook's Voyages

Navigation

10.10.1774

For longitude
you need to know
the time at Greenwich

and the time
under your feet. Four
minutes difference

means one degree;
an hour, fifteen.
The moon can be used

when it's there to see.
Much better is
Harrison's 'Watch'

which our Commander
has called his
'never-failing guide'.

Today our
reading – South
twenty-nine / fifty-seven,

East one sixty-eight /
sixteen – locates
one more island.

The world is made
to yield its secret
places. Five leagues

in circuit
we measured, and rowed
ashore knowing

we were the first
ever to set foot there.
Cabbage-palm,

wood-sorrel,
sow-thistle and samphire
we brought on board –

also fresh water.
Captain Cook
has named it Norfolk.

The Puzzle

George Vancouver, 29.7.1775

Home after three years he thinks
Lynn is as it was – alarming

tides and muddy vacancies.
At sea, weary on long watches,

sick of the salt meat, homesick,
he sometimes tried to remember

the Customs House, and sketch it.
One oblong box he drew and then

another above, topped by
a roof like a lid with a spire

for handle – three dormers on
the long side, two on the other.

But which way did it sit – short
side towards the Ouse? It troubled

him that he couldn't be sure
just as it pleased him to know that

his father was there, in charge.
Now he learns his father is dead

and his brother Controller
of Customs. In America

England is fighting a war.
There is, it seems, more than one

real world, and while you are in one
the other goes on without you.

Postscript
Hawaii, 14.2.1779, and the days that followed

A theft began it
it ended in mayhem
on one side seventeen dead
five on the other
none of it intended.

King's Lynn's linguists
Burney and Vancouver
were sent to parley
for the Commander's body.

Cook was Erono
the god on his floating island
who in legend promised
'I shall return.'

One had his head
another his hair
a third his legs
the feet and jaw were missing.

Piece by piece
he was accounted for
wrapped in cloth
returned under a cloak
of black and white feathers
for burial in the bay.

Men kill their gods.
The gods make promises
they can seldom keep.

Creation etc.

Psalm

Every Dog has his day
but this one taketh the Prize
therefore buy Him a deserving collar,
feed Him and walk Him.

His Yap in the high country
driveth home the sky-flocks,
his clattering Feet
are the claws of the pelting rain.

A distant quake is his Growl
in the deserts of Kadesh,
his Whine warneth Lebanon's leaves
of the burglar Time.

Dog the heavens call him
whose Bark and Bite alike
shall be praised for ever
in the temples of man.

Applause

Bristol University, 12.7.01, with thanks to Andrew Bennett

My life in summary
and only nice things said
it could be my funeral

except that
vertical in scarlet
I'm listening to it

allowed even
after the hand-clasp
and the gold-tasselled

velvet hat
to go away home
with family and friends.

'You were a callow youth
Curl Skidmore'
the Orator quotes

my other self
saying of another
self – thus proving

he's read my novels
and meaning I suppose
to suggest

distances
travelled, obstacles
overcome. Rewarded

(and glad of it)
only for being myself
I confront

Zen's other
and unfamiliar
hand-clapping puzzle –

not what is
the sound of one
but the meaning of many.

Washington

i Horace (2001)

Summer arriving late
your poet's remembering takes him
where marbled Lincoln looked down
the long reflecting water

and you and he, Cynara,
walked and talked three days
over that hallowed ground.

Let me tell you something you know:
while satellites were reading
the innocence of your lips
Caesar in his White House
was enlisting yet more legions
for memorials in stone.

That was the heart of Empire
which Time, in time, must teach
the flavour of defeat.

So remind your poet, Cynara,
he has no need of brass
nor the brashness of marble.
Libitina will crush him,
but words outlive the mind
that sets them free.

ii Suetonius (1974)

Forced to resign the Button,
his staff assembled,
a helicopter on the White House lawn
waiting to shuttle him
into the five o'clock shadows,
the Quaker boy who became
instrument of America's will
to be world policeman
world judge
and world executioner
makes his farewell speech
about love of mother for son,
father for daughter,
and how from the deepest valley
stands forth most clearly
the grandeur of the highest hills.

iii Catullus (1963)

'Ask not
what your country can do for you
but rather
what you can do for your country' –

how it rang in your ears
Caesar's worthy wank
before Fate grew bored with it
and cut him down to size.

They say the habits of vice
are hard to break
but so are the habits of virtue
especially those
of the faithful dog.

Here, therefore, Catullus
to cure that malady
is what you had better recite
each morning at sunrise:

'Strong gods
if you value me at all
teach me to bark after passing cars,
to bite the postman's ankle,
and especially, nightly,
to howl at the moon.'

His Round
Allen Curnow, 1911–2001

'Home' for the boy had meant
somewhere between England

where God was still living
and the ground under his feet.

As a man he wrote of islands,
talked tides and distances,

and seldom bought his round.
Not Prospero, but like him,

he made words work and had
'an abominable temper'.

His project was to catch
the heron's deliberation

lifting itself over mangroves,
or on that opposite coast

the careless way a gull
could be tossed in an updraft.

These were his annotations
on a world that exceeded

all it could say of itself.
He fished for the brown cod

and had a name for those
who thought it inferior eating.

He summoned his dog by car horn,
looked hard into sunsets,

and called himself 'an old man
who wouldn't say his prayers'.

Stubborn, still owing his round,
he was towed at the last

headlong into the westerly,
tottering, leashed to his Dog.

Gotland Midsummer

July is when the fingers
of evening and morning touch
under the blanket of night

and the straw-headed children
of the children of the Vikings
go nearly naked into

the nearly saltless Baltic.
They find wild strawberries
among grass at a wood's edge

and thread them on a stalk
to be eaten after herrings
with coffee black as tide wrack.

Thatch is spiked against witches
and tumbled stones remember
an invasion of Danes.

This island of ruined churches,
abandoned farms and windmills
is Stockholm's secret playground

where Lars Ardelius built
his theatre in a barn
and every summer's drama

opened like a wildflower
attended at the wayside
by butterflies and moths.

No record, no reviewers –
such stuff only as dreams are
made on, rounded by a sleep.

Cat/ullus

Zac's dead
buried with his brother Wallace
beside the carport
under the ponga.

Zac of the goldfish eyes
and nice-smelling fur
who when I had a problem with a poem

slept on it,
who lived to put his paw-print
on a valued citation,
who in his dying days
jumped to swipe at a passing moth
and missed.

Zac the radical,
Zac the bed-crowder
the window leaper
the lateral-thinker,
Zac the head-first rat-eater
is dead,
is 'laid to rest',
has met his match.

Frater, ave (etc.)
Black Zac
Zac the Knife.

Creation etc.

i The Annunciation

Angels are never average and seldom avenging
but was it a kindness to whisper
a victim and a victory over Death
in Mary's marvelling ear?
The light creeps crab-wise over a sky it paints
in blue-eyed blue, and it's we
cousins of the fur and the stalk must write
an End-of-Term to be delivered by
that silence behind the silence of the stars.
In the beginning was indeed the Word
and it wasn't ours. Ours will be simply the last.

ii The Death of God

Whitman and Nietzsche we watched
dancing together in a high wind of Self
on the cold horn of the moon.

'Oh the great Noontide,' they sang.
'Oh the warm South of the Future!'
We were looking back at them from that very Future.
God was dead, but so was Zarathustra.

iii A Note on Sectarian Conflict

What 'came next' was always the problem.
If there was life after death
there had to be somewhere to go.
We called it Heaven
and made it nice – then 'nice' became the problem.
Who wants bad guys fighting over the hammocks,
damaging the palms?
Another place was needed. We called that Hell.
Really our wars were over the sorting process –
wheat from chaff, sheep from goats.
If signals from Headquarters had only been clear
there need have been no burnings.
Faith showed faint cracks. Downstairs engendered
anxiety, then rejection – and even our Club Med in the Skies
began to lose trade. Who'd ever been there
and come back to report? – apart from the One,
and look what happened to Him!
It's been a hard road.
But hell! – who ever said it was gonna be easy?

iv Heaven

By e-mail
two below-the-belt
digital pics
one full-frontal
one between-buttocks
and the message
'Remember me?'

He imagined it
circling the globe
stopping among the stars
(those supreme flashers) –

a cunt on the move,
a cunt in space,
in heaven!

'Holy Mother!'
(is what he said)
'This might be anyone.'
He messaged back
'Send me your face.'

There was no reply.

v Dog

In His Museum of the Universe
Dog has everything that is / was / will be
in exact replica
even the passage of time.
Things (stars, for example, bugs)
are born, grow up, grow old and die –
imagine that!
In the long lovely lonely
heavenly afternoons
(each one lasting for ever)
He strolls in the galleries
watching the fall of heavenly rain
on heavenly gardens
but pauses sometimes to listen
for the yells from Hell
which He's told are loud
though out of earshot.
He thinks of inviting them up
but there'd be no end of trouble.
He plans a new universe
– more colourful, various –
but He's a lazy Dog, and jealous:
people disappoint Him;
Time is unstable.
He needs another medium
but He's at the end of His rope.
Some other Dog will do it.

vi Messiah

Jesus claimed he was the Son of God.
He was not. I am.
Only through Me is there access
to my Father's chain of Mansions
called 'the Life after Death'.

This is known as yet
to hardly more than a dozen
(and Dwayne will betray me).
After my Death and Resuscitation
we plan to change the World.

vii Dogma

Stillness came to the garden –
so many greens!
and it occurred to him without beauty
there would not be much to speak of,
much to love.
A face, stars, islands,
a vastness
of darkness and light,
a few wrenching bars –
these made sadness possible,
compelled regret.

Last night
straining to make his ears
attend to the silence
he heard it in the distance –
a dog barking,
and then a half-asleep voice
(his own) with laughter in it:
'Dog, are you there?
Good dog. *Dog*!'

viii Philosophy

Dr Johnson kicked a stone
Bishop Berkeley sulked alone
Swift went swiftly mad, or so
it seemed, so bad his vertigo
Reason earned John Locke's applause
Hume the doubter doubted Cause
Kant knew Reason on its own
can't account for Johnson's stone –
that turned on a light for Goethe
to write *The Sorrows of Young Werther*.
Our skein is paid out by the Fates
the Dog Star guards the Pearly Gates
the Roman Church upholds a proof
that God is there, although aloof.

I dreamed I met a man in space
he had a brain and not much face
he used a small machine for talking
it said his name was Stephen Hawking
I said 'I know that Space is bending.'
He quacked 'It's worse than that. It's ending.'

Vincent

Old girlie Brother Ignaz
who liked the swish of cane
on bent-over buttock
in that long-ago classroom:
'Boys, please – some flightless birds. Bernard?'
'The emu, Brother.'
'The emu, yes. Michael?'
'Ostrich?'
'The ostrich. Thank you. What about you, John?'
'The kiwi, Brother.'
'The kiwi, of course. Vincent, any more?'
And Vincent, pausing, holding his eye:
'How about a shag, Brother?'

Poetry and Philosophy

Here's another grumbling letter from Wittgenstein.
'No reason of course,' he writes, 'why you should give thought
to my thoughts of you, and indeed, I know you do not.'
'Indeed'? He 'knows'? What kind of 'knowing' is that?

'When I gave you lunch on Tuesday . . .' He calls that lunch? –
a pot of tea and a bun? Didn't he know
I'd have to go off, find myself a loaf of bread,
a plate of ham, and thou beside me chatting in

the Gardener's Arms? 'You call my practice "a theory",
but it's not a theory precisely because it's a practice –
a habit of mind, a way of conducting oneself
in relation to language.' The bread and ham were delicious.

It was raining. Across the pub yard I could watch
how water runs through thatch, along a stalk *then down*,
along a stalk *then down*, and finally out at the eaves,
half the thickness of the thatch still dry.

You'd dropped off in your chair, and Yes, I thought,
what a fuss he'd make over the phrase 'dropped off'
and nothing at all of the thatch. 'I think it better,' he writes,
'that we do not meet again.' He thinks he means it.

Wellington
Remembering Baudelaire's 'Spleen'

The gods of weather who dislike this town
cast their cold shadows over its hillside graves
and in the damp ears of suburban dwellers
whisper that death is just around the corner.

A neutered tom fed hormones for eczema
curls and uncurls himself on a threadbare carpet
hearing, as I do, in the rain-choked gutter
Jim Baxter's ghost complaining and composing.

The hot pipes grumble and a clock strikes chill.
I'm tired of playing patience with a pack
that smells of landlady's soap. Darkness comes down.

Listen! The rain has stopped. Now you can hear them –
the Jack of Hearts and Queen of Spades exchanging
sinister gossip about their long-dead loves.

A
U
C
K
L
A
N
D
Low sky
spiked,
rain in sheets
followed at once
by High Blue –
and bright!

Then murk again.
I think it in headline:
ANOTHER SHOCK DOWNPOUR!

Doused
silver and green
the city glitters.
We burn in the gaps.

Still jet-lagged
our visiting Poms
are pinked in a day
their rug-styles ruined.

Do they love Auckland?
Doesn't matter. I do.

373

Dunedin

Remembering James K. Baxter, 1966

Evening where Taieri moved
between dark McCahon hills

fog threatened. You were back
in your aquarium town

wearing your flesh and blood
as if it belonged to you.

Would I get out? Would
it close on Momona?

In the womb we were all
fish. Once was enough.

Any bad-coloured sky
I'd have risked climbing,

scaled any barnacled chain –
yet there you went, at home,

submariner for God
telling the squid and the skate

'Open your gills, my brothers.
Enjoy the life of the Deep.'

To Karl Miller at 70

I see you
flanked by two women
one smiling, in green shoes

the other, head down,
devising (was she?)
your displacement.

Admonitory (unfair?)
you once reproached
my curling lip

your own wit
the Celtic kind, oblique,
leaving its object

uncertain whether
the nip he'd felt was wound
or caress.

Scholarship Scot
among the Simons at Downing
you took

bookish London
by the back door
making space for yourself

who could construe
ahead of time
Heaney's invisible

mending no less than
the magic of Gazza's
dancing steps.

Last week I dreamed
you'd married Rebecca
West and lived at

H. G. Wells,
a confusion you at least
will comprehend.

Karl
in those dingy precincts
of U.C.L. as in the

airy offices
of Bedford Square
you made me welcome

'for which much thanks'
and to my namesake
these birthday greetings.

Shapely Fact Number Poem

'B = T, T = B QED'
                    – John Keats

I X I = I
II X II = I2I
III X III = I232I
IIII X IIII = I23432I
IIIII X IIIII = I23454321
IIIIII X IIIIII = I2345654321
IIIIIII X IIIIIII = I234567654321
IIIIIIII X IIIIIIII = I23456787654321
IIIIIIIII X IIIIIIIII = I2345678987654321
IIIIIIII X IIIIIIII = I23456787654321
IIIIIII X IIIIIII = I234567654321
IIIIII X IIIIII = I2345654321
IIIII X IIIII = I23454321
IIII X IIII = I23432I
III X III = I232I
II X II = I2I
I X I = I

Beauty

Apollo was a god
with a golf course,
Hyacinthus a Greek kid
from the Valley,
then Venice Beach.
They met on Santa Monica Pier
and for the billionaire
it was (as he put it) 'a broken heart

at first-sight – *Wham*!'
The boy caddied for him
(meaning for money),
learned to pilot his helicopter,
and was taken on a world cruise
crewing and (the word was) screwing.

I met Apo some years after
at a pool party –
a Hollywood crowd,
Dustin, Clint, Meryl,
the usual suspects.
He was drinking hard
but seemed contained
wanting to talk to someone
who wanted to listen.

'What's your name?' he asked.
When I told him Ovid
he said he liked my scripts.
'As for my thing with Hy –'
(had I asked?) 'It wasn't sex.
No. It was Beauty' –
which I write with a capital B
because that's how he said it,
frowning, intense,
precise: '*Beauty!*'

No one could quite believe
the official story:
two guys, one fit, one flabby,
throwing a discus
on the old boy's ranch.
It split the kid's skull.
By the time an ambulance came
he was in heaven.

The local police were puzzled
by that flower
with the letters AI
fingered in blood.
To them it was Greek –
meaning it made no sense.

Apo was a known big-hander
to their Holiday Fund
and they let it pass –
which makes it a story
let's say for Elmore Leonard
or one of those *noir* movies
of the 1940s.

But I come back in my thoughts
to the old aesthete
in the deck-chair that evening
by his Brentwood pool.
I'd been looking at his collection,
stunning things
mainly in steel and glass,
and such elegant spaces!
'Not sex,' he insisted
squeezing my arm.
'Sex is nice, my friend,
but it's everywhere,
ordinary. What Hy had
no one else I've known
(and I've known some
believe me) has ever had.
I call it "*Beauty*".'

And then, in one of those
transformations
by which booze can put
iron filings into the voice
and gimlets in the eyes:
'What will *you* call it
Mr big-time pisser
in other people's beds
when you write about it
in your next *shitty screenplay*?'

Bald Caesarion

Bald Caesarion
among the hairy Caesars
trailing your gown or your coat

in the groves of academe
at Rome's far-flung remove
no one would ever guess
you rode once hell-for-leather
bareback, bees in your hair.

He was twice your age
and smelled of horse
that beast of mythic proportion
you rode to the gate for the meat.
Oh indeed the sun shone down on the dark green scrub,
the white road, the brown dam water.
It shone on you!
It had never seen in our region
two such in such disguise –
a boy and a horse.

Reaching for meat
wrapped in newsprint twisted about with rope
you saw too late
bees had swarmed in the box.
Can we say it was then
wheeling, flying homeward lashed by stings
you learned your horse had wings?

What if next day your face waxed like a moon
and your eyes, half-closed,
half-saw indulgent smiles?
You had trailed a plume of demons over the land.
Pride with an indignity was joined
and bald Caesarion, lacking Caesar's glory,
would gather to himself
a mythic story.

On Turning Seventy

I think it came to me in sleep
that when at Anzac dawn parades
old soldiers weep
it's not as they will say for fallen comrades

but for the young self full of sap and fire
as distant now and caught in coils of time
as one the bullets of a half-forgotten war
stopped in his prime.

Of Irony

On matters of food, Horace,
you advise a middle course
between Wolf and Dog. Wolf stands

for greed and excess, Dog for
scavenging meanness. Your friends
who dine on peacock because

its feathers are beautiful
you deplore; but equally
you disdain Aviedenus

who gives his guests five-year-old
olives, rancid oil, and wine
that's turning to vinegar.

Measured, not frugal, pleasure
receives your thumbs up, Horace.
And now Ianus our once young

rebel against everything
especially Irony (that
compromiser of passion)

recovers his poet voice
silent almost a decade
by mimicking you, prophet

of the bourgeois life! Ianus
may rail against Irony
but he shows us what it means.

Even Newer English Bible (2)

Big Daddy-in-the-Sky
your PR's good –
we're backing you to win
down here as you won up there.
Please feed us
and go easy on us
as we go easy on
those other bastards.
No honey-traps –
we want to stay out of trouble
because you've been
the Big Cheese always
and likely to remain so
for the foreseeable future
amen.

Lost Dog

d o g o d o g o d o g o d o g o d o
o d o g o d o g o d o g o d o g o d
g o d o g o d o g o d o g o d o g o
o g o d o g o d o g o d o g o d o g
d o g o d o g o d o g o d o g o d o
o d o g o d o g o d o g o d o g o d
g o d o g o d o g o d o g o d o g o
o g o d o g o *d o g* o d o g o d o g
d o g o d o g o d o g o d o g o d o
o d o g o d o g o d o g o d o g o d
g o d o g o d o g o d o g o d o g o
o g o d o g o d o g o d o g o d o g
d o g o d o g o d o g o d o g o d o
o d o g o d o g o d o g o d o g o d
g o d o g o d o g o d o g o d o g o

Maui

He'd tamed the Sun.
Death would be next –
Hine-nui-te-po
who slept at noon
legs open under ferns.

'There,' he told the birds,
'is her unlocked door.
I will enter
and Death will die.'

The story doesn't end well.
'Someone at the door, Hine' –
that was twittering Piwaiwaka
who prided herself
on having the ear of Death.

Hine squeezed her thighs.
Some say no harm was intended –
it was her shudder of pleasure
killed him pushing headlong
into that Darkness, as once
into the World of Light.

Waitangi, 2002

Summer has come. It's time for the national act.
This year Prime Minister Helen's returning.
We're not to shout at her, we've had our warning –
one more display of traditional disrespect
and she's gone for ever. Off our mana flies
to Ngati Whatua, Waikato, or the tribe of the south,
Ngai Tahu, who often get the biggest bikkies.

In bush around the Treaty House cicadas
are loud – and that's permitted. It's their way.
Ours is different. Mike Smith, no chainsaw today.
Dun Mihaka, you must stay inside your trousers.

Tame Iti, no dancing about and spitting
Tuhoe style. Titiwhai, please guard your mouth.
Today we do it nicely. Bring your knitting.

Full of itself the tide floods the mangroves.
Unpainted boards, carved heads depicting anger,
reflect on stillness. The pied shag goes under
for a long count as if she has something to prove.
From lookouts on the hills the ti-trees sign
that everything is tika, everything couth;
that the circus is coming; that it will soon be gone.

Catullus 65
Allen Curnow, 1911–2001

Grief – or if what's expected and accepted
cannot be grief, then call it incomprehension –
has kept me from the company of the Muse
and the sweet children she bears me, Rodicus,
because my brother poet has taken his swim
this time in Lethe's waters, and already I feel
his forgetfulness leaving me, leaving us all, behind.
Never again will I see him dragged by his dog
as if *he* wore the leash, nor wait for the end
of a witty sentence broken by the lighting of his pipe.
But something of his voice will sound in my lines
as the morepork, heard in a dream, tells us we're home.
And though I cannot send you poems of my own
I offer this by my older friend Catullus
so you'll know my boast of verses wasn't idle.
Let it come to you, as it does in the Roman's trope,
like an apple given to a girl, hidden in her clothes
and forgotten until it rolls to her mother's floor
and has to be explained, and cannot be.

At Wagner's Tomb

i Nietzsche – the Mistake

Student in a strange city
he asks to be directed

to a café. Now he sees
sequins, gauze, feminine forms –

no tables, just couches, doors,
and those insinuous shades

patiently waiting. Also
a piano. He goes to it,

sits, and plays from memory
a *Tristan* duet – music

that is unlocking his soul,
teaching it to speak and sing.

The chords surge to their climax
of sex, then death. He gets up,

explains the mistake, thanks them
for polite applause, and leaves.

ii Ludwig II – the Young King

Affairs of state weigh heavy.
His wedding to the Duchess

Sophie is again put off.
His Ministers, the papers,

the people, complain of his
gifts to ungrateful Wagner

who lies about relations
with Cosima von Bulow,

is quarrelsome, difficult,
ever in need. Forgetting

promises made to himself
Ludwig indulges a taste

for hussars, stable-boys, grooms –
writes desperately to Wagner

proposing abdication
'to be with you for ever'.

The reply is not unkind
but the king understands it.

He wants to punish Wagner
but how and not harm also

that music he loves more than
life itself? In the dark hours

he hears the Rhinedaughters' song
and longs for death by water.

iii Wagner – Dog

News from Dresden catches him
in Marseilles. Minna is dead.

He sends instructions for her
burial. He will not attend.

There is *Die Meistersinger*
to complete. An infected

finger gives him pain. And then
a wife abandoned in life

in death should not be reclaimed.
Returned to Geneva he learns

his dog Pohl has died. All night
demons pursue him, obscure

griefs and remorse. Next morning
the dog is dug up. Weeping,

distraught, the Master gives him
a collar worthy of such a

faithful friend; also a fine
silk coverlet. Reburied

under a suitable tree
Pohl will have a monument

in Jura stone. Days follow
of unaccountable tears.

Die Meistersinger resumes.
He dreams of Minna. She smiles.

iv Hans von Bülow

Music was my God, Wagner
and Lizst the Saints. I married

Cosima, daughter of Liszt,
and conducted for Wagner.

How far does loyalty go?
Here at Tribschen by the lake

preparing *Meistersinger*
for Munich, I learn my wife

is pregnant – and not to me.
She used to fear my rages.

No more. This truth I wanted
not to know, turns me to stone.

Enslaved now to her pity,
double slave to his music –

how I love and hate them both!
I watch her unhappiness

lift a moment as a phrase
floats down from the music room

where the great man is working.
Intelligent devotion –

that is what I lose in her.
That is what the Master gains.

v Wagner & Cosima: Liszt

'If our fake Abbé bangs out
one more Ave Maria

or another Mephisto
Waltz, I swear I'll go insane.'

'How can you speak so cruelly
of my father?' 'The father

who abandoned you, yet kept
you and your mother apart?'

'My parents' passion was grand –
it matched his fame and her rank.

So did their hate. He asked once
"Are we dining or weeping?"

But my father loves . . .' 'He loves
nothing but the Roman Church

and his horrible Princess.'
'Richard, he loves your music.'

'Alas, I cannot love his.'
'You called him a great artist,

said he'd initiated
a new epoch in music.'

'Listen to him, Cosima.
An epoch? – in *fingering*!'

vi Nietzsche – the Renunciation

Passion's advocate who fears
his client, he turns his back

at last on Wagner. Requests
to come again to Wahnfried

he ignores. He travels south
away from the rain, away

from the loud tread of the gods
into that region where man,

godless, might govern himself
under the dance of the stars.

'What is good is light,' he writes
'and runs on delicate feet' –

yet he weeps hearing the music
that once was 'heaven on earth',

weeps recalling their brilliant
conversation and laughter.

But it's Cosima, her eyes,
voice, he will remember when

madness comes, babbling of her
even at the brink of death.

vii Joseph Rubenstein – the Pianist

'I am a Jew. Please save me,'
he writes, and Wagner responds.

Eleven years he spends in
the 'Niebelung Chancellery'

making copies, transcribing
the Master's works for piano,

in the evenings playing Bach,
Beethoven, Liszt. Playing whist!

'Why does he stay?' Cosima
asks; but when he leaves, Wagner

calls him back. 'Herr Rub' in her
diaries. And then 'Malvolio'

and 'the Israelite'. Insults
there are, but also purpose,

excitement, talk. And music –
such music! Walking one day

they meet a stone-breaker. 'Why,'
the Master asks 'does he not

see me, yet greets you warmly?'
And Rubinstein: 'I give him

a coin sometimes.' Cosima
takes note. The Jew gives money!

At Wagner's death he will lose
his Star, his reason for life.

Once more Death's conscript, this time
he will answer the summons.

viii Cosima – Wagner

That morning 'making' (as he
said) 'the two-headed eagle'

she'd felt they were one body.
Now in the palace gardens

of their neighbour and patron
their accord was of the mind.

'Can you not make us one soul?' –
she meant, perhaps, in music,

but he pointed through the trees
to the tomb already built

that would house them both, as if
death alone, or God in death

could make their union perfect –
and indeed when the day came

she pressed herself against him
hour after hour, believing

she too should have died. Decades
would pass before she joined him.

This morning his music floats
from Wahnfried across the lawns.

The palace grounds are a park.
Silent, a stream glides under

trees and bridges, past man-made
islands and moss-green marble.

Flowers are laid at their tomb
on which no word is engraved.

The Red Tram

2004

One

Auckland

After a night of storm
the right-hand buoy's
gone. The sea's

ruffled but
settling. Old Jim swims
as usual, goes home,

lies down as
usual, and dies – not
usual at all, but

at eighty-something
what can we
say? The veteran

wallower has done
his last circuit.
At Friday's full

tide we have drinks
in his honour by
the sheds. Someone

brings a cake. Away
left the sun pulls
in its horns as

lights come on across
the water. There
goes a white cruise

liner rounding North
Head like a hospital
ship in

wartime, and look,
great uncle Webb's
paddling home from work

to Cheltenham in
the canoe he called
Topsy. That was

sixty years ago.
Tonight's moon is
coming up big

over the Hauraki
Gulf. We agree
when the new

buoy's anchored
we'll christen it 'Old
Jim's'. We drink to that.

The Season, Tohunga Crescent

1 *Early September*

The plum tree is
white with blossom
and visited by
wasps (two sorts), monarchs
bumble-bees, large flies
and honey bees (just a few).
Do all these pollinate? Does it matter?
The butterflies seem to compete
with the bumble-bees
and drive them off.
I want plums of course. They come at Christmas.
It's an old tree, capricious
unpredictable. Mrs Nature tells me,
'You will have to wait and see.'

2 Mid-September

The greenest green
creeps up against
the whitest white
which accepts defeat
and scatters
over the lawn.

3 October, constantly

Click smack snick
quick snack
another snail
is whacked
and tenderised
in the garden.

4 Mid-November

Enamel
the small plums
are the tree's
green buttons.

Newly wed ducks
just in from the Wild
are quarrelling
on next door's pool.

Our neighbour's
confused.
Should he play
Tony Soprano?

On the swan plant
the monarch's offspring
are illustrating Ovid –
soft into hard,
black and white into
green and gold.

5 *Early December*

A fledgling thrush
hurls itself at reflections
in my glass door.

Usually they're stunned
and recover
but this one's beak is broken.

All afternoon it hunches,
ruffles, shivers
under the hedge.
I can't settle
or stand its pain.

'What's an axe for?' I ask,
and put myself
out of its misery.

6 *Mid-December*

The Ovid story continues.

This one
shrugs off green and gold
not easily
and pumps itself into
orange and black.

On the bank, flax spears
convert to flowers
and the jet-feathered
tangata whenua
(white wobble at throat)
beaks into them.

7 *Towards Christmas*

Now, as plums ripen
an old war breaks out,

beady-eyed beak and claw
against hand-clap and shout.

Pick or peck?
No contest!
Either I gather early
or they do.

8 *Year's end quarrel*

Between thrush and blackbird
I detect division.

Thrush considers me
beneficent cat-chaser
turner of grub-soil
provider of plums.

Blackbird knows
it owns the plum tree
and that I am a thief.

Legs: an Acknowledgement

Lost in my head
I don't think about
my legs until

they catch my eye.
There they are, feet, ankles,
crossed calves, up

on the desk like
a puppet's, the strings
let loose. Someone

might throw them
out. I see them
with other off-cuts, two

long white discards
in a hospital bin –
or on the

run through a dark
wood looking for the
rest of me to

carry as before. Legs
were always a
part of my

self – the jumper,
goal-scorer, the
middle-aged rambler –

and never given
a thought. I know
there's a tribute

owed to them, but
shyness gets in the way:
they're sportsmen

and we've never
talked. I feel we should
get together,

discuss things,
think creatively
about our future.

The Tree: a Story

1 *The Writer*

'My neighbour tried to arrest me.
I was on his drive, under his tree
sheltering from the rain.
In the struggle I hurt his mouth.
It bled. He called the police.

'When they came for me,
six of them, in three cars,
I was feeding the cat.
Puss had seen it all
but would say nothing.
The thrush said a great deal
(too much in fact
mostly about the rain)
and was not understood.

'At the station an officer
two-fingered my statement.
He said my neighbour thought
I was poisoning his tree.
I said I thought
my neighbour was mad.
I was charged with assault.

'I showed the judge how my neighbour
held his arms out wide
and chanted spells
to protect his tree.

'My neighbour told the judge
his tree had been unwell
and lately depressed.

'The judge wondered
whether it could be the spells
causing the problem.

'I was found not guilty.'

2 The Neighbour

'Why was he crouching under my tree?
It wasn't raining hard.
Couldn't he have sheltered at home?

'Every time he looks at my tree
a branch turns red
and sheds more leaves

which are for the healing of the nations.
Either he has the Evil Eye
or a bottle of Something Deadly.

'He says he is a writer,
but who is the Writer of the Book of Life?
I say it is the Tree.

'I tried to hold him and he hit me –
hard, in the mouth.
He lied about that in Court –
said it was an accident.

'The police had his measure
but His Honour was weak –
possibly influenced by Dark Forces,
who can say?

'The Tree is also a River.
I fear for the future.'

3 *The Cat*

'My chances with the thrush are not good,
I know that, I'm a realist –
but after rain there's what we in the bird business call
a window of opportunity.
I was keeping a low profile, getting in close
when he had his stupid scuffle with the neighbour
and that was the end of it.
They were rolling on the ground, scratching and biting
and of course the thrush took off.

'Straight afterwards
he fed me tinned tuna, my favourite.
Guilt probably –
he's so transparent. It's pathetic.

'I feel I was the meat in the sandwich.'

4 *The Police Officer*

'We knew that arsehole from way back.
He'd given us no end of trouble in '81
and then wrote lies about us in the papers.

'His neighbour may be a screw loose but so what?
You can't go about poisoning plants
and punching tree-freaks
just because you're an "intellectual".

'We parked at the top of the street
and marched him up to the cars,
all six of us
so everyone could see who was in charge
and that he was an arsehole.

'It's called "Law and Order", isn't it?
But what's the use
if the Courts won't back us up?'

5 *The Thrush*

'It was raining.
There were worms
and snails.

'Because my wings were wet
I was nervous of the cat.

'The human was crouching
against the trunk
licking drops
off the end of its nose
when the other one came.
They coupled on the path.'

6 *The Judge*

'An interesting case
turning on the question
of "reasonable force".

'There was no doubt in my mind
the accused had the right
to free himself.
The neighbour was half his age
and somewhat eccentric.

'I gave my judgment in writing.'

A Cow is . . .

A grass processor
on a bone frame
with bagpipes underneath
fly-whisk at the back
and at the front
soft nose, beautiful eyes
and the breath of meadows.

A cow is also beef.

She is milk, she is meat.

The cow follows me
into my dream.
I like her hairy neck-ridge
under my hand.

This is a courtroom –
possibly a church
with green windows
and wooden walls.

Notice there's no
bucket, and no cups.

See how the cow
hangs by one leg.
She grins at the throat.
She vomits ribbons.

History: the Horse

Recall those wartime
draught horses pulling
carts around our suburb –

milk, bread, firewood – like
the record of something
irretrievably

lost, the way for example the
beast would stand, one
rear leg resting

poised on a hoof-point
like a ballerina –
or, square-foot, head-down,

nose in a chaff-bag,
or in the roadside trough
blowing through nostrils

before drinking, as if
to test by the ripples
that this really

was water – tail swishing
between shafts; the regretful
blinkered eyes

and lashes; the mane
like human hair but
coarser; the rakish tilt

of the cart, its iron
wheels grinding on the roadway;
the clop-clop

clop-clop and the carter's
cry; and those great dropped
muffins my mother

sent me with spade
to scoop from the street for her
vegetable garden.

It's as if to return
reporting, 'I've seen the past
and it worked.'

Patience, inwardness,
strength, a body warm to touch,
that smelled good, this

was 'horsepower'.
Nothing with an engine
would ever so engage

feeling and thought,
the pleasure and pain of
planetary kinship.

The Red Tram

Sometimes I climbed the aromatic tree,
macrocarpa I think, with close easy branches
across the road from the chemist while
my mother finished her shopping.

Life went on under the macrocarpa.
Women stopped to talk about the War,
trams lumbered by on their steel rails,
poles flashing at the junction.

My father was at work at the post office –
he had a book to write in, and a rubber stamp;
my sister was at school, my grandmother
at home doing the housework.

Now my mother and father both are dead,
my grandmother of course, even my sister;
the tram rails are torn up, and the macrocarpa
cut down, cut down –

and I am there still, close to the sky
listening to housewives talk about the War,
watching the pole flash and the red tram
clank off into the future.

Speaking Plain

1 *Now and then*

You used to mow your own lawns –
not any more;
you used to Hoover your own house –
now a woman comes.
When one car wasn't enough
it was all you had –
now you have two and don't use them.
As the bills come in you pay them;
as the rubbish goes out, you buy more.
In a hungry world you eat well;
in a crowded one, you have space.
It has cost a lifetime.
Enjoy!

2 *Irene*

Somewhere in a grave
in a coffin the size of a shoebox
lies my third sister
who lived one hour.

Irene she was called,
or was to be called.
I see her as a redhead –
something I was told
or imagined.

Many tears were shed.
To me she was a puzzle –
a sibling coming
and then gone.

Suppose she too had been
a troublesome writer.
I see us together
a sentence beginning
'Irene and I . . .'
'I and Irene . . .'

She's smoking,
tossing her red hair,
laughing at my
bad-taste jokes.

3 *The Grandmother*

This space was meant for 'Nana'
but she kept bursting out of it –

her shoes with holes cut
to suit her bunions,
her bandaged
unreliable knees,
her singing
(especially her singing) –

impossible!

I tried to make room for her,
provide comfort and entertainment
(especially entertainment)
but it was no use.

She's stolen a packet of my father's DeReszkes
and gone to the pictures.

4 *Piano*

'*Third* finger! *Third* finger!'
That was the voice
from two rooms away.
I'd used second finger
or fourth.

That's how it was
having your teacher in the house
while you practised.

Not that the note was wrong,
just the finger.
How could she tell?

I was her worst pupil,
her biggest disappointment –
perfect pitch
and some failure of hand and eye.

Never mind, Mum,
you trained my ears.
They're listening still.

5 Dad

This spring my dreams are
nowheres, otherwheres,
places I've never been –
or if familiar
it's usually childhood,
my father in his garden.

He has his back to me.
Something's unresolved
between us.

'Look at me, Dad –
I'm older by five years
than your final count.
Speak to me.'

He goes on planting.

You

Our friends' wedding:
I'd lied, called it a funeral
to get army leave
so I could be with you.
It was a surprise, a present
and your blush of pleasure
cheered me like a crowd.

So here we are on the step
above 'the happy couple'
who will one day divorce –
looking into the future
which is now.

Ten friends together
in that photograph.
Fifty years on
and four are dead.
Who will be next?
Who will be last
and put out the light?

It's time to tell you again
how much I loved the girl
who blushed her welcome.
Forgive my trespasses.
Stay close. Hold my hand.

Two

That fear makes killers

1 *The Bandusian Fountain*

Remember how thunder
out of a cloudless sky
turned our poet religious?

It couldn't have come of nothing:
this was invisible Power
shaking the earth.

He was shaken –
chided himself for a fool,
abased himself

before the gods
promising prayers
and acts of reverence.

All that I could accept,
but not his sacrifice
of the kid I called Picasso.

I used to heel my hand
against Picasso's brow
and he would push

practising manhood,
goathood. Now
we have only a poem

and that splash of blood
by the Bandusian spring
to remember him by.

2 *O!*
Aeli vetusto nobilis ab Lamo . . .

O Oilman Caesar
ignoble heir to another, taller Caesar
who first sent men and missiles across the desert
but not as far as yours –
even into Baghdad, even Tikrit
searching for the Evil One's
hidden unspeakable weapons;

O Texan Caesar
tomorrow (the Raven warns)
a hurricane will close your capital down,

keep cars from streets, trains from tracks
and civil servants at home.

Gather, then, your slaves about you;
kill a pig, broach the wine cask,
summon the dancers –

while you may
O celebrate your greatness!

True Tales from Ovid

1 *Global Warming*

Visiting his father Phoebus,
Phaeton wears shades.
He finds the big guy busy
with charts and timetables
attended by Days and Seasons.

The boy asks
can he borrow the car.
Phoebus, uneasy
but thinking 'quality time',
consents.

Big mistake!
It's all wheelies and burn,
smoke and exhaust flame
along the Skyway Highway.

The gardens of the East
degrade into desert.
The Ganges shrinks;
fish fry in the shallows.
When the crash comes
(officer Jove in pursuit)
the polar caps
are already cracking.

Man-centred Ovid laments
another teenage statistic.
The World, he seems to imply,
can heal its own wounds.

2 Soham

Pyreneus was caretaker,
the school his domain,
certain girls (nine in all)
his inspiration.
It was a Sunday,
rain threatening
when two came by.
He pointed to the black cloud,
invited them in for shelter
and locked the doors.

According to Ovid
they should have escaped
and Pyreneus in his wild pursuit
crashed and burned.

So why these forlorn bodies
hidden in a field
and this hangdog in the dock?

3 Rugby World Cup semi-final Sydney, 15.11.03

George Gregan
is the Gorgon's
head,
every All Black
an Atlas
turned to stone.

4 The Wall

Metamorphosis:
how time changes even
the meaning of a story.

Pyramis and Thisbe for example –
lovers from the same
suburb or village
cruelly divided
by a wall.

Are we Black and White,
Jew and Goy,
Ossie and Wessie?

No, my love
we are Palestinian
and ready to bleed.

The Advance of English – Lang and Lit

1 Shakespeare – Sonnet CXVI

Trust me –
I'm backing myself here.
Love doesn't budge.

2 Marvell – 'To His Coy Mistress'

IF there was time . . .
BUT there isn't . . .
SO
we better fuck NOW!

3 Wordsworth – 'Tintern Abbey'

I used to come here
when I was a kid.
Sometimes my sister came too.
It was nice.
There was the river,
and the rocks for climbing.

You miss those things, don't you
as you get older.

4 Coleridge – 'Kubla Khan'

You have to get the map of it:
the river came up here, out of the ground,
and five miles further on
it went down again.
That's where old K.K. built his brothel.
He put in some nice gardens,
walls and stuff.

I was going to tell you quite a story
about old K.K.
but that pusher from Porlock knocked
and by the time I got back to my desk
I'd forgotten what it was.

5 Keats – 'Ode to a Nightingale'

Just listening to that bird
makes me feel as if I'm pissed
or high on something –
and then the fucker flies away.
Bugger!

6 Tennyson – 'The Lady of Shallot'

This creepy woman
she had a thing about windows –
instead of looking straight out
like you or me
she used a mirror.
Crazy, man!
And then one day a real hunk went by,
Lance Slot, I think he was called,
and she looked straight at him
and sure enough – she died!

7 *Eliot* – The Waste Land

I
Yes it's spring
but London's hell –
all these dead people
and me.

II
Rich and poor
I find them equally
obnoxious.

III
Autumn's no better.
Sex can be really disgusting
but I do like the River.
I go there
and hum a little Wagner –
weialala leia
and so on.

IV
But imagine drowning in it –
that would be ghastly.

V
So in my head
I head for the desert –
dry throat
crops dying
voices, thunder . . .

oh God!

Sweet and Sour

1 To Auntie Huia who made the kete in which
Dr Glenn Colquhoun sent me his poems

He calls you his Auntie
and me his Godfather.
Does that make us rellies
or just partners in crime?

He's your scribe who prescribes,
you are surgeon to the flax.
Your kete is a poem
and I treasure it.

I think of you up there, 'up North'
on the Hokianga
where the sands are blond
the sea has blue eyes
and the soul is Maori.

How is your heart, Auntie Huia?
Listen carefully
to what he tells you about it.

Moko can be skin deep.
I think the one on his arm
goes all the way to the bone.

2 Patriot

'Let me introduce myself.
I am a patriot from a Shithouse
in the South Seas
known as New Zealand.

'You think your Shithouse
is worse than mine?
It may be
but I don't live in your Shithouse,
I live in mine.

'Why do I live there?
Let's call it a habit, an addiction
like smoking.

'When you hear our national anthem
please remain seated.
If our flag's raised
tear it down, burn the bastard.

'Do this for me.'

3 *City fathers*

'*The Mayors of Auckland and Manukau cities are combining forces to
advance the cause of the Eastern Corridor Motorway*' – News

John Banks

The part of us
that's human
dislikes him.

The part that has wheels,
accelerator and brakes
voted him in.

His thank-you gift
will be another scar
across the face of our city.

Sir Barry Curtis

The speech machine
will go on orating
without grace or thought
conscience or content
grammar or grampa
as long as coins are fed
into the slot marked 'coins'.
If, after a pause,
speaking is not resumed
insert more coins and

wait while the tape rewinds.
Do not kick or shake.

4 *In that country*

In that country
poet spoke for people
against the invader.

Between bombings
when sirens were silent
poems were broadcast.

When newspapers lied
people queued for poems
and read them on trams.

Oh for such a contract
to write only the truth,
even to die for it –

how much better than
to be civil servant
to Propriety, our master.

Sentry Duty

1 *Derrida*

He thought the whole fucking discourse
should have been preceded
by 'a long learned thoughtful meditation
on the presupposition of Yes'
but I said No.

2 *Where do the Great Composers go when they die?*

A black hole
in the galaxy of Perseus
has been humming

(scientists report)
in the key of B flat
but at 57 octaves
below middle C
inaudible
to the human ear.

Come in, Beethoven.
Are you receiving me?

3 *So the Ancient Egyptians were right*

A star
in the constellation of X
has eaten two of its planets
and exploded.

Our sun could do the same.

Great Ra
source of our life
source in time of our deaths
we abase ourselves,
we salute you!

(And please, watch your diet.)

4 *Sun Block*

Less melanoma may mean
more rickets
and vice versa.
So the bow-legged cowboys
confront the twiggy blondes
with leather faces.

There's no gain without loss.

5 *Petit Mort*

Little Death, Little Death
where have you been?

I've been up to London
to fuck with a queen.

6 *Gerard Manley Hopkins*

He made an appointment
with the Blessèd Virgin.
There were one or two
details of doctrine
he thought it important
they should discuss.

She stood him up
and it was raining.
She may think it
doesn't matter,
but (off the record) he told me
he was *not* impressed.

7 *How to Rhyme in 2003*

Here we're debating
schools of creative wraiting.

Day after day
graduates rush to say
in the same indignant tones
'We are not clones!'

Africa: an Autobiography

I
Geoff Walker at Penguin
is one of many
wanting my life
but the story's well known.

My father was political
a revolutionary of sorts
a forty-a-day man
with a gunshot arm
and paralysed hand.

My mother
a concert virtuoso
gave up the circuit
to teach (among others)
me.

My sister's affairs
with officers and aristos
were legend.

My granny?
She was Dame Nellie
and a peach in the kitchen.

I published my first novel
at fifteen
and went off somewhere –
to Africa I think.
The rest is history.

2
I was born on grass
among flowers
and volcanic stones.
Those blacks and whites
falling from the window
were notes of music.
Death was not in the picture.

3
Over the road
was the school
and beyond the school
the hill.

From the hill
I would see the harbour,
from the harbour
the world.
Oh dear!
There would be no going back.

Africa, expect me!

4
Who will argue with a war?
It was a story.
People died.
Our side won.

5
Love
is no end of trouble.
There will be no escape
not even in
Africa.

6
Children will be
children are
children have been
and look
here comes Death
with a bag on his shoulder
marked 'Africa'.

America

There's a prescient movie
maybe by Robert Altman
that ends with toads
falling from the sky –

a storm, a downpour
an Old Testament pelting
of tumbling toads –
and in case you should think
his story's slipped
into the realm of the unreal
he has a boy, a quiz-kid,
one who knows everything,
smiling, saying 'Yes, this *happens*!'

Nine-eleven was like that –
minute shapes that were bodies
all arms and legs
hurtling down.

We'd picnicked
on the white stone slopes
above Mausanne-les-Alpilles
and came home to it,
to watch it like a movie,
its horror, its rough justice.

New York seemed to be burning.
'Yes, this *happens!*'
Americans
were falling from the sky.

Three

Horae Secularae

Matins

This minute after midnight
is when the cells of the body
turn into pumpkins
and want to go home.

Humour them.
They'll sing his praises
better and together
in the morning.

Prime (**London**)

Sir fox in the garden
lifts and directs his ears.

I'm silent, I'm still
but his nose
is telling him something.

So we face one another
in the dawn,
I wanting to affirm
a kind of kinship,
he with nothing to add.

Terce (**Memory**)

Phoebus burning the curtains
pushing marmalade fingers
between the blind slats –
fuck off!
Must to thy motions
lovers' seasons run?

(But that was in another
century, and besides
the wench is dead.)

Sext (**Gotland**)

Mrs Martin
('House' to her friends)
wings in from Pinetops
to the summer structure
of straw and mud she's stuck
almost at man's reach
in this doorway's shelter.

At the whirr of *her*
three yellow beaks
open.

I call them Gold,
Frankie and Myrtle.

All through lunch
she comes and goes
taking it on the wing.

Nones (Uzès)

Sunbrowned
among sunflowers
I'm fraternising
(as is my habit)
in particular with one.

Round-faced and
smiling into the lens
they're looking
(as is theirs)
all one way.

A battalion! A host!
Yelloluiah!

Vespers (London)

I shedding tears
under thatch
at the Globe Theatre
not at sad stories
of the death of kings
but at beauty.

The grass withers
the flower falls
but the lordship of the word
is for ever.

Compline

Praise be to our God
we call Getaway
who made heaven and earth
and on the seventh day slept –

who will not answer e-mails
phone-calls, prayers
and will not wake
even at the Trump of Doom.

The Masterwork

On turning 70, Hokusai
(or was it Allen Curnow?)
told his neighbour across the street
'I begin to understand
the mysteries of my art.
Another decade will bring me
nearer Reality.'

On turning 80 he told his wife
'Be patient, my love.
Beyond understanding
comes control. A further decade
will give me that.'

At 90 he told himself,
'Understanding, control
have given me freedom at last.
Tomorrow
I begin my Masterwork.'

Next morning
as the sun rose, he died.

Karekare

1 *Lone Kauri Road*

The dead man's bach
goes for a price.

One summer I stayed there –
sent him a sketch
of the view from his deck
that made the valley
a glass bowl filled with ocean
up almost to the rim.

Would it spill over?
Can he see it still?

Down there's the road
he walked in a poem
at evening, for mussels.
Those voices if you listen
may be the stream's
quoting his lines.

Or are they saying,
'Sold to the highest bidder!
Gone for a song!'

2 *Streams*

Even the cheerful ones
have a death wish –
or is it no more
than a craving for salt?

One here has created
a step-down path
with lingering glades.
Another, to meet it,
takes a long-fall short-cut
down a rock-face,
after which, joined by a third

beyond the road-bridge,
they amble as one
seaward through dunes.

Sometimes a wide lagoon
forms and disperses –
or the flow bears south
before turning again
and rushing the exit.

The moon has a hand in it
but the west wind is God.

3 *The Giants*

The lower jaw's gone,
chain-sawed off
and top teeth taken.

Some bogus ethnic bone-man
using electric drills
will carve them.

The black hulk
speaks weight –
forty tonnes
unsupported by water.

It presses into sand
wanting to bury itself.

Scarlet thins to pink
and spreads in shallows.

Blow-hole, anus, eyes
all are shut.
The fluked tail alone
answers to
the motions of waves.

You've read of giants?
Down this long smoking coast

Karekare to Whatipu
twelve lie dead.

What are they telling us?
Such a lovely day!

Without

Crossing Cook Strait
going home to be
ordained in the

parish of his
father, while seas wished
by and the wind

had its say in the
wires, it came to
him there was no

God. Not that
God was sulking or had
turned His back – that

had happened
often. It was that God
wasn't there, was

nowhere, a Word
without reference or
object. Who was

God? He was the
Lord. What Lord was
that? The Lord God. Back

and forth it went while
stern lifted, screw
shuddered, stars glowed

and faded. The
universe was losing
weight. It was

then he threw his
Bible into the
sea. He was a

poet and would
write his own. Happiness
was nothing

but not being
sad. It was your
self in this one and

only moment
without grief or
remorse, without God

or a future – sea,
sky, the decks
rolling underfoot.

Takapuna

Janet Frame 1924–2004

So old friend you've come to it at last
(Ron Mason's line, and now an echo of Yeats!)
How does it feel to feel nothing?
No one will ask you to read, no unmarked sheet
will ever again reproach you.
You can 'become your admirers'.

Somewhere along the way your brain got sparked
but your hair stood up for you.
You wrote of shame without shame.
'Madness' was the house of your self, the house of cards
falling whenever someone opened a door.

Remember the day of our disaster?
We sat in the hut and I criticised your poem.
Clumsy, literal, your junior in years and in pain
I'd thought it was what you wanted.

There were winged things in the garden, and wilting leaves,
earth smells, compost, beans.
You sat in all your radium intensity,
in the brightness of mercury falling.
The thing you'd wanted was love!

I remember the walk home,
the glass veranda, matting on the walls,
and the view to Rangitoto.
Sea lanes were open
all the way to the World, those dark rough paths
we knew we'd have to travel.

Histories of the hive, the swallow's flight,
the archives of the ant, even an ode of Keats –
all, I know, confirm it: the thing that happens
dies when it happens.
The thing that doesn't happen lives for ever.

Ode to the Eight Immortals

and remembering one over the eight, Denis Glover

One who could sleep on horseback;
one who, invited to the Court of the Emperor
arrived with two flagons – his 'contribution';
one, a Prime Minister, big spender of public money
especially after the dandelion port;
one – young, rich, handsome, well-dressed –
who had everything to lose
and the determination to waste no time
in losing it;
one, a devout Buddhist who swore off all meats
but kept wine as his path to Enlightenment;
one a thirsty poet whose subtlest haikus
were costed in bottles;

one a calligrapher who, for just half a flagon,
could do you mist, mountains, waterfalls
seen through the branches of a fir tree;
and finally a poor man, a man of no consequence,
whose eloquence in his cups was inebriation's
finest flower –
these the poet Du Fu celebrated
as the Eight Immortal Drinkers
deserving commemoration
and eternal honour.
Let's raise our glasses then, in salute to them all
and not forgetting our own unquenchable Denis
laureate of the grain
Nobel of the grape.

Brit Lits

1 *A-Mo and B-Mo*

There are two poets for example
Andrew Motion and Blake Morrison
edited together
The Penguin Book of Contemporary British Poetry.
I call them A-Mo and B-Mo
but I confuse them.

One has a fruity voice,
writes biography
and addresses poems
to Her Majesty the Queen
and members of her family.

The other has written a book about his father
and a book about his mother
and a book about a small boy
beaten to death with a brick.

But is A-Mo the Laureate-biographer
or is it B-Mo?

It should be easy.
One of these two I've met –
but was he B-Mo or A-Mo?
I'm not sure. I forget.

2 Alzheimer's

I can confirm I was not one of her friends –
never lusted after her red-gold hair
as she cycled along St Giles,
never talked about Sartre as cattle crowded our path
through the Port Meadow to the poplars at Binsey,
nor joined her swimming party and removed my clothes.
I was never privileged to see the squalid house
she kept with John, nor ever made use of the loo
with its encrustations her friends so starkly record.
As for her very last years, my sharing of those
was the anodyne cinema version.
John's books about her dying I'm afraid I declined.

But it's true – I can say I met her.
Once was a dinner at Auckland's White Heron Motel
when, late in an evening of stammer and startling chat,
our linguist, Forrest Scott, asked her to dance.
From Oxford she sent him a friendly thank-you card
calling him Foxy Trot.

And there was that final meeting
thirty years on at a literary launch in London.
She didn't know she'd ever been to Auckland.
Her back was pressed to the wall, eyes full of fear.
Her friends were tigers. Was I one of her friends?

3 Health Warning

My friend Miranda
who wrote about Robert Graves
was given the scarab ring
of poetry's worst witch
his mistress, Laura Riding.

Miranda's car was stolen,
her dog put down,
her flat suffered 'rising damp',
her mother fell ill
and her husband decamped.

'Is the ring safe?' she asked.
'I kept it outdoors on a twig,'
its former owner confessed.
Miranda has gifted it
to the Robert Graves Trust.

4 *Iris again, Auckland 1960s*

John banging on about the Beatles
and doing a Ricks
on 'Eleanor Rigby' –

I telling Iris
the green brooch at her throat
(knight killing dragon)
was on the jacket
of *The Italian Girl.*

No, she assured me, it wasn't.
'But you've *seen* a connection.'

And then she said something
I've remembered forty years:
'*Looking* is the death of ego.'

'Not the death,' I corrected,
'but maybe an *escape*.'

She smiled
that blue-eyed white-witch smile
that had trapped so many.

My Fellow Writers at Eaglereach

1 *Their names as a poem*

Aminatta Forna
Ronnie Someck
Marcel Beyer
Ghada Karmi
Raja Shehadeh

2 *That geography and history can't be disentangled*

Aminatta
south London Sierra-Leonese

Ghada
north London Palestinian

Ronnie
Iraqui Israeli

Marcel
Wessie who moved against the tide
to live in the East

Raja
Palestinian Palestinian
who refuses to budge

3 *Family matters*

Aminatta
whose father was hanged by his political rivals

Marcel
whose parents
must have played their part
in the great German silence

Ghada
whose parents were driven out of Palestine
by the Israelis

Ronnie
whose parents were driven out of Iraq
because they were Jews

Raja
whose father, a judge
was stabbed to death
in a street in Ramallah.

4 *Descriptions*

Aminatta is glamorous
Marcel glossy
Ghada beautiful.

Ronnie is large
Raja very small.

What they have in common
is language
a voice.

5 *What they leave behind, and bring*

One recalls his mother
first-year immigrant
lacking Hebrew
sewing workers' overalls
in the Rekem factory

One tries to imagine the rope

One wonders what his
father said to his mother
when Hitler said . . .

One speaks of her mother
creating Jerusalem
in Golders Green
even to the red-tiled floors
the meals, the talk
even to the tears

One remembers the knife
the body on the slab
the Israeli police
indifferent
because it wasn't 'political'

6 *Here, now*

Together at
Eaglereach, N.S.W.
they become
walkers
wallaby watchers
picking golden wattle
listening to wind
up from the Valley
catching the scent
of eucalypt.

They laugh a lot.
Things go on.

Calgary

Flying in
to read and sign books
I see the brown barren plain
spelling FLAT
in any language
and every direction –
and the long straight highway
drawn with a ruler
going all the way
 to Shirley Nowhere.

And this
an immense graveyard
seen closer is a suburb –
nice houses
pale and tight as gravestones
with no trees.

Later, in the city
that is every pull-down push-up quick-fix city
someone says
'This place was built on oil.
Nothing above ground
could have paid for it.'

Letter from the Mountains

to the late Lieutenant-Colonel John Mulgan, M.C.

I wanted to write you a poem –
twenty attempts and more
all dead in the water.
'If poetry doesn't come
as leaves to the tree – forget it!'
That (more or less) was Keats.
Courage may be a madness,

a disease afflicting the young.
Your work behind the lines
took lives, and cost lives –
and then you took your own.
Yesterday, a birthday
(my seventy-first) I climbed
the steeps and puff of a trail

to the top of a mountain.
A penance? Maybe a test.
Air was thin. Conifers
sighed and whispered
arcane intelligence.
Only chipmunk and squirrel
understood that language

of place and season.
I thought of you dealing
death among the pines

of the Pindus Mountains.
Was it there you decided
history wouldn't dictate
the end of your story?

You don't know me, it's true.
We learned the same suburb
through the soles of our feet,
sat in the same classrooms –
but decades apart.
I've seen in you a self
time never taught me,

a shadow unexplored –
but if you decline to live
in lines of mine
I have to honour that.
If there's a secret, it's safe.
You are still your own man.
Be at peace, soldier.

Banff, Canada, October 2003

Rapallo: an Economy
for Massimo Bacigalupo

I
Think sea
cypresses and saints –
this is what we sailed from
to invent the world;
this is where the world returns
to discover itself.

Stone piled on
stone:
endless renewal.

Like the seasons
Rome came and went;
like God
it issued large instructions
largely ignored.

2
I am history
banging on,
a broken shutter
hanging by one hinge
in a window
of the Hotel Villa Cristina.

Fishermen sailed out
and back at evening;
soldiers who marched west
marched east again.
Now it's tourists
arrive and depart.

I see the storm
before it strikes;
I watch the violinist at midnight
hitch up her skirts
and change her shoes
before climbing the salita
to Sant' Ambrogio.

Behind my back
sleep happens
and waking
and sex.

3
Between double cannon
and phoenix palms
a four-frog fountain remembers
the poet Pound
blessed and burdened,
a vision of the earthly paradise

locked behind blue
clouded eyes.

4
This morning
Vagabonda III
sails us out into
the horseshoe bay.

Puccini is a province,
Liguria a personality,
pasta a saint.

Flowers are politicians
promising the earth.

Ashore
Venus in a swim suit
rides pillion on a Vespa
and the marble Virgin
retires defeated
to her stone shell.

5
It's the lesser gods survive
on hill-slopes
among grape and olive.
They are in the roof beams,
under floor tiles and altars;
they live in the wren's nest
and the fox's den;
they speak in the squeak of a bat
and the chatter of swallows.

The messages are simple
and ample:
obey the season
and the seasons of the blood.
Look hard.
Live as well as you can.

On Fame

Quid dedicatum poscit Apollinem

Who asks the gods for glory
and that his books may be read
throughout the world, should recall
the one whose prayer was answered,
who lived ten years in hiding,
lost friends, family, everything
but fame itself and a fortune.

How joyful to have your words
say what they mean! Be content
with that, and that you write for
those who can read, and can rune.

Best wines for finest palates.
Look for no other reward.

Four

Haiku

1 *The lesson*

Mamuko's Master
a famous scholar of Zen
fell from a mountain.

It's said he strayed from
the beaten track to reach for
a lovely flower.

Mamuko, noted
for sexual adventures,
read in this sad news

his Master's final
lesson: 'See in my death the
story of your life.'

2 *In Tsingsi District Prison*

A flute complaining:
Ho, the patriot, listened.
'None but a lover'

(he told his leg-irons)
'locked up and far from his dream
could make such music.'

He was right of course.
I was the flautist, you sole
object of my song.

Since Time must visit
your face and curb my fingers'
deftness on the stops,

let's praise our blind love
that gave the nation-maker
(he said) new courage.

Love etc.

1 *Fragment XXXI (Sappho), poem LI (Catullus)*

Has he a name
this man I make
equal with the gods because
his place at your table
confirms a rumour?

He bends to listen
catching word and breath in one
and your easy laugh –

how it stills my tongue,
blinds me,
runs over my skin
like wind over wheat.

You are his, then, Clodia
and I am nothing.
All my past
he takes without knowing.
All my future
you give him with a smile.

2 Ode I/iv – to Venus (Horace)

'Intermissa, Venus, diu ...'

No Venus
you've had more than your share of this poet.
There's not a part of his being
you haven't camped in,
colonised.
Enough of that.
Hasn't he earned a rest and the right to smile?

Look, here's a Christian girl commanded to love,
and there an atheist wanting it for himself.
Confound them both –
set them at it in a hayfield.

As for yours truly,
leave him to his late-night paper and pen –
or if you haven't quite lost
your taste for tease and torment,
demand he pay you back-rent, a page a day,
and if he should fail, if he should come
empty-handed and whining to your door,
let loose on him by way of encouragement
the remembering dogs.

3 'My Recurring Dream' (Verlaine)
'Je fais souvent ce rêve ...'

It's of a woman
never quite the same
but always the same
who loves me,
understands me,
sets my heart racing
and can make me calm.

About appearances
hair colour for example
I'm uncertain.
I can't quite catch her name –
hear it only as a tone
soft and sonorous
like the names of the Romantic dead.

Her eyes see in and through me,
her voice is a silence
that speaks of silence.

My lover, I thought at first.
Now I know she's my death.

4 Poem LXXVI (Catullus)
'Siqua recordanti benefacta ...'

Catullus, you seem to think
your steadfastness should earn you
reward in your final years.
So now you ask the gods
no longer that she be faithful
or even love you –
only to give you strength
to free yourself from bondage.

'O gods, O greatnesses' you pray
as if you believed indeed
the Silence of space had ears –
'in return for my piety

443

and virtuous observance
rid me at last, I beg you,
of the disease of love.'

Do you really not know you ask for
what's already granted?
It's the habit of love, Catullus,
not the fact of it
that burdens you still.

5 'The Portrait' (Baudelaire)
'Je te donne ces vers . . .'

I give you these lines
so that if in some future time
when you and I are dead
my work should find new readers,
your ghost, wanting only rest,
will be called on to explain
that moment when you turned
your back on me
and walked away.

'Why did you do it?' they'll ask,
and you, lacking speech,
will have no answer
but re-enactment.

This gift I owe you my love,
my dark-eyed angel,
because you it was gave me cause
to perfect my art.

Take it. It's yours.

6 Elegy II/xiii (Propertius)
'Non tot Achaemeniis armatur . . .'

If you insist the heart is the source of feeling
then hear my heart when it speaks.
If Cupid must be the deliverer of love

then yes, his shafts have delivered.
However you wish me to decorate the fact
love it is indeed dictates these lines –
and not to foster growth in the Sacred Grove,
nor to charm wild beasts from their lairs
into the path of hunters,
but to praise this woman beside me.

Even an ugly man
can bring beauty to his bed;
a fool will win a countess
if his desire for advancement
burns like a passion;
and I, who care so deeply
for wit and discrimination,
have found and loved them in her.

Great Jove-of-the-Arts
as long as compliant others
are there to praise and serve you,
from you I won't receive
the laurel crown;
but while I have her ear
and her approval
I shall not need or want it.

7 *'Evening at the Green Café' (Rimbaud)*
'Depuis huit jours . . .'

At the Green Café in Charleroi
I order rolls and butter
and ham.

Eight days
I've worn my boots to shreds
on stony roads.

Now look at me –
legs stretched out
under the green-painted table,
reading the wallpaper
and happy.

Here comes the smiley girl
big tits, bright eyes
the sort not frightened to fuck
bringing the rolls, the butter, the hot ham
(pink and white, with a whiff of garlic)
all on a hand-painted platter.

She pours me beer from a jug –
plenty more where that came from!

Down goes the sun.

I tell you . . .

Stone Figure
Archipel de Tanimbar, Ile de Yamdena,
Village d'Alusi Karwain, seventeenth or eighteenth century

Necklace, ear-ornament
and bob of hair
say female

but it's the hips and knees
confirm. Patient,
vulnerable –

yes but dependable.
She's there. She *is*
and can be

counted on. Eyes
steady under the bows
of brows are

intent on distance.
Village matters concern
her, this

goddess of the fields,
focused,

benign. Imagine her
not in the full
blaze of sunlight but
at evening in

broken shadow, or
at the full of the moon
still and

silent. Invite her
indoors? No. You
know she wouldn't

come. Her work's
unfinishing. Those eyes
will never close.

The Black River

2007

One

The Art of Poetry (i)

'Where is your theory?'
he asks. 'What
is your aesthetic?'

I give him the
pied stilts stepping
it out on the bay

in low-tide light,
the bottle-brush bush
shaking with

warblers at work.
I explain I'm no
respecter of

birds that can't
sing, dogs that won't
bark, rudderless yachts;

that I salute
sooner the prisoner
poet who made

a life of observing
the ant. 'My
theory,' I say

'is the warblers
working, the stilts up
on their stilts, the

'world looking hard
at the word and the
word at the world.'

Auckland

There are dreamscapes
                and realscapes.

              This one I suspect
                    is real
though the sun is walking on water
and the sea out at the yellow buoy
                      is silk.

           An orange container-ship
is rounding North Head.
                Green Rangitoto
pictures itself
and is not displeased.
              Moehau, deep blue
insists on distance.

              Swimming back
on my back
                I become again
the connoisseur of clouds –
feathers and fleeces.

              A gull drifts over
                  a tern
                  a gull again
white on
white
on blue.

              A low-altitude
                Exocet shag
                (late for lunch?)
hurtles across.

           This is the life that goes
                godlessly on
a poem without words
a gift without conditions
                a present
without a past.

Oxford

the nice old stones
the green lawns
the clever children –
clever and polite.

I was old
a visitor
an old lion

but in youth
how tempting
if a door had opened
a word been said
to step inside a moment
and wake middle-aged
drowning in honey.

Three Poems from the Languedoc

1 *St Maximin*

The swallows are
gone, also the white
snails from fennel

along the roadsides.
The sunflowers have
been harvested.

The summer Swede
has gone back to
winter in Malmö.

The engines of
the *vendange* are doing
their last best

up and down the
lines of vines. A good
season, they say.

At the bar in
the little café the
village drunk

is joined by
the waitress. *Le patron*
entertains them

with his pierrot
act, but stops to
make us a seafood

risotto with
mushrooms. Don't be
deceived by oilcloth

and unemptied
ashtrays. This is France
and he can cook.

2 *Talking to Bill*

I'm telling Bill
Pearson about the
Department, my

surprise that it's
gone, all the ones I
thought of as rocks

in a landscape –
Mike Joseph, John
Reid, Betty Shepherd,

Prof Musgrove, Allen
Curnow – where are they
now? I think

John Reid may be
dead. I tell Bill
Allen has gone to

live in Australia.
Even as I say
it, it seems

unlikely. I give
him a farewell hug.
He submits,

flinching. It comes
to me only slowly
that they're all

dead, even Bill.
I go to the window
and look out.

A medieval village
in moonlight looks
back at me.

Am I too dead?
Not yet. Only dreaming
and in France.

3 *Curtailed*

Battered, dirty,
fur torn out in
patches, the little

hang-dog stray
stands shivering in the
lane, wolfing scraps from

a bowl. His Good
Samaritan stands
back and watches.

Next seen, he's
drinking from the mill race.
He hobbles on

through the woods
past the château
hurrying on tender

paws as if he has
somewhere to go.
That path will take

him into the
nowhere of the garrigue.
The mind finds

happy endings
for him and doesn't
believe them.

Four Poems
each beginning with lines supplied by Sam Sampson

I
      Each cubicle, every theoretical base
offers an age of wishful thinking
         from which we deviate
'at our peril'.

      The oracle however
knows what it knows, and
      undercover
            will keep it so.

To guard it
singing its praises (but only in private)
          is sound.

Take this key
and listen.

Look and lock.
Hold your head high.
          Speak as if
it didn't matter but in the knowledge
      that a wrong note may be death.

There will be more in the morning.

2
        You go winding from
distance, old mind-wanderer. Re-
           found fabrications
              won't wound
    but the hand
          that forged a folly
may also make you a fortune.

No it was not a mistake
         rather
that I wound back

     the clock of what I knew
disunderstanding you.

You know about the whole in my heart
and that I am a swimmer.
           Forgive
    me my passes
my pauses
my paws-on-you
        as I forgive those
that put their tresses against me.

It may be marred in the mourning.

3
'External' – enough to give some space
      (and then some)?

        No brother –
it was 'eternal' you know you

meant
            and let it be so
while it lasts.

Upstairs
still holds His breath
        but if it's true
                    (and it's true)
we made Him in our image
        it can't be for ever.

Listen then for the mighty wind
        the big exhalation
                    the sweetness
(will it be?)
            of the cud of the Lord
chewed these millennia
        let out at last
in a relenting sigh.

Give over God
is our daily prayer.

It may be four in the morning.

4
After a number of years
            the landscape changes
            but not Guantanamo Bay
where we squat unshielded at stool
        under a tin roof
        and waterboarding
            is the sport of choice.

'Go, Condaleeza!' we cry
            but the heavens are empty.

You wanted an eternity?
        My friend, you have it!

        There will be more
in the morning.

Into Extra Time

I

There are times (not many) when your whole life seems
an open book. Whatever takes place takes words
        and the words are telling you

something. A biographer's wanting your life?
You read her letter as a word of warning.
        You want to improve your French?

Why not say so in verse? You battle your way
to the yellow buoy and feel an undertow –
        the lovely pull of language!

Nothing it seems is empty quite of meaning,
and meanings not given their due in nouns and
        verbs are inclined to complain.

But when the thought comes to you from a poem
by Jaroslav Seifert that – for all your words –
        what you really want is death

you say the time has come to stop this scribbling.
It's late. You'd like to sleep, but behind closed eyes
        the words, like rats, are working.

2

Your books have read you too often. The songs of
your youth have forgotten you. This world's an ear
        that listens for something new.

Your pictures that have stared down at you so long
see scarcely even the one that once you were –
        and sometimes the yellow buoy

as you swim towards it murmurs to its chain
'Here he comes again,' but without excitement.
        How easy for Captain Oates

to 'step outside for a moment' through that door
marked 'Hero's End'. But did he hesitate there
        in the battering white-out

straining to catch a voice calling from within
'Oates, don't do this! Come back!' and hearing nothing –
       nothing at all but the wind?

Elegy
24.1.06

I
'Forgetfulness'
      that's the name of the ferry
      but the process has begun
      before you reach the wharf.

'Asphodel'
         that's Death
      giving itself airs –
a lovely name
a kindly aspect.

        Or might it be
'Narcissus'
after one who died of love
      for his own fine face
        for his own
sad story?

2
So you arrive in the dream
with a handwritten pile
      from which the wind tears
        page and page and
pages –

     so much remembered
       so finely
forgotten.

3
It's the worm-eaten sheets
           torn, stained, blotted
               the ferryman
likes best.

'Have a seat there.
Make yourself comfy.'

        I hear him on the wharf
            the pirate sea-dog
John Silver
he his own parrot
cackling
           'Missing a word
             'a world
           'missing a word
'missing.'

4
'Elysium' –
have you been there?

     You pass through the needle's eye
          cross the black river
in silence
(and I think in pain)
         to a sunlit field
           of yellow
nodding heads.

            'Daffodil.'
       'Asphodel.'
'Narcissus.'

5
          Forgotten
all is forgiven.

6

Today would be my mother's
one hundredth birthday.

                            She's there
somewhere
                   the ferryman
                      assures me.

                   He tells me
she was reluctant to go
but silent –

               stood in the prow
                    no tears
and never looked back.

The Rower

Did grandfather Stead
(she wants to know)
row for Oxford

or Cambridge – or
(as sometimes asserted)
for one then

the other? These
claims for him I long
ago dismissed

but she's heard there's
a pewter mug inscribed
with his name

that proves it was
Oxford. I remember
a tall man

'well spoken', who
came only at Christmas
and gave me

always a half
crown. Catholic, a
sinner perhaps –

everything he'd
ever owned lost or
spent – he was found

dead in his bed in
a rooming house in
Mount Eden

arms crossed
over his chest in
an act of contrition.

I tell her I think
he's rowing still
on the black river.

S//crapbook

i Good, better, best . . .

'Frightened, bored, yes
and short of rest –
but you knew
what you had to do.

'How vivid the colours were! –
and what a story!

'Peace can be good, it's true
but war is better
and World War best.'

ii Bella

Isabella
is a-born
in London.

Already
she's forgetting
what she knew
back then.

I ask her, 'Bella,
before the Big Bang
what was?'

She won't tell.

iii And you may lay to that . . .

Down Under
is Over and Above
and quite Beyond
the call of dooty
which may be why
John Silver's long-johns
are lacking a lag
and Blind Pugh
(the one who won
the Black Spot)
was really Reilly.

iv Why I didn't get to Jan and Dieter's party

Because of the plums
in my pocket
and the birds
in the plums.

Because of the
time of the tide

and the hangover
(all my own).

Because of
the hard drive
and liking the look
of 'alone'.

v Summer

     You start with something
unusable
and build.

     The language if you listen
will tell you
where you must go.

     Now the rains are falling
the flies have come indoors
and are restless in the heat.

       They are little gods
(but you knew that)
            secretive
          unwilling to say
where they go in winter.

vi Meanwhile in Oxford

At this very moment
it may be
          Ian McEwan
      is performing delicate
             surgery
upon the brain
of Raine.

vii Seven poems each beginning with a line by Colin McCahon

1

How could I forget her face?
but will she like
the way I remember it –
that sad sack
with a speech balloon
saying 'This
is the King of the Jews.'

2

Rita, when we were at Clifton
remember those breakfasts
Weet-bix and milk
followed by brown toast?
And Lilburn
at the harpsichord?
Wonderful days!

3

Sadness holds our hands
and won't let us
beat off the flies
which are very bad this summer.

Our bicycles are parked
by the garage
ready for another adventure.

4

Anne and Rita read each other well.
'So that's what you think of me,
you bitch,' says Rita.
'And you think I don't know
what you did with Colin,'
Anne replies.

I zap the flies
with Mortein
while summer throbs on.

5

Sadness later but who so loved you then
as Mrs Tumbril
the lady next door
who used to shop for you on Thursdays
and bring in the milk.

Yes, she was an angel –
dead now, of course.

6

The bicycle boys may now rejoice
as I do
at the plan to pave Ferry Road
all the way to the wharf
Rita.

7

I thought we had lost you
but found you in the laundry basket
not hiding
or not meaning to
just dreaming of that blue hood I gave you
and your speech balloon.

viii The secret of Zen

I met a young man who said
he'd 'found' some of my books
from long ago – Molière,
Verlaine, I've forgotten what else
or he'd forgotten.
                    He said he supposed
he should return them. Was it a question?

He seemed to value them
because they'd been mine.

What could I say?
I'd have liked the Verlaine
but didn't like to ask –

and isn't letting things go
the secret of Zen?

ix Two Sparks

1
Philip Larkin was not
Phar Lap
            but each was good
of its kind

2
William Faulkner
            was less
                    than happy
but more
        than Kentucky fried
Dickens

x Professor Bob

Last night's walk
was with Bob Chapman.
'Quite frankly . . .' he said

as he used to
say when he was a
living legend.

He showed me the
map of a village. We
were to walk

its perimeter
but found ourselves
in that bushy

hollow by the
Stanley Street courts.
'*Quite frankly,*' said Bob

shaking his jowls
and blaming me. 'You're
looking well,' I

replied, 'especially
for one so recently
deceased.'

Agent *Arc-en-Ciel*

No the tui won't shut up
        and there's no pleasure
    in its three and then a fourth
harsh
unlovely notes.

      Agent *Arc-en-Ciel*
returning to the scene of her crime
goes through it one more time
    and asks herself (*se demande*)
      why the plan failed.

      The skies are livid.
It's ten kilometres back
      as the blow flies
and they fly a lot.

Here in the north she believes
    are many lawyers
    their signs on the grassy verges
'Avocado'.

      She may yet need one.
Meanwhile
    she's dreaming of Paris.

The Art of Poetry (ii)

Poetry is sometimes
a lightless cave
a river through it and the talk
of water on stone.

Like blood
it belongs in the veins
closed to the public
open to need.

Words have their secret
ways of conjoining
of signing and
complaining.

Even under
a blue-eyed day
they can be the dark
living of the leaves –

as they were once
when you first
heard them in the womb
singing.

Remembering Anactoria

The return

Already the second month
and still I'm surprised
by colour
lushness.

When they sent me away
what I remembered most
was tamarisk
beside the little gate,

the three steps down to the sand,
and the sound of waves lapping
when the moon rode them
so lightly
between the white weatherboard house
and the dark hulk
of Rangitoto.

Memory

It will be the same
when I die.

Wherever I travelled they asked
'Where is your luggage?'

I told them
it was all in my head.

Later, alone in my room,
I unpacked an island.

The abstract

Remember
how Anactoria walked
under willows at evening
where the Ngongotaha Stream
runs out into the lake?

It was long ago.
A poet
laboured at verses
to capture what cost her
no effort at all.
He failed of course.

She was an abstract of Beauty,
the melding of Nature and Art.

She was Anactoria
without need of verses.

The exile

This is how it was
in Crete
when I walked for sure
over the bones of soldiers
and saw children
playing among flowers
who fled
alarmed at my tears.

The funeral

Closing my eyes
while your soul was prayed for
Anactoria
I thought I caught for a moment
a sight of you
in the house of Death.

You were running from room to room
hunting for your rings
your necklaces of gold
your 'things'.

Honours are declined

Look at me once.
Note well what time and the sun
have done,
and look away.

Here on the page
I'm just as I was.

You say there should be laurels.
Let the page have them.
This late summer
I'll settle for the shade.

Theology

Heaven was it
or hell?
     the river brimming that night
and M. Le Crapaud
         the toad at his table
     one of those lights set in turf
marking the path to the floodlit
Pont du Gard.

          Mottled
      wattled and bloated
        a brown sack
without excuses and
sick with excess –

and still the moths
came to his light
and still he gulped them down
        manfully
        toadfully
a duty
an on-going effort –

a scene it could be from Dante
the Glutton required to eat
        to repeat
       for ever
     his one particular
sin of the Seven –

cruel of course because
nothing in Nature
had prepared him for a place
      where the moths
     would *keep coming*

   where the Lord's Bounty
would *go on so!* –

    world without end.

Black River Blues

for Mahinarangi Tocker

    Chanterez-vous quand vous serez vaporeuse?

Will you sing
when you're only a ghostly thing
when your self is no more
than the squeak of an unoiled door
a creak in the floor?

Will you sing then
lyrics to furnish a room
cantos of doom?

Where will you go when you die
what will you say to the sky
as your smoke goes up the chimney
and your world has a tear in its eye?

Will you sing when you're gone away
down to the end of the ever
to row on the black river

– will you? Will you sing
when you're *not here* and *no more*
than the squeak of an unoiled door
and a creak in the wooden floor?

Kentucky, 1853

Today it a do-nothin day
cept my Daddy
he hitch up the hosses
take the white folks to church.

That Miss Flora she say to me
'You know what my name mean, boy?'
I tell her, 'Yes, Missie,'
(coz she tell me befoh).
'It mean flower, Miss Flora.'

That Miss Flora
she look right through a Darkie
right through
all the way to heaven.

One day I trimmin vines at the House
see through the winder
she wearin no dress.

I don look, I don look away
scared to deaf
she see me seen her.

Today my Granny
talkin bout that place
she call 'Faraway'.
She say to me, 'Boy
you's gwine be big man.'
She eyes wet but she
grinnin like a hoss.
'Big man. Big man.'

Free Will

for Ann and Anthony Thwaite

The wind billowed the drapes at 4 a.m. at
Gloucester Terrace and it was Shakespeare. He was
          there also at Low Tharston

where the moorhen with her red beak and green legs
had nested among 'vagabond flags' and reeds –
          and in Oxfordshire again

under those low black beams he told me he'd heard
an overheated groupie, once, at the Globe
          tell actor Burbage he should

knock at her door and say, 'It's Richard the Third'.
Shakespeare was there before him, astride, at work,
          when a servant tapped to say

'Ma'am, Richard the Third is waiting in the hall.'
'Tell him,' said Will, 'that William the Conqueror
                    comes before Richard the Third.'

Embarrassment

1

It was one of my many mistakes
                    disconcerting the stars
                        bringing a blush
                to the pallors of winter.

No one answered my calls
                            not surprising
given that the heavens were empty
                the exchanges abandoned
nest eggs
broken on the face of the moon.

And these were my better years
        when everything stood up for me
                    and spoke in tongues.

How much worse had it been?

I will tell you.

2

                            Jerk-off
                            ejaculate
                there was a lot of that

hard-on
masturbate
ejackoffulate

                    some praying too
and trying not to
                        trying hard
(on).

3
Buying anything
was painful –

                  tennis racquet
                     bike.

               You pretended
the choice had been made
long ago
you'd had the brand before
always used it –

                  (like Janet
                in a whisper:
'I'll have the same')

That's how I found myself
              with a chain guard
          the sort of 'men's' bike
            a lady might ride.

It was just another
embarrassment.

                I lived with it.

4
It was to be an evening picnic
on the slopes of One Tree Hill
              ewes bleating
for lost lambs
             tui in the flax
         making their late raids
on the inarticulate.

             Do you remember
what the wind said –
           the phrases so exact
        the timing / the intonation
so nearly perfect?

5

And the bible
that was one huge

         embarrassment –

         all that palaver
pretending to know how everything
began
and why
and for whom
         and how it would end –
       and what you had to do
           to be 'saved'
who to pray to
what to say.

Sometimes the words were nice
        and the music
        (I liked singing)

     but the whole fat lie of it
the hypocrisy
the honey –

        O Lord!

6

Later you would write:
        'Fearful
      of the embarrassment
        of a refusal
he created
embarrassment
        by not
asking for
what was plainly
on offer.'

7

Innocent days!

Now we know wines
far places
exotic cuisine –

look down from our high
chairs
(holding a glass)
at cities that glitter
in the vast
continental
dark
like stars
(like cities).

We are gods.

Get in touch with yourself,
sailor.

Embarrassment
is a failure
of democracy.

La Sainte Famille

The donkey stands
head bowed ashamed
of her enormous

ears, while the foal
who certainly loves
her tugs at her

udder. Their friend
the black ram with curled
horns who secretly

believes he's
Joseph to her Mary
shares with them

the shade of over-
hanging trees. Today
the mistral

gusting down the
corridor of the Rhône
is beating

the last of the
poppies to bits. No
green is greener

than these spring
vines, no grey greyer
than olives in

flower, nor blue
bluer than the
windswept skies of

Provence that will
make you at evening
the gift of stars.

History

I

Pirandello
                               at his café table
                            in the Via Veneto
                                asked why
he had joined the Fascists:

'If you knew how demeaning
democracy was
you would understand.'

And then:
'What times we live in, my friend!
                              Did you know
                the Principessa di Piemonte
has been inseminated
artificially?'

And later
under the arcades
                    of the Piazza Colonna
                        the poet Ungaretti
his blue eyes between slits
                    moving back and forth
                    like praetorian guards:

'When war comes
so does greatness.'

2

16 May 1940

                        As Prime Minister
I address you
Signor Mussolini

assuring you
                    I have never been a foe
                        of Italy's greatness –

assuring you also
                    that this appeal is made
in no spirit of weakness
or fear.

                        France has fallen.

                        Britain fights on –
                        if it must be alone
so it shall be.

                        We can
your country and mine

inflict on one another
cruel harm.

I beseech you
in all honour and respect
let it not happen!

3
11 June 1940

'I have told his Majesty it is time
to draw the sword.'

That was Il Duce
and this was war.

I switched off the set

The typist had run
behind the sofa
and was hiding her tears
in the cushions.

Through the open door
I could see the Via Veneto
deserted.

They had all run
to the Piazza Venezia
to see him
hear him.

One man
dwarfish in black
led two little girls
twins with bent legs
through the empty tables
outside Rosati's.

4
January 1942

I could talk about pain
                              but what do you say
when you write home?
                              ('Hullo Mum
                              here's my regulation
                              24 lines marked
"Verificato per Censura".')

I got this wound
near Sidi Rezegh –
                    Musso's arsehole we called it.
                              Now I'm in Bari
a prisoner of war
and they've cut off my leg.

I was prepared for death
                              not for the fight it is
                              to stay alive.

                    You have to fix
               your mind on something –
force it to stay with you.

                              Today
an Eyetie's kind greatcoat for blanket
I'm remembering
                    the Devonport ferry
               green water under wharf piles
and that jump I'll never make again
as the ropes grind on the bollards.

                    I give it all my thoughts
('and you too, Mum')
all my love.

5
                    Count Ciano is anxious.
The Signora Mussolini
                              goes about

dressed as a bricklayer

          or a peasant
      her shot-gun shouldered.

She complains that starlings
      are vanishing from pines
         in the garden
of the Villa Torlonia.

'Because you shoot them, Signora'
Ciano suggests.

              She insists
           it's an omen.

'The war is not going well.'

6
19 July 1943

             I was once
this madman's hero.

All morning he shouts at me
         waving his arms
          at war maps.

         In North Africa
          in Greece –
I have failed him –
Italy has failed him.

          This lavish villa
        all blacks and whites
like a cubed crossword –
it's a nightmare.

          The peacocks
scream in the garden.

         Hitler rants on
        interrupted only

                              by news
of the first air raid on Rome.

1500 dead
                    but from the Fuehrer
                         no sympathy.

How do I tell him my Grand Council
wants to sue for peace?

7
24 July 1943

Black steps down
                         to a green door
                         half hidden by
                              honeysuckle –

rooms light
white and
                         almost empty
                         but for Ezra's
chairs and table –

pale wood
hand-made

                    thuk thuk of olive press
                         plof of bucket
                              dropped
into the well –

                    long views over olives
to the Golfo di Tigullio –

                         murmur of bees
in lavender
like these rumours
of a *coup d'etat* –

                         and Ezra gone
                         (gone mad)

to Rome

'to save

               'the Duce
               'the Dream.'

8
11 January 1944

Ciano's dead
but you knew that –
               not even the Duce
could save his son-in-law
                    or wanted to.

I used to see him
at the Acquasanta Golf Club
                    wearing whites
and once
         at the Countess Pecci-Blunt's
                cocktail party
with his film-star friends
               his face already
a handsome bronze
cast
for history.

           They say he died bravely.

It was done at the firing range
outside Verona.

            Those militiamen
            were rotten shots.

An officer Furlotti
finished the job
with a shot to the head.

9
May 1944

               I'd been in Egypt
                  with NZDiv
but Cassino was my first battle
my first wound.

When I rejoined my unit
             we'd moved on to Sora.

                I was up a tree
by the railway station
filling my rucksack with cherries
            when shells came over.

I saved the cherries.

It was at Avezzano
we found the twenty-two
dead civilians –
           a reprisal for sabotage.

        The Teds were just three hours
ahead of us
and retreating
      blowing the shit out of everything
              as they went.

They were laid out in a line.

I counted them:
              three old men
           a dozen women
            seven little kids
with skinny legs.

10
28 April 1945

When we came for them at the
farmhouse

                    the Duce's girlfriend
couldn't find her knickers –
they were lost in the bed.

'No time for those,' I told her.
                    (No need for underwear
                    where they were going!)

We stopped on the empty road
                    beside some gates.
You can see his name there now
on a black cross
with the date of his death.

                    Down through trees
I could see the lake
reflecting the sun.
                    It felt like spring.

          When we brought out our guns
she tried to get in the way
frantic:
                    'Mussolini must not die.'

          She took the first shots.

'Aim for the heart,' he said
pulling his lapels apart.

                    When I saw them next
                    they were lying
                    in the Piazzale Loreto
A woman had fired five shots
into his head –
'For my five dead sons.'

                    Another squatted
                    and pissed on his face.
When a drunk kicked out his eye
                    we fired in the air
                    and drove the
                    crowd back.

                        It was then
we hung them by their ankles
from the ruined roof
                    of the Esso forecourt.

Her skirt fell around her face.
                        Our chaplain
                        Don Pollarole
stuffed it between her legs
wanting (he said) to hide
Italy's shame.

I I
8 May 1945

Now the great storm
                        has rolled over us
                    with its iron wheels
what is there left
to pray to
but the rain?

Spring comes at last.

                        Il Pape
is a man in a mirror
shaving before breakfast

                    the Mother of God
                    and all her Angels
are broken stone

                    and we are the dead
                            i morti
in mezzo ai fiore
with nowhere to go
                    with nothing left
                    to say or to do.

12

late July 1948

Returned to Milan
                              buying petrol
in the Piazzalo Loreta
I recognise those iron bars
                              painted red now
where the bodies
                      hung by their heels.

On a blank wall
                      VIVA IL DUCE
blurred by the rains
of three or four winters
                              is legible still.

I remember the shame
                      of the days that followed
                      how every eye was averted
from the hanging meat
in the butcher's window.

                      Was it that we had cheered
                              his greatness
                          or that our cheers
had created it? –

                          that jutting jaw
                      the strut of a Caesar –

had we remembered our history
we might have foreseen
                          a Roman death.

13

26 June 2004

I follow the anchor chain
down into dimness.

Another summer
and the scene is unchanged

                    the sun the same
                        the sea still
            greenly transparent.

                    Rapallo
looks back at us
at our white yacht
                    Vagabond III
indifferent that once
Ezra sailed in her

                        that one
                century has passed
into another.

Massimo
                too young to remember
                            knows
                what he inherits.

It is his.
It is history.

My Sister and M.S.

A catheter was the last straw. My sister
made 'a rational decision' – it was time
            to die, but she misjudged

the dose – or was it the hours those drugs would take?
'Saved', she was told her medication would be
            watched – no more hoarding her pills

– and to help her beat her Black Dog there would be
counselling. She was marking time now, hanging
            fire, but it wasn't all waste.

Sometimes we visited her in that Home for
the Helpless – sat in the sun looking over
            the lake, our backs to Bedlam;

sometimes wheeled her to see a James Bond, or
something romantic. Talking about the past
            she laughed so much I worried

she might fall out of her chair. Death came in its
own slow time. She was laid out in her son's house
            all the grandchildren Maori

and Pakeha goggle-eyed until someone
turned on the TV which stole their attention.
            At her funeral I thought

I couldn't speak, then spoke, remembering a
photo of her in school uniform with three
            friends, and another up north

on the farm with cousins. She looked so pretty
and friendly, someone you'd like to meet at a
            dance or take to the pictures.

Small boys avoid big sisters but mine in age
against all the odds in that battle with her
            body proved that grace could win.

'Daddy's Girl', I drafted these lines for you on
the warm stones of a Mediterranean
            beach, on our father's birthday.

Menton, 6.6.06

Versions of Two Poems by Victor Hugo
for Tony Axelrad

Demain des l'aube . . .

Tomorrow as dawn whitens the landscape
I'll set out, because I know you expect me.

Through the forest, over the mountain I'll go.
I can't remain so far from you any longer.

Lost in my thoughts I'll tramp the roads
Seeing nothing, hearing not a sound,
Alone, unrecognised, shoulders hunched,
Too sad to notice whether it's day or night.

I won't be looking for the gold of sunsets
Nor at the distant sails coming home to Harfleur,
And when I get there I'm going to lay on your grave
This wreath of green holly and flowering heather.

Les Contemplations, IV, xiv

Pendant que le marin . . .

While the sailor, doubting his calculations,
Asks the constellations to show him the way;
While the shepherd, frightened by moving shadows,
Seeks the faintest star to light his path through the wood;
While the astronomer places a single orb

Among a million brilliant points of light –
I must ask something other of the vast pure sky.
But what a black hole that dark sapphire has become!
How can I now, so late, learn to distinguish
Night itself from the blue-robed angel of death?

Les Contemplations, IV, x

My Father (a fantasy)

My name is No Man –
also known as
Norman.
        Oh, and
Odysseus.

Penelope's upstairs
at her loom
'not speaking'.

This morning I feel it –
the sea's great gate is open.
I've said goodbye to the dogs,
Bark and Bite.

I feed the hens
and stand among them hearing
the dying fall of
their disconsolate

conversation.
It's as if they know
any time soon
my men will come for me.

The asparagus
are spearing,
the crop of runner beans
will be good this summer –
and I will be gone.

C.K.

for Margo White

There's a Stead I
recognise only by
his picture

in the papers
and what's said of him
behind the lines –

has my name, my
face, my (such as they are)
achievements –

doesn't smile
often, and when he does (they
say) watch out! –

doesn't suffer fools
(or anyone)
gladly . . . 'No, no,'

I protest
'this is not the man
who eats my lunch, reads

'my newspaper, sleeps
in my bed' – but who's
listening?

The world's sure it
knows you better than
you know yourself.

One day I'll meet
the bastard, surprise
him, introduce

myself. 'Hullo, C.K.
I'm Karl. We haven't
met.' 'Let's

'keep it like that,'
he says, unfriendly,
and turns away.

The Art of Poetry (iii)

This tiny flower
Kay tells me is a viola
purple with a yellow centre
bloomed once
and a second time
in a crack between concrete slabs
on the path to the back door.

With care
I pinched and pulled it out
to plant in a pot

beside a grape
(also self-sown, also transplanted)
where one more time (surely the last)
it blooms.

Read this however you will
like the flower
it means what it says
and does what it is.

Two

S – T – R – O – K – E

hullo death
is that you
with the hole in the head
or just another Picasso?

*

jump
the letters are jumping
watch the words jump

as in McCahon
JUMP

*

the leaves next door
are raging

how I love the world
and will be sad
to see it go

*

words have given me access
to the inside
of the inside
of the mind

whose mind?
mine

the mine of the mind

⋆

god is dying in the desert of the mind
no god   no god

god is dying in the desert of the mind
no good   no god

god is dying in the desert of the mind
no god   no god

JUMP

⋆

ward 81
late beyond any o'clock
'what's your name, nurse?'
'winnie'
'ah'
and winnie:
'sorry not to have told you.'

⋆

rain
on the white rose
in the green garden

the rose
should not mean
but be

the rain also

*

in Xanadu did Karlson Stead
a stately pleasure dome decree

DOME

thank god for the wound
you are stripped

*

remember the world
when it was new?

it's old now
seventy-two

but full of reminders

*

I think
therefore I am

I think
therefore I think
I am

therefore I am
(I think)

and a voice
out of the nowhere
of your head:
'oh darling
your dark days
are only beginning'

*

stripped
disclaimed

misnumbered
unremembered
you have become
the unencumbered
whipped
soul
of the noun
and the verb

*

doctors
go walking
down cool green corridors

soft-soled
nurses are numbers /
numbness

ward is a word and
patient
is pain
is pen

*

the train in the night
the rain on the roof

spain

the train in the night
the rain on the roof

plain

(mainly)

*

since the little river
in the dark interior
blocked or broke –

8 daze
and clearing

★

waking
to make a note of
my best friend Shakespeare
met in a dream
carrying his
caesura
and 'a vagabond
flag upon
a stream'

★

mort lock
mort lock
mort lock

JUMP

★

choices   discriminations
this word / that word
meanings and their song

the mind as
source and sieve
the heart
hearing itself –

you're alive, Karlson
you're writing!

★

of men and of angels
sounding brass
and a tinkling cymbal

of men and of angels
sounding brass
and a tinkling symbol

but the JUMP
will move mountains

*

then I saw clearly
now
through a glass darkly
last
will be not-at-all

but the lordship of the word
is for ever

*

every man is an island

do not therefore ask
for whom the head aches

it aches for thee

*

the lore
long ago learned
is the loam

(DOOM)

is the loom

(DOME)

and the lordship of the word
is for ever

*

no wish
to be part of the past
fuck history
give me the now
(please)
give me it
now

*

eavesdropper
(leavesdropper
on the drenched day)
and the bro in the next ward
'nurse –
any chance of a smoke?'

*

and mid-May's eldest child
the tui
full of chips of sound

(and full of remainders)

*

when it comes to
Menton   Uzès   Rapallo
memory
is future tense
and may deceive

we call it hope

*

hullo Mum
yes it is
it's me
couldn't you tell?

I know but I'm old
you see
and not very well

*

reluctant
to walk out on
the comfort
of my own body

*

look there
Onegin's
on his knees!

sarcastic sardonic
aristocratic ironic
superior Onegin
is on his knees!

*

a clean sheet?
no!
life's rough on the sheets

and would I want to be dying
(if I were dying)
regretting anything
but the things not done?

*

faith   hope   the JUMP
these three abide
and the greatest of these
is the JUMP

Some Early Uncollected Poems

1951–61

Elegy

Ian Lamont

Earth, you are frozen now,
The dead-cold centre of a doom-darkened winter.
Yet from this spiny row
Of waxen, wasted willow-sticks must grow
New life in spring.
The sun will be warmer then
And velvet leaves will spin
A net of new-born comfort round old signs.
Persistent sapling shoots in lines
Of contradicting green
Will not admit
That dead-brown death has even been.

1951. Previously unpublished

Feuilles d'automne

The sparrows understand but do they fear?
Does the threat of what's to come grip them within
And freeze the last warm pleasure in Autumn's sin
Or are they careless that the cold is near?

The mood descends upon my willing mind.
On the rock wall, ivy is dying;
On the green lawn, yellow leaves lying
Can scarcely stir themselves to greet the wind.

Rocks laid bare beneath the barren stalk
Call scenes of time and darkness to the eye.
The lily, a golden brown, has decided to die;
Soon rain will be the garden's whispered talk.

I know that spring will come at winter's death,
I know the sun will rise and set the same,
But on my winter page is scored a name
And how will that change, though summer soon draws breath?

Kiwi, 1952

Kaiwaka

Remembering the General Store, post-office above
And matchbox church below, the bridged stream
Speaking the moon's mood in supercilious whispers
Or the sun's incandescence when cicadas click,
I salute Obsession's sister, Memory.

In this image returning to mind the wind whispers
To pine belts, whistles in the wires of time above,
Or plays with smoke where cattle-trains clatter and click
On the track, and passengers, each carrying a memory
Turn blank walls of their eyes to the blink of the stream.

Here once my hands cupped water from the stream
And today seems fresher for that cool memorial.
The roads in brief embrace of dust, above
The field where a long-distant past echoes
Among stumps in the remembered hollow-voiced chock

Of the axe, are the cross of more recent memory
The great uncle spoke of, though his teeth clicked
In his head, and his words were a hesitant stream
In a youthful land, under storm-clouds of war above.
How much of that scene has changed? Wordless, it whispers

As if preserved from time and the machine's clack
It is to remain for ever, hearing grasses whisper
And milk-cans clatter, so that all memory
In each generation shall include the symbol stream,
Bush on distant hills, and the hawk hovering above.

Published under the title 'Settlement' in the *New Zealand Poetry Yearbook*, 1953,
and *A Book of New Zealand*, ed. J. C. Reid, 1964

Sonnet for a New Zealand Soldier Killed in Korea

Perhaps you hoped to lose an old despair,
      A discontent, or earn the praise that lies
      In a cause the headline news-page glorifies;

Or seeking money and a change of scene, you saw
Reason there, and armed against chaos to share
      The 'heavy burden'. Knowing what death denies
      You may have steeled yourself in colloquies
Of liberal thought – small comfort when the heart's laid bare.

Fed on the manufactured truth, you stilled
      An older boredom in the gamble of guns and shells
And paid the debt calmly when your loss was billed.
      Your epitaph is the age-old cry that tells
How you died 'fighting for peace' – words fogged in sighs.
In the arms of our hate you were strangled by a knot of lies.

Jindyworobak Anthology, 1953, and *Craccum Literary Supplement*, 1953

That Particular Morning

Frost on the angle-iron of roofs
And sun sliding diagonals of light
Into my room. From the window
Maybe you watched the migrant birds
Like night-hopes, gathering to leave.

Did you decide then not to disturb
The morning of my dream, leaving
Me deep asleep, hearing
Only the discord of waves
Rising with a wind from the sea?

Craccum Literary Supplement, 1953

Logging, Mangawhai

All day the shouts, cracking of leather whip
Over bullock team, and the tree's loud groan:
Until, down what remained of the old slip
Through bush to ruined mill, the kauri was won

Free of its home. And when we had stripped the log
Clean of its limbs, and only the drag

To the road remained, there was time for rest,
A bottle or two, with talk of bush-bound days
When whine of pit-saw carried over the crest
Of hills tied tight in green, and falling trees
Split with the cracking of whips. Not now those teams
Creeping like a disease along the seams

Of the mountain range. Still on these higher slopes
The bush grows thick, where wild board dives
For cover under fern and supple-jack ropes.
And there the oldest hand, lean, with the sly
Humour of his age invited us back
In time, his gang, without home but a brown shack

By rushing water, and no town worth the name
Within a hundred miles. We could not play
For long our part in that past: it was a game
Of make-believe from which we turned away
To finished roads, glad now to see the town,
The shops, the stop-banks, sprouting where trees had grown.

New Zealand Poetry Yearbook, 1955, and *Verse For You*, book 3, ed. J. G. Brown, 1958

Sonnet

You are the music of another time
Strung on the frame of now and harping long
Over the quickstep shapes and shaky mime
The age strikes poses in. Beauty among
The crones and crooners of despair, your eyes
Beg each a pardon though your face is proud.
Knowing the willing ear is also wise
Yours is the voice of truth that dares aloud.

And this, the music which we will not face,
Accuses us who'll bray sooner than bat
One eyelid praise before such sounds of grace.

Sing, then, your endless swansong to our flat
Accompaniment. Time banks these notes of truth.
Unrecognised, you are our vanished youth.

New Zealand Poetry Yearbook, 1955, and *Kiwi*, 1955

Man Alone

Under the clean sky at evening, beyond gum trees and the
                                    cut smell of grass,
I take the clay track to look for friends, and praise of
                                    friends, and pass
Propped by a trunk, untempted by airs that tempt me, the
                                    hut of a man
Whose name I do not know. His lamp is lit, scattering
                                    on books that run
Shelf-wise along a wall, erratic light that holds the
                                    hut contained,
He shadowed by it, not looking out, having
                                    retained
Against the drum-beat of the sea, against the voices that
                                    float above it and call,
Against the garrulous, egotistical gull of the heart, a
                                    roof and a wall.
Unknowing, he sits in judgement on me, whom I have
                                    never met,
And draws, lovingly, deliberately, the casual consolation of
                                    a cigarette.

1950s. Previously unpublished

'Like to a vagabond flag . . .'

Each day is wedded to what might have been,
The ghost that takes the other offered hand
    Born in impossible duality.

Each hour lies bedded in a present dream
Where two roads offer one unutterable end
    Through fate or time's duplicity.

Words light our shadows on a vital screen,
The different means that parallels the end
    Present, but past all possibility.

Death lives in living, laughs at the dying wish
That once attained puts on imperfect flesh.

Numbers, June 1955

Shelley looks to the future

'This will abate. Then will come the time
When artifice is lauded like the birds,
Age mould its passions into carefree rhyme,
Priestship in poetry, monument in words.

'Now is the time to dream that golden day:
Labour that sings, youth in dancing pairs,
Love mending all uncoloured, bookish ways,
Sunlight in markets on the heaped-up wares.

'These and the grace of hands that through each sense,
Translating dream to object, myth to song,
Grant to the ear their music, eye their dance.'

'And still the poet dream? Against what wrong?'

Meanjin, Spring 1955

Noviciate Sonnet

She wore the novice habit, a dull grey,
Waited nine months on her incubating soul
(The righteous hatch to open), assumed the role
Of penitent for crimes. Enormously

Self-pity's belly grew, as is its way.
Big Bible words banged down inside her head –
The thrust and charge of lust condemned, the bed
A place of prayer, fearing the dirt of day.

Yet sleep had human hands to lift the curse,
Led her through fields and over rustic stiles,
Uncorked the bottle, opened the book of verse
And showed how love was made beside the streams.
'Sister,' the holy Mother cried, 'you smile!'
'God,' she replied, 'is good to me in dreams.'

Arena, 43, 1956

The Shadow

I walk Muriwai beach
West of Auckland, and think
Its black, light-speckled reach
Of sand a proper place,
Where no one goes to sink
His wordy poet's face
But stalks his shadow where the seabirds cry.

I might have made my mark
With those self-righteous men –
Pitched voices in the dark
Who light the Coming Age;
Might have obeyed the ten
Commandments of their rage,
But stalk my shadow where the seabirds cry.

And then I've tried the part
Of sad-eyed clownish lover,
Backing the clownish heart's
Hunch, and never winning;
It's time all that was over,
Time for a new beginning:
I stalk my shadow where the seabirds cry.

Sydney Bulletin, 12 December 1956

Lord Gannet, Mrs Shag

Lord Gannet glides along his arc of air,
White-into-yellow neck, and eye to spear
The sea for fish; swooping, makes eating look
An art he's learned out of some ancient book –
This aristocrat, measuring the bay.
See where he brings precision, and the way
Each glide is broken by a plummet plunge,
The shimmering downward foil a fencer's lunge.
Few fish, or small, his lordship takes, the sport
Being one armorial ancestry has taught,
And food (at least to every delicate eye)
A matter less of weight than artistry.

Old Mrs Shag squats heavy on a rock
Watching for bargains. Water takes the shock
Her flopping forward makes, and ripples clear
Round where black back and tail now disappear;
Then yards away is broken by the stretch
Of struggling bill, gulping down the catch.

New Zealand Listener, January 1956, and *New Zealand Poetry Yearbook*, 1956–57

Homage to Ancestors

Already forgotten the men and women whose journey
Half round the world to find a pair of islands
Set my life here; neglected their names, whose hands
Pointed to mountains stepping from the sea,
Who rowed ashore with pigs, fat sacks of grain,
Sharp implements to beat a stubborn ground
They could not own, hearing always the sound
Of chipping surf that shared their own frustration.

Forgotten but not lost, who nourish soil
In rainy Kamo under their crumbling stones,
First layer of whatever our blind toil
Shapes without plan. To them may words atone
For what seemed failure, and for small success,
Among these hills they tore in their distress.

Landfall, December 1957

Afternoon with Piano

outside the thin rain falls
      on steaming leaves
the curved and buttressed walls
      dry under eaves

down urn-flanked steps she runs
      among the trees
mist and the fragrance stun
      her velleities

and still the notes repeat
      from the hot room
ravel's *boléro* beats
      on the afternoon

mad she whispers mad
      her satin stained
shoes crushing fruit gone bad
      in the summer rain

delicate fingers play
      across her mind
the steps are ivory keys
      not left behind

and still his casual grace
      inflicting pain
tears and her ruined face
      and the drifting rain.

New Zealand Poetry Yearbook, 1956–57

Choruses

I
I have led my five senses like hungry children
Into the world of poems, and there fed them.

I have shot my spirit like an arrow into the heavens,
For it knows no satisfaction in the life of things.

I have plunged my mind into the clear well of science
Like a dry sponge, hungering to cool my brow.

Yet I know no power great as Necessity.

II
Necessity, goddess, you who stand alone
We offer nothing at altar or graven stone;

Knowing you deaf to prayer and sacrifice,
Moved neither by pity, nor a price;

Yet pray that you, whom even Zeus needs,
Press not too heavily on our frailest deeds,

For we know no power great as Necessity.

III
We see the hands of Admetus bound on rods of her will;
We see his tears that water a barren hill.

We listen for a last departing breath
Signing the marriage of Necessity and Death.

We hear the praise of a thousand years of men
And in their words Alcestis live again.

Though we know no power great as Necessity,
Goodness like a fountain for ever spills
To loose your name, Alcestis, among the hills.

From a version of Euripides' *Alcestis* written with Iain Lonie. See notes, p. 521.

Afternoon with violin

High on the afternoon a violin
Its note now sure, now broken by gusts of wind,
Runs to the ear or falls short in the yard –
Music uncertain of the path it takes.

As once a drone out of a baritone throat
Came reaching down to me on a hot morning
Under the cabbage tree – a swarm of wasps
Backing and filling round their industry.

Some bird notes, too, at night touch and are gone,
Startle on rough roads or across fields,
Leaving the homeward traveller seeming to hear
Danger disguised as a silence.

Murmurs hidden deep in busy streets,
Mutters in empty rooms, the fear and desire
For what it is suggests itself and is gone –
Deep in a day of dreams, a violin.

Meanjin, Winter 1957

England

1 *Laica and other Victims*

Bristol buzzes. Autumn chills the skies.
The night is shot through with a dog that flies
A thousand miles up, yelping data down.
Our earth has shed her first real tear and cries
To lose a little dust she called her own.

Today a plane crashed at the edge of town.
Now midnight murmurs as the fires burn down
Where fifteen souls, hot rockets from the blaze,
Shot their way out into the large Unknown.
Like arrows after them go prayers and praise.

Flags are run up on emptiness, and Earth
Labouring always to bring shapes to birth,
Acquisitive of scrap, and hating most
All that flies free of her compelling girth,
Hunches in frost beneath our newest boast.

2 *Mr Empson meets his Muse*

I cannot see the thing I am
But touch its edges as I can
Watching with imperfect sight
Its shadow in a solemn light.

I cannot know the thing you are.
Lips, movements, eyes, familiar
(Each you) in separation call.
No man's at one time true to all.

The thing you see, the thing I see –
Neither is really you or me,
But each as apprehended through
The differences of me and you.

Yet let me praise you, formed to please,
Who breed such ambiguities.

3 *Gloucestershire*

'If I should die think only this of me,
  That there's some corner of a foreign field . . .'
                        – Rupert Brooke

Up to my ears lounging
In English grass that evening
I might have been a Georgian
Trying to reconcile
One silent, ripening field
With what I knew of the world.

I could do no better than they
At the end of England's day
Thinking about myself
And good beer, and clean sheets,
Watching that predator
The tawny owl drift over.

Light thickened as Macbeth
Let slip another death;

The witch of Wooky Hole
Was stabbed and turned to stone.
Everything had that look.
It had happened in a book

Nothing moved in the lane.
Down there an only train
Had stuttered through
The hole in England's heart.
Alien, too clever by half
Would never be clever enough.

Up to my ears lying
In a foreign field not dying
It might have been myself
Happy to be where I was
At the end of England's day,
Not wanting to go – or to stay.

4 *A Song for the Season*

Autumn breaks along the blood,
Down the ditches leaves are flowing,
She who teaches solitude
Shakes her red-brown hair and goes
Singing down a blade of wind.

Touch red hair that tumbles free,
Touch the freckled face of water;
Grant the brief ascendancy
Of the voice that echoes after
All the love that loss accords.

You beside him in this wood
Make the song he makes your own,
That it may be understood
Yours the tousled head of autumn
Floating from him like a leaf.

5 *West Country Prose Poem*

Holding it high the priest in starched parchment presents
Christ with a silver cup for the best sportsman of the year.
The effigy looks down and cannot accept it. He supports
the east wall. Subdued by the impeccable, the indulgent,
I pad out pursued by an anthem. Grass is green; graves
have *gravitas*; the thatched pub, its beams and its brass,
are open to the sun. A branch line has burst into leaf.
Nothing is exactly vertical or horizontal, nothing un-
pardonable. A Sunday news-board announces a new tax
on cigarettes. Is this new? Undeterred, I light one. In
ancient Rome one might have known how to conduct oneself.
Where is the world? Where are the keys to my car?

6 *There was a girl . . .*

There was a girl went thinking in a gale –
It was her way – or on a train, not seeing
The flying trees and whiteness of white birds
In a turned field. Like Carrington perhaps

In the Gertler portrait, she remained in the mind.
Daily she put them down, her thoughts like things
Or trackside flowers through which the trains went racing
To an end that might be bunting or the stocks.

Did she paint her nails because her name was Never?
I met her once, wearing a page of Shakespeare,
Placing cherries in the snow, moving with grace
Through a dream of squirrels in a bookish wood.

7 *Der Rosenkavalier*

The marchioness weeps in her brutal mirror –
Youth has cast its eyes another way.
In spite of age, the baron's ribald error
Has called the lovely maiden into play
Who weeps to learn the world so rich in wrong.
A mocking pity smiles upon their song.

This sequence is previously unpublished. Dates are uncertain, except that the first is 1957 when
the dog Laica was sent into space in a Russian rocket. And I have confirmed that a Britannia
crashed on the edge of Bristol in November 1957.

Curaçao

Willemstad's Dutch façades teach colours to meet and debate.
A black waiter brings ice-cream on a yellow plate.

The Caribbean breaks low on the old fort wall.
In there Ethel and the Doctor are swimming in a glass pool.

The road-bridge swings aside, lets pass another ship.
The waiter returns across the marble, helps me decide on a tip.

He and the mop-girl are at home. I am nowhere at all.
The blue sea breaks and breaks, white on the orange wall.

I lack a language. Colours all speak of the weather.
Goggled at, Ethel and the Doctor swim coolly together.

A lizard translates itself from a shadowy groove
To a sunlit patch of marble, and is not seen to move.

Somewhere deep under the reef I think an angel fish
Pauses in bright shafts, hangs weightless, without a wish.

Previously unpublished. Date probably late 1959

Eden

On the floor our fire
In white skin alight
Barely visible may be
To him on the street
If he should strain to see
Us, getting it right.

Never mind if he stare –
We have our licence,
And what he half-sees
He half-creates –
The undefeated Pair
Doomed to pass through the gates
And meet him there.

Previously unpublished. Date probably 1961

A New National Anthem

To be sung to the tune of 'God defend New Zealand'. Written April 1960 for the departure of an all-white All Black team for a tour of South Africa, captained by Wilson Whineray and managed by Tom Pearce.

Boss of men in football socks
Keep backs white, and golden, locks;
White and woolly as our flocks
Pearce, defend Apartheid!
Kaffir, Coloured, keep inside
While we watch the scrum's blind side –
Nothing nigger, nothing pied:
Pearce defend Apartheid!

All-white All Blacks rally here,
Meet Erasmus' searching stare,
Show your finger nails and hair –
Pearce, defend Apartheid!
Welcome Whineray and all,
Keep your blue eyes on the ball,
Plug your ears if Kaffirs call:
We defend Apartheid!

Previously unpublished

Invocation

Suburb or Sabine farm, no human talents
Create, though they regulate as best they can,
Your order that answers, in feather, fin and flower,
Motions of our two first orbs. See where tides
Advancing under the causeway flush the Bay.
Light silvers the ferns, domestic grass pricks up
To meet the mower's onslaught, and my timber house
Creaks on its jacks. That once I crossed
The rust-red river, heard steel speak and saw
Scavengers wait on the dying; that I command
At peace diagrams of dissolving stars
Or proceed, white-coated, against the militant Crab –
Such purpose itself commends. But my blood must keep

Even as Caesar's, your lyric measure precisely,
Or lose itself among the abstract spaces
Where no bird builds, no predator patrols
The grainy shallows,
Nor sap rises to inform a tree.

Previously unpublished, apart from a fragment of it which appeared, some time after it was written, in *Crossing the Bar*. It was intended for the opening of a collection of poems.

Notes

WHETHER THE WILL IS FREE (1964)

Published by Paul's Book Arcade after I had despaired of the famously dilatory Leo Bensemann, who had accepted it for Caxton, ever actually doing it, though it was printed by Caxton for Paul's Book Arcade. Acknowledgements to *Landfall*, *Landfall Country*, *New Zealand Listener*, *Kiwi*, *Arena*, *Sydney Bulletin*, *Universities Poetry* (UK) and the *Penguin Book of New Zealand Verse* edited by Allen Curnow.

'Night Watch in the Tararuas' won first prize in the undergraduate poetry section of *Borestone Mountain Poetry Awards* for poems published in 1954 (Stanford University Press, 1955).

'À la recherche du temps perdu': This is a revision, omitting one poem, of what appeared as 'Three Poems in Afterthought'.

'Whether the Will is Free': The word 'doved' here was commonly heard when I was young meaning 'dove-tailed' – fitting perfectly.

I have radically revised (rewritten might be more accurate) 'Dialogue on a Northern Shore'. The acknowledgments to *Whether the Will is Free* say that it was broadcast, and then telecast on the NZBC programme *Focus*. I have no memory of the telecast.

'Winter Song': I have restored the Yeats epigraph that was in an earlier version of the poem sent to Charles Brasch in April 1958.

'Pictures in a Gallery Undersea' appeared first in *Landfall* 50, June 1959. In *Landfall* 56, December 1960, it won the *Landfall* Readers' Award, voted the 'best poem' in the magazine's first fifteen years of publication. The fiction section was won by Frank Sargeson, and the non-fiction was shared by R. MacD. Chapman and Bill Pearson. Allan Phillipson, who did a PhD thesis on my poetry at the University of British Columbia, has persuaded me to restore the epigraphs which were omitted when the poem was reprinted in *Crossing the Bar* and *Straw into Gold*. In 2006 the Hocken Library gave me copies of my correspondence with Charles Brasch, which included an earlier, slightly longer version of the poem, and the following explanation of the epigraphs (my letter dated by Brasch 5 July 1959):

> i. The muse has (always) blonde hair; sometimes – as in 'The Twa Sisters of Binnorie' – she is drowned and her hair is played upon by a minstrel (hence the Aeolian harp); at other times she drowns the minstrel. (See [Robert] Graves *The Crowning Privilege*, the first few pages of [the Clark Lectures, No. 4] 'Harp, Anvil, Oar'.)
>
> ii. This comes from [Paul] Valéry's 'Cimitière Marin'. The marble in ii is the marble of London, but it has the quality of a graveyard in which the shadows of the past are still active.
>
> v. This is the first line spoken by Cinna the poet in [Shakespeare's] *Julius Caesar*, before he is lynched by the crowd. Obviously appropriate to this section.
>
> vii. Again from Valéry's 'C.M.'. Could be interpreted a number of ways, all appropriate to vii: Will the ombres of the poem continue singing, though dead? Will modern England sing though its past is dead? Will the persona of the poem sing when he is gone from the life of London? Etc. etc. 'Sing' in each case suggesting literature, poetry, more than anything. This line of course also ties up with 'Binnorie, O Binnorie' and the sister who tells her tale though drowned.

The same line, 'Chanterez-vous quand vous serez vaporeuse?' returns in my work half a century later as the opening lines of 'Black River Blues': 'Will you sing / when you're only a ghostly thing?'

'Chorus' is from a translation of Euripides' *Alcestis* by Iain Lonie and C. K. Stead, first performed by the University Players, University of New England, in the Armidale Town Hall, N.S.W. in 1957, and subsequently broadcast by the ABC. Another of the choruses now appears in this volume's 'Early Uncollected' section (pp. 511–12).

CROSSING THE BAR (1972)

Published by Auckland University Press/Oxford University Press, and reprinted in 1974. Dedicated to K. Some of the poems were reprinted from *Whether the Will is Free*. Acknowledgements as for *Whether the Will is Free*, plus *Mate*, *Poetry Australia*, *Critical Quarterly*, *New Statesman*, *London Magazine*, *Punch*, *Commonwealth Poems of Today* (ed. Howard Sergeant) and *The Oxford Book of Twentieth Century New Zealand Verse* (ed. Vincent O'Sullivan). In an earlier form this collection was called *Bald Caesarion*. Caesarion was Cleopatra's son to Julius Caesar (also bald). He was probably murdered on the orders of Augustus. I didn't feel I had got the title poem right, so only its opening lines appeared. It surfaced again, however, the whole poem this time, but slightly revised, in my 2002 collection, *Dog*.

    Crossing the Bar won the Jessie Mackay Award for poetry which was at that time the major New Zealand award for poetry. It was later replaced by the New Zealand Book Award for poetry and became an award for a first book. The poems in the first section reflect, mainly obliquely but sometimes directly, my concern at that time about the Vietnam War and my involvement in the anti-war movement.

'You have a lot to lose' was commissioned by the Poetry Book Society for the Commonwealth Arts Festival of 1965 and I read it first at the Royal Court Theatre, London, during the Festival readings. It was set for voice and orchestra by Doris Sheppard and I have a note to say it was performed by the NZSO though I have no recollection of having heard this performance. In 2007 Professor Douglas Monro of Victoria University, who is working on Sheppard's life and music, sent me a copy of her piano score for the song-cycle. He tells me that in Radio New Zealand's sound archive there is a recording of a performance by Bruce Chandler, tenor, with the National Orchestra/Alex Lindsay String Orchestra, dated 16 December 1969.

'A Small Registry of Births and Deaths': This appeared first in the *New Statesman*. The reference in the penultimate section to Lyndon Johnson's 'Birds' comes from the fact that his wife was known as Lady Bird Johnson, and I think two daughters had parallel 'Bird' names. 'Even without his gall', and the nation watching his heartbeat, refers to the fact that Johnson had his gall bladder removed at this time, giving some anxiety to his few remaining supporters. The 'side-burned sage' in the final section is Matthew Arnold.

'Crossing the Bar': Brumel in this poem is the Russian Valery Brumel, world record holder at the time (1965) for the high jump. It springs partly from the fact that I was a high jumper at school.

'With a Pen-Knife': I have written at some length about this poem and its subject in an essay called 'Poetry and Politics (and a beating)', in *Book Self* (AUP, 2008), pp. 103–10.

'Meeting of Cultures': The 'fire-crowned bishop' is an African bird.

'April Notebook': Like most of the poems I wrote at this time, this one is full of the atmosphere of the Vietnam War and the protests against it.

'Like': Vines of flowers such as the ones described here lined the drive in to Balmoral Intermediate School when I went there in 1945, so one was welcomed in by the waving wings of dying butterflies.

'Putting it Straight in London': Anyone interested in what is 'true' and 'untrue' in this poem should look at Dr Gerri Kimber's interview with me in London in 2006, in *Book Self*, p. 361.

'On the Publication of Frank Sargeson's *Memoirs of a Peon*': For a later, more complex view of this novel, see my *Kin of Place: Essays on 20 New Zealand Writers* (AUP, 2002), pp. 51–64.

'What Will it Be?': The alternative last line when this appeared in *Punch* read 'Lord, what waits for Logue, for Lowell?' Of the four nominated poets the answer to the question has now been found for three. Logue remains very much alive.

'Myrtle': The myrtle plant is sacred to Venus.

'A Charm': Tusitala was the name given to R. L. Stevenson in Samoa, and Vailima (five rivers) the name of his property there.

QUESADA (1975)

Published by The Shed – i.e. this was my own experiment at publishing my own work. Dedicated to Aristide Caillaud. For acknowledgements, see the notes below to *Poems of a Decade*, where these poems reappeared. This collection won the first New Zealand Book Award for poetry. It was part-product of my receiving the (as it then was) Winn-Manson Mansfield Fellowship to Menton, France, in 1972.

'The Swan' is an attempt to translate Baudelaire's 'Le Cygne' as accurately as I could while keeping the formal rhyme scheme. The same is attempted with Apollinaire's 'Le Pont Mirabeau'.

'For a Children's L.P.': 'Ecology' – In fact the filling of Hobson Bay, Auckland, referred to here, was stopped and the bay has been preserved.

WALKING WESTWARD (1979)

Also published by The Shed. For acknowledgements see *Poems of a Decade* where these poems reappeared.

'Breaking the Neck': It was 24 January (my mother's birthday) I think 1981 that I broke my neck in the surf at Karekare. It was what's called 'a stable fracture', so only almost rather than actually serious – but dramatic at the time, and extremely painful. The section 'Long before . . .' was later translated into German by the German-born Dutch writer Elisabeth Augustin, and that translation appears in the sequence 'Yes T.S.' in *Geographies*.

'Twenty-two Sonnets': Sonnet 1 – This records the death of Prime Minister Norman Kirk. The Maurice addressed in the first line was Maurice Duggan who died three months later.
   Sonnet 8 – This piece of literary game-playing, which (mis)quotes, first, Shakespeare's *Macbeth*, and then, at the end, the lines from *Henry IV*, part I, which are inscribed on Katherine Mansfield's grave, sprang from a note Maurice Duggan wrote me signed

	Shadbolt	X
Maurice	Gee	X
	Duggan	√

To which I responded, signing my note

	Sinclair	X
K.S.	Smithyman	X
	Stead	√

The event with Allen Curnow and the bantams was not invented.

Sonnet 9 – I took the young man's word for it that he was the son of a 7th Fleet Admiral and had gone to jail sooner than to war in Vietnam. Some friends of his age thought he might be a CIA spy.

Sonnet 19 – This is an attempt to achieve a close translation of Baudelaire's poem 'Correspondences', but adapting it to the form of the sonnet.

'Walking Westward': The title poem became part of a plan (indicated in the later poem 'Scoria') to write a sequence of five long poems that might, in the end, be published together. This one was all contemporary in time, but ranged about in space. The second, 'Scoria', was to be fixed in space (Auckland/Tamaki-makau-rau) but range about in time – history and pre-history, human and geological. The third, 'Paris', was to be a literary-cultural-intellectual place-and-time, a location of the mind as much as, or more than, 'real' Paris. When that section finally appeared, however, it was in a completely different form from the first two, a sign that the work was taking its own path. The fourth part was to be 'the Wars', but pieces of what would have gone into it have been used in the sequence 'Voices' (the Land Wars), the novel *Talking about O'Dwyer* (the Battle of Crete) and the poem sequence 'Crete', and more recently in the sequence 'History' (Italy) in *The Black River*. There are also elements (World War I) in my novel *Mansfield*. What the fifth part, 'the Smoky Athletes', was to be has become hazy over time, but the image itself came partly from Dante's Paulo and Francesca episode, where the rather nice but unfortunately illicit lovers run endlessly in Hell pursued by the hot winds of lust. Also the stylistic intentions of this sequence had been overtaken by the long poem 'Yes T.S.' in *Geographies* – so the five-part long poem was never completed.

'Uta': The original fifty poems from *Walking Westward* have been somewhat culled, revised and rearranged here into the semblance of a narrative. I wrote these 'translations' knowing no Japanese but using scholars' (principally Waley's) transliterations, notes, grammars and glossaries, in the way Pound used Fenollosa's. I was less concerned with exact fidelity to the sense of the original than with catching something of their spirit. I cut down the Uta form from its fixed 5, 7, 5, 7, 7 – a total of 31 – syllables to as few as I could make it while still preserving the bones of the original statement. And I imposed on myself the (I suppose arbitrary) discipline of retaining the original Japanese line-order, which is often altered in translations to make English sense.

GEOGRAPHIES (1982)

Published by Auckland University Press/Oxford University Press.
Acknowledgements to *Islands, Landfall, New Zealand Listener, Pilgrims, Poems for the Eighties* (Wai-te-ata Press), *London Magazine, London Review of Books* and the souvenir programme of the International Poetry Festival, Toronto, 1981.

'Scoria' was the second in the planned sequence of five long poems (see the note to *Walking Westward* above). The person referred to in the section beginning '"Owairaka" (said Robinson)' was a teacher of that name (he was 'Mr Robinson', and I have no idea of his first name) at Maungawhau School, Mt Eden, when I was in standard 4 (1943) who was unusual, and to whom I remain grateful, because he gave us many Maori stories and legends of the region which remained with me and came back when I was writing this poem. I have no certainty about their provenance or authenticity, but I think Kendrick Smithyman (who liked the poem very much) traced at least one to John White's *Ancient History of the Maori*.

The section beginning 'Aspire to no forge nor flight' describes my high jumping on the front lawn at home (later I was Mt Albert Grammar School champion), and thus relates to the title poem of *Crossing the Bar*.

'Yes T.S.': Some of my intentions, described above, for five long poems were anticipated and used up in this sequence tracing a late-twentieth-century writer-and-academic's reflections, observations and anxieties in the course of a not untypical literary tour/circumnavigation. A few revisions and rearrangements have been made for reasons which are purely stylistic/aesthetic. 'Did a nightingale (etc.)' – I later discovered the source of the cock-crow in Bloomsbury was a kindergarten/nursery where a few farm animals were kept so city children could experience them – 'the poetry of fact' again.

'17.10.32' – I crossed the Channel on my 48th birthday and record the (as it seemed, and still seems) extraordinary coincidence that I read the passage quoted from Jean Rhys's novel *After Leaving Mr Mackenzie* in my Paris hotel that night.

'Il faut demeurer . . .', etc. – Here I am experimenting with writing French verse, translating it into English, and then the other way about, English into French, with no certainty of grammatical or lexical correctness. However, the 'je est une auto / elle suis Rimbaud' comes not out of grammatical ignorance but is a parody of Rimbaud's 'je est un autre' – literally 'I is another' and meaning, I take it, that the self is somehow alien – which is how I was feeling at the time.

'The Clodian Songbook: 15 Adaptations': My note to these in *Geographies* indicated that they are not translations but that each gets its start from a particular Catullus poem – in order (the Catullus number in brackets): 1 (1), 2 (2), 3 (4), 4 (5), 5 (7), 6 (8), 7 (11), 8 (12), 9 (13), 10 (15), 11 (16), 12 (17), 13 (18), 14 (22), 15 (101).

POEMS OF A DECADE (1983)

Published by Pilgrims South Press, Dunedin, in both hard- and soft-cover, this collection was mainly a reprint of 'April Notebook' from *Crossing the Bar*, together with all the poems of *Quesada* and *Walking Westward*, and the few new poems included here. One sonnet was added to the sequence that had appeared in *Walking Westward*. Acknowledgements (which included the poems from *Quesada* and *Walking Westward*) were made to *Cave, Education, Islands, Landfall, New Zealand Listener, Poetry New Zealand, Poetry Australia*; to the anthologies *A Cage of Words* (ed. Harvey McQueen), *Oxford Twentieth Century New Zealand Poetry* (ed. Vincent O'Sullivan), *New Zealand Writing since 1945* (ed. Vincent O'Sullivan and MacD. P. Jackson), *Fifteen Contemporary New Zealand Poets* (ed. Alistair Paterson), *Mystical Choice* (ed. Helen Shaw), *New Zealand Love Poems* (ed. James Bertram), *The Penguin Book of New Zealand Poetry* (ed. Harvey McQueen and Ian Wedde) and *The Oxford Book of Contemporary New Zealand Poetry* (ed. Fleur Adcock); and to Margaret Hayward's *Diary of the Kirk Years*.

PARIS (1984)

This was published by Auckland University Press in association with Oxford University Press, with illustrations by Gregory O'Brien, a student in my 1983 Creative Writing class who at the time had never been to France. This was the third of the planned five long poems (see notes to *Walking Westward* and *Geographies*). Its location is, as intended, a place as much of the mind as of geography (space) and history (time) – 'the Paris of Paris that's nobody's dream but your own'; but it presented itself in long lines and in twenty ten-line stanzas, very different from the open forms of 'Walking Westward' and 'Scoria'. I have no idea why this should have been the case, and it certainly followed no precedent. It might be argued that these are almost-Alexandrines – the traditional French form – but if so they are somewhat rough-hewn, and that thought was not in my mind at the time. Though the poem draws heavily on memories of visits to Paris, it was all written in Auckland. There are some things in poetry which simply happen – are *so* – and nothing to be done but note them.

The 'Denise' quoted in 3 was the poet Denise Levertov with whom I read at the Toronto Harbourfront Festival in 1981.

BETWEEN (1988)

Published by Auckland University Press and dedicated to Allen Curnow. Acknowledgements to (NZ) *Islands, Landfall, Listener, Poetry New Zealand, Rambling Jack* and *Tango*; (Australia) *Poetry Australia, Scripsi* and *Sydney Morning Herald*; (Canada) *Ariel* and *Malahat Review*; (UK) *London Magazine, London Review of Books* and *PN Review*. Some appeared subsequently in *New Zealand Poetry, 1972–86*, edited by Mark Williams.

'After the Wedding': I renamed my cousins in this poem, in case they didn't want to be made use of in public by their writing relative, though it now seems they wouldn't have minded. The two referred to as Elspeth and Caroline were Jane and Elizabeth Worsfold, though I think cousin Colleen Bowmar was also part of the mix in this poem. A lot of the background to this and similar Northland poems may be found in my novel *The Singing Whakapapa*.

'Two Dates from the Auckland Calendar': 12.9.81 was the date of the final South Africa–New Zealand test match of the infamous 1981 Springbok tour; 4.4.86 was the police/military assault on the Ngati Whatua (and supporters) occupation of disputed land on Bastion Point.

'Deconstructing the Rainbow Warrior': The French bombers, Alain Mafart and Dominique Prieur, were travelling on false passports as a married couple with the surname Turenges. French pronunciation facilitates a bad pun here; and the poem mocks French literary theory and the critical methodology of 'Deconstruction'.

'Paris: the End of a Story': The poem opens with the often replayed scene of the Saigon chief of police executing a Vietcong prisoner in the street.
'Ludwig' is the philosopher Ludwig Wittgenstein (1889–1951).
   One of Wilfred Owen's best-known First World War poems mocks 'The old lie: Dulce et decorum est / Pro patria mori.' And the inscription on the Tomb of the Unknown Soldier in Paris reads, 'Ici répose un soldat inconnu mort pour la patrie.'
   Horváth – Ödön von Horváth (1901–38), Hungarian-born, German, then Austrian, playwright who offended the Nazis with his political plays. He dreamed his destiny awaited him in Paris, went there, and died as described in a rainstorm.

'From the Clodian Songbook': As with the Catullus poems in *Geographies*, these are not translations but sometimes versions, sometimes approximations, sometimes poems which use the Roman poet only as a stepping-off point for going in a different direction. The persona is neither Catullus nor myself, but a shifting fictional identity somewhere in between. The starting point for each, putting the Catullus in brackets, are as follows: 1 (3), 2 (6), 3 (9), 4 (10), 5 (14), 6 (21), 7 (24), 8 (26), 9 (27), 10 (32), 11 (34), 12 (40), 13 (42), 14 (44), 15 (46), 16 (49), 17 (58), 18 (92), 19 (96), 20 (107). There is no overlap in source poems between this set and the set in *Geographies*, so the two could be fitted together to make one sequence, but I have preferred to retain the books as collections belonging to their time of publication.

'Kin of Place': Ken Smithyman's first book was called *The Blind Mountain*. I bought it as a student before I'd met him and found it contained a sonnet to Graham Perkins who was best man (I was groomsman) at my sister's wedding. The book title I helped him select was *Inheritance*, 1962. Ken and I became colleagues when he joined the Auckland University English Department as a senior tutor. A childhood spent partly in the North was what made us 'kin of place'. Ken's poem about our meeting on a beach with wives and children and his showing a shell he'd discovered is 'About Verbs', published in *Earthquake Weather*, 1972, p. 58.

'The Radiant Way': This sonnet was a sort of farewell to the academia of the period when French literary theory was fashionable. It takes its title and theme from a novel by Margaret Drabble.

VOICES (1990)

Dedication: To the memory of my grandmother Caroline Karlson, née Flatt, 1881-1954. This sequence was written in response to a commission from the Hon. Dr Michael Bassett, Minister of Arts and Culture at the time, to write a poem for the New Zealand 1990 celebrations commemorating 150 years since the signing of the Treaty of Waitangi. Rather than one poem, I wrote a sequence, taking significant, and insignificant but typical or exemplary, moments out of those 150 years. I used traditional forms – sonnets and formal stanzas – mainly five-stress lines, and often patterns of rhymes and half rhymes. The reason for preferring this more conservative style was that I felt to use the freer forms that had become characteristic of my work over the previous two decades might draw attention to the poet rather than the occasion, to virtuosity rather than to substance, and I felt the poet should be largely absent, or anyway not too clearly present. I thought also that the poems would fulfil their commission better if they were simple and direct enough to appeal widely, and perhaps be used in senior classes in schools. The result is therefore untypical and, some would argue, a little flat-footed. In their defence, however, I note that when quite a large part of the sequence was given a very good radio production they were shown to have some considerable dramatic potential, i.e. they worked as *voices*.

'1820 The Missionary': Based partly on John Butler. The story about the visitor frightening the 'natives' by pretending to be a ghost comes from Edward Markham's journal.

'18 October 1836 The Catechist': This is based on the experience of my great-great-grandfather, John Flatt (grandfather of my grandmother to whose memory the *Voices* collection is dedicated). But in fact more happened than merely the theft of his horse and clothes. One of his party, a Maori girl, Tarore, was murdered. I have used this well-documented event in my novel *The Singing Whakapapa* (1994). In 1977 Tarore's grave at Waharoa was marked and a new inscription unveiled by the Maori Queen, Dame Te Atairangikaahu, saying that Tarore's Luke Gospel, taken by her killers, converted the Arawa tribe to Christianity and thus 'brought peace to the tribes of Aotearoa'.

'1840 The Treaty': 5 February The Girl – a representative figure; 5 February The Printer – William Colenso; 8 February The Settler – a representative figure; 8 February The Chief – a composite figure of several who spoke on that day; 15 April The Governor – William Hobson, recounted by Colenso; 21 May The Governor – William Hobson. In the last, the exigencies of the sonnet don't allow room to make clear that Captain Pearson was arrested in Port Nicholson but escaped to sail north and warn Hobson what was happening there. Hobson felt the Wakefield settlers in what was to become Wellington were taking the law into their own hands, and resolved to make Auckland the capital.

'1840 The Dream': John Logan Campbell, 'father of Auckland' and author of *Poenamo*.

'1848 The Radical': Thomas Arnold (brother of the poet Matthew). In the first sonnet he is sailing to Otago in the *John Wickliffe* with William Cargill and family. Arnold is sailing partly to get over his rejection by Miss Henrietta Whatley ('Etty'). 1848 was the year of revolutions in Europe, and Arnold's reflecting on an account of events in Paris that has come to him from his friend the poet Arthur Hugh Clough.

'1849 The Settler': Based on a story told to me by my grandmother about her grandmother.

'1860 The Pakeha-Maori': Based on the conclusion to F. E. Maning's *Old New Zealand*.

'1860 The Soldier': An imagined British soldier in the Taranaki land wars.

'1861 The Boy': Based on an early recollection of William Pember Reeves recorded in his biography by Keith Sinclair.

'1864 The Warrior': An imagined warrior who has made his escape from the battle of Orakau which came to be known as 'Rewi's last stand'.

'1869 The War': 12 April The Raid – This was by Te Kooti's Ringatu warriors on the stockade at Mohaka. The people named, and events, are real. 14 April The Colonel – Colonel (later Major-General Sir George) Whitmore dined at the Auckland Club on that date and talked of war and the future.

'1875 The Girl': The speaker here is about eight years old – based on Helen Wilson's autobiography, *My First Eighty Years*.

'24 January 1884 The Visit': This was long after Te Kooti's war and the massacre at Matawhero, for which he was held responsible, and after his pardon. The speaker is Adela Stewart, author of *My Simple Life in New Zealand*.

'1889 The Gentleman': A fiction based on a news report in the *New Zealand Herald* of the time.

'1889 The Empire': A fiction, some elements of which are derived from T. E. Y. Seddon's *The Seddons*.

'1908 The Actress': The first two stanzas are based largely on Ngaio Marsh's autobiography, *Black Beech and Honeydew*. The third I suppose attributes my own preoccupations to her.

'August 1915 The Commanding Officer': This is Colonel William George Malone, killed at Gallipoli after the taking of Chunuk Bair, 8 August. Malone kept a diary which has been published.

'1917 The Mother': Based on my great-grandmother, Annie McDermott, daughter-in-law of John Flatt, who figures in the poem dated 1836.

'Cornwall 1918 The Expatriates': the painter is Frances Hodgkins, the writer Katherine Mansfield. Both lived in Cornwall in 1918, and I have imagined their almost-encounter.

'1925 The District Nurse': Derived from several books on medical practice and conditions in New Zealand in the 1920s and 1930s, in particular *King Country Nurse* by Frances Hayman.

'1929 The Immigrant Artist': This draws in particular on *An Artist's Daughter* by Jane Garrett about her father Christopher Perkins, though the Wellington observations are my own. The poem reappeared in *Big Weather: Poems of Wellington*, edited by Greg O'Brien and Louise White, 2000.

'1932 The Student': Based partly on an anecdote in Elsie Locke's *Student at the Gates*, though I make the student more divided between the attractions of opera and Marxism than Locke appears to have been.

'1939–45 The War': These six sonnets are a fiction based on fact, including some of my own recollections. 'Tiny' is General Bernard Freyberg, VC, Commander of NZDiv, and 'Monty' is Field Marshall Bernard Montgomery, Commander of the British Eighth Army in the Western Desert.

'1945 The Explanation': This is based on a real incident in which Colonel Humphrey Dyer, then the (Pakeha) CO of the Maori Battalion, shot a wounded Maori soldier – an act for which the soldier's family subsequently put a makutu (curse) on him. This became the central event in my novel *Talking about O'Dwyer*, and when I came to investigate the facts I found a much darker version of what happened. The account given here is what comes to be called, in the novel, 'the sanitised version'.

'1945 The Anniversary': The voice here is my own. My father, J. W. A. Stead, was Auckland President of the Labour Party at the time. The late leader is Michael Joseph Savage, and the remark about his never having framed a sentence anyone remembered is from John A. Lee's *Simple on a Soapbox*. Lee was the rival expelled for criticising Savage, but outlived him by many years.

'1947 The Orchestra': My cousin who played the oboe in the National Orchestra was Ngaire Stead; the cabinet maker who played the flute was Victor Cater, father of my school friend Don. I have taken a slight liberty here – the two may not have played in the orchestra at the same time.

'1951 The Wharfie': This is fiction based partly on Glen Catton, a deregistered wharfie, father of another of my school friends, Barry, and partly on Jim Henderson's *Gunner Inglorious*.

'Christmas 1953 The Queen': Her Majesty was in residence in Government House, Auckland, when the Tangiwai rail disaster occurred on Christmas eve. In the choir of children who came to sing carols to her in the garden on Christmas morning was a plump schoolboy called David Lange.

'Rome 1960 The Athlete': Murray Halberg won the 5000 metres at the Rome Olympics. Specs Julian and Peter Snell were fellow athletes in Auckland, and Arthur Lydiard their coach. Snell won the 800 metres at Rome, and the 800 and 1500 in the Tokyo Olympics four years later. The story about praying to the gods was told to me by Maurice Shadbolt who had it (he said) from Halberg.

'1971 The Revolution': This is the sexual revolution of the late 1960s, associated with the protest movement especially against the war in Vietnam.

'31 August 1974 The Private Secretary': The Prime Minister is Norman Kirk, the secretary Margaret Hayward, and the poem draws its facts from her *Diary of the Kirk Years*.

'25 July 1981 The Clergyman': The speaker is watching the break-in at Rugby Park, Hamilton, during the infamous Springbok Tour. This was the only occasion when protest actually prevented a tour match being played. After that the Muldoon Government got tough, the protest increased, and there was something close to civil war in the country. I was awarded my (to date) only criminal conviction for my part on that day, and a fine of $250 and costs.

'10 July 1985 The Secret Agent': This is the bombing of the Greenpeace ship, *Rainbow Warrior*, in Auckland Harbour by agents of the French secret service, to prevent it monitoring nuclear testing in the Pacific. The speaker is Captain Dominique Prieur who with Major Alain Mafart was convicted of manslaughter and sentenced to ten years' jail. More significant agents escaped, and the French Government used economic bullying to force the transfer of Prieur and Mafart to serve their sentences on French Pacific territories from where they were soon repatriated home to France and freed.

'1990 At the Grave of Governor Hobson': Here the author speaks in his own persona, and the forbear referred to is another great-great-grandfather, Martin McDermott, whose grave is still easily found across the road from Hobson's.

STRAW INTO GOLD: POEMS NEW AND SELECTED (1997)

This was a selection from *Whether the Will is Free* to *Voices*, with new poems written since *Voices* and published for the first time. The new poems have been cut down in number and rearranged into groups for the present volume.

THE RIGHT THING (2000)

This collection was published by Auckland University Press and re-issued by Arc in the UK in the same year with a very slightly altered selection of poems. 'I've seen the future and it's OK' appeared only in the Arc edition and 'Even Newer English Bible' only in the AUP edition. Acknowledgements: (NZ) *Landfall*, *New Zealand Listener*, *New Zealand Books*, *Salt*, *Sport*; (UK) *The Forward Book of Poetry*, 2001, *London Magazine*, *London Review of Books*, *New Writing 7*, *PN Review*, *Poetry Review*, *Times Literary Supplement*; (Australia) *Sydney Morning Herald*; (Canada) *Malahat Review*; (USA) *Cumberland Poetry Review*.

A large part of this collection was written during 1996–97 when I was Senior Visiting Fellow at St John's College, Oxford.

'Encounters' was written for Peter Porter's 70th birthday volume, *Paeans for Peter Porter*, 1999.

'Ravidus the Bookman' appeared first in *Poetry Review* and then in *The Forward Book of Poetry*, 2001. In *Areté*, Autumn 2001, an unsigned piece claimed 'there are those who believe' that the model for Ravidus was sometime Faber fiction editor, and subsequently *Observer*'s books editor, Robert McCrum. *Areté* then goes on, clearly tongue in cheek, to show why this could not be so, in particular because Ravidus in the poem is said to write 'execrable prose'.

'The Other Place' is how Cambridge is referred to in Oxford – rather than naming it.

'Lessons in Modern History (i)': '1956 West' – It was Lady Eden, the British P.M.'s wife, who said it was as if the Suez Canal was flowing through the sitting room at Number 10. Why did I give her a cockney accent? I suppose because that was as absurd as the stories Sir Anthony told to explain the British and French invasion of the Suez Canal. The whole affair was shameless and mendacious.

'1956 East' – Mr B and Mr K were the Russian leaders Nikolai Bulganin and Nikita Khrushchev.

'Lessons in Modern History (ii)': 'C.K.' – The Cuban missile crisis.
'1963 HiJKL' – Jack and Jackie were the Kennedys, Lee was Lee Harvey Oswald who shot Kennedy, Lyndon was Lyndon Johnson, and the second Jack was Jack Ruby, who shot Oswald.
'1965' – This was when the United States decided the line between North and South Vietnam was an international boundary and that therefore 'an invasion' had occurred.
'1968 made . . .' – Bobby Kennedy, Martin Luther King, the Tet Offensive in Vietnam and Lyndon Johnson.
'1974' – Tricky Dicky was Nixon's nickname.

'Hollywood': I was working with Donaldson on completing a movie script of my novel *Villa Vittoria*. See below, the notes about 'Rapallo: an Economy' in *The Red Tram*.

'Nine Nines': 'Sylvia' – Sylvia Plath was born 27.10.32; C.K.S. 17.10.32.

'Crete': Drafted 1998 during a visit to the island in the course of working towards my novel *Talking about O'Dwyer*, and finished immediately afterwards during another stay in Oxford. It reappeared in *Gifts: Poetry for Senior Students*, edited by Harvey McQueen, 2000.

DOG (2002)

Acknowledgements: The sequence *King's Lynn and the Pacific* was published as a separate book by the King's Lynn Poetry Festival in 2003, in a paperback edition and a hardback of 50 copies signed by the author. *Dog* (the complete collection) was published by Auckland University Press in 2000 and re-issued in the UK by Arc in 2004.

Acknowledgements: (NZ) *Landfall, New Zealand Listener, Metro, Moving Worlds, New Zealand Books, Sport, Under Flagstaff: An Anthology of Dunedin Poetry* (ed. Robin Law and Heather Murray); (UK) *Areté, Leviathan Quarterly, London Magazine, Nonesuch, Stand*; (Australia) *Island*.

'King's Lynn & the Pacific': at the King's Lynn Poetry Festival, October 2001, I received the Festival's fourth Poetry Award. This gives the recipient £1000 and requires him or her to spend a brief time in King's Lynn and an equal time in one of the ports with which Lynn (as the locals call it) traded at the time of its maritime heyday, and then to write a poem (or poems) based on that experience. The first recipient, Peter Porter, had written about Lynn and the Netherlands. Kit Wright had gone to Portugal. My immediate predecessor, Pauline Stainer, had gone to Iceland. I decided it was time to bring my own region into the picture. Although there may not have been ships that sailed from King's Lynn to the Pacific, its seamen certainly did – most notably James Burney (younger brother of Fanny Burney and son of the musician Charles Burney) and George Vancouver.

James Burney (1750–1821) joined the Royal Navy at ten (which meant that such childhood as he had was spent at Lynn), and later sailed with Cook's second and third expeditions to the Pacific. So did George Vancouver (1757–98), who later gave his name to the city and the island of Vancouver in Canada, and whose statue stands on the quay in King's Lynn in sight of the famous Customs House, which first his father, then his brother, had charge of as Collector of Customs. Both Burney and Vancouver attended Lynn Grammar School. On the Cook expeditions they visited New Zealand more than once, and other places in the South Pacific, including Tahiti (Otaheiti), Tonga and Hawaii. Both were involved in the drama of Cook's murder. Both had successful subsequent careers – as naval officers (retiring with the rank of Rear Admiral) and as writers on the subject of maritime exploration.

'The Captain's Servant': Boys must have attended Grammar School at an early age in the eighteenth century. The usher who told young Jem Burney 'murderer's tales' and then was found to have committed a murder was Eugene Aram. Seventy years later Thomas Hood wrote a melodramatic poem about him, 'The Dream of Eugene Aram, the Murderer', in which he is portrayed as revealing his guilt by telling stories of murder to one of his pupils. Hood probably meant the pupil to be Jem Burney.

'In Principio': George Vancouver was seven years younger than James Burney, who had risen from captain's servant to midshipman by the time both were signed up for Cook's second expedition. Both sailed from Portsmouth on Cook's ship, *Resolution*, Vancouver as a trainee. In Cape Town Burney was promoted to lieutenant and transferred to the second ship, the *Adventure*, under Captain Tobias Furneaux.

'Bread etc.': Omai, who was taken to England as an example of the Noble Savage, and was for a time a great success there, meeting the King and moving in high society, is the subject of a book, *Omai: Pacific Envoy*, by my sometime colleague Eric McCormick. Burney, who managed the Tahitian language better than Omai managed English, befriended him. Omai made a great impression on Fanny Burney, and also on Dr Johnson. Cook, who had known many such 'savages' and failed to detect any special 'nobility' in this one, returned Omai home on his third voyage to the South Seas.

'Tonga': The words are as Burney transcribed them, and show he had a good ear and memory. The notes to Beaglehole's edition of Cook's *Journal* (Vol. III, Part 2) show how the words would now be written ('O sisi tu O sisi tu matala', for example, the opening line) and suggests what they probably meant. My version is a free rendering.

'Navigation': Harrison's 'watch' was a clock resistant to all vicissitudes of sea travel (pitch and roll, extremes of heat and cold) and thus able to keep Greenwich time, while daily readings of the sun fixed local time. The difference established the longitude exactly and thus overcame a problem in navigation which had caused many ships to be lost. On his second voyage Cook took an approved copy of Harrison's watch made by Larcum Kendall. He referred to it as 'Mr Kendall's Watch' and reported its success. I have used Harrison's name since he deserves the credit. The other three chronometers taken on the voyage, made by John Arnold, all broke down.

'Postscript' jumps forward several years to Cook's third voyage and to his death. The facts are compressed. Vancouver was involved in the fighting at one point, though not where Cook was killed, and took a blow on the head defending Thomas Edgar, Master of the *Discovery*. Burney watched from the ship. Next day two armed boatloads, one commanded by Burney, the other by King, went ashore to try to recover Cook's body. Bern Anderson, in his book *Surveyor of the Sea*, says Captain Clerke, who was now in charge of the expedition, used Burney and Vancouver to negotiate because they were the two with some command of Polynesian languages. Because Cook was thought to have been the god Erono, his body was prized, as the relics of saints have been by the Christian church. It had been divided among the chiefs, and probably only the threat of war caused any of it to be given up.

'Applause' goes with my grateful thanks to the University of Bristol for the award of an Honorary Doctorate in Letters in 2001, forty years after I completed my PhD there.

'Washington': This is a poem about public eloquence, and the titles indicate no more than a style in each case. The 'Cynara' with whom I spent three (innocent) days in Washington was Elizabeth Knox. The 'Quaker boy' was Richard Nixon whose farewell speech, especially given my contempt for him and my joy at his departure in disgrace, struck me as oddly eloquent. The 'Caesar' whose 'worthy wank' rang in my ears in 1963 was John F. Kennedy.

'Vincent': This story about a well-known New Zealand poet was told to me, admiringly (as it is recorded here), by a contemporary who was in the class at the time.

'Auckland': The shape of this poem mimics the shape of the Auckland Sky Tower.

'Beauty': This is a (very considerable!) recasting in modern terms of Ovid's story of Apollo and Hyacinthus.

'Bald Caesarion': See notes to *Crossing the Bar* (p. 521) for this poem's history

'At Wagner's Tomb' followed a visit to Bayreuth with Kay in 2001 to hear the Ring Cycle.

THE RED TRAM (2004)

Acknowledgements: (NZ) *A Heady Brew* (Café Poems), *New Zealand Listener, New Zealand Books, North & South, The Waitakeres: Ranges of Inspiration* (Waitakere Ranges Protection Society), *The Second Wellington International Poetry Festival Anthology 2004, Sport*; (UK) *PN Review, Stand, Times Literary Supplement*; (USA) *Cumberland Poetry Review, Fulcrum*; (Italy) *Da Ulisse a . . . La città e il mare dalla Liguria al mondo*, ed. Giorgetta Revelli, 2005; (France) the poem 'Stone Figure' derives from an entry written for *5000 Ans de Figures Humaines: Cent Regards sur les Collections Barbier-Mueller*, Mona Bismarck Foundation, Paris, 2000.

'The Advance of English – Lang & Lit': The first poem parodied, Shakespeare's Sonnet CXVI, was wrongly listed in this collection as Sonnet XXXI, because I looked it up in the *Golden Treasuryof Songs and Lyrics*, where it is numbered XXXI – the 31st poem in the anthology!

'Love etc.': Although I have indicated the Latin and French poems from which this sequence takes its beginnings, they are not simply translations, and in fact I have allowed myself complete freedom. Some are close to the original; some rework similar elements into a different statement; some take off from the original and go in a different direction. None pays any respect at all to the Latin and French forms. The Verlaine is almost close enough to be called a 'translation'; but then the final two lines are an interpretation of the original rather than part of its text. And both the Verlaine and the Rimbaud are formal sonnets in the French. I stress that although I know French reasonably well and have read quite a lot of French literature, I am no linguist. I am certainly no Latinist. I use these precedent texts to make what I hope I can claim as my own poem, creating my own fictional persona.

'Rapallo, an economy' was accompanied, in the Italian anthology acknowledged above, by a note, part of which read as follows:

> My first recollection of Rapallo is from 1972 when I lived for eight months in Menton as Katherine Mansfield Fellow. I had driven with my wife and three small children across to Florence and Venice, and on the way back stopped at Rapallo and wandered about hoping I might chance to see Ezra Pound. I might well have been looking in the wrong place, since Pound, in those years, had left his wife Dorothy and was coming and going, between Rapallo and Venice, with his long-time friend Olga Rudge; but at that time I was not as well-informed about Pound's life as I became later on. He died the following year, 1973.
>
> I returned to Rapallo in 1984, with Kay and our two daughters, and it was then I discovered the famous *salita* and the climb up to Sant' Ambrogio and what had been Olga Rudge's house. The town figured in my novel *The Death of the Body*, published in London in 1986, and subsequently translated into several European languages (but not Italian).
>
> My next visit was to attend the fifteenth annual Ezra Pound conference and to write a piece about it for the *London Magazine* (April/May 1994). It was here I met the distinguished Pound scholar Professor Massimo Bacigalupo of the University of Genoa, who has remained a friend. Here also I met Mary de Rachewiltz, Pound's daughter to Olga Rudge. It was on this visit I conceived the idea for what is the only thriller I have written, *Villa Vittoria*, published in 1997. It did not make me a large amount of money, as thrillers are supposed to do (very little in fact); but it did arouse the interest of the New Zealand movie director Roger Donaldson, who works in Hollywood, and I wrote a script for it which remains, thus far, only a script. [See the poem 'Hollywood' in *The Right Thing*.]
>
> The novel begins with the unveiling of a bust of a famous (and famously deplored) American pro-fascist poet, Sterling Grant, by his former mistress. Forbidden photographs are taken of the invited guests, revealing that a corrupt banker, supposed dead, may be still alive. Names have been changed but Grant is clearly Pound, and the banker, Roberto Calvi, of the Banco Ambrosiano scandal. The 'thriller' takes off from there, and becomes also a love story. Place-names are also changed, but the places are easily recognisable. The Hotel Villa Vittoria, from which the photographs are taken, is based on the Hotel Villa Cristina on the Rapallo seafront.
>
> The same hotel, given its real name, figures in the poem, somewhat derelict, one of its broken shutters 'banging on' in the wind, speaking in the first person and representing a long history.
>
> *Vagabonda III* in section 4 is Professor Bacigalupo's sailboat, successor to *Vagabonda I* and *II* on which Pound was taken sailing from time to time by the Professor's father who was Pound's doctor.
>
> The poem speaks in part from the perspective of the New World. Rapallo represents Italy and the ancient culture from which the modern world has emerged, and to which we must return, in the mind or in reality, if we are to understand ourselves. What the broken shutter sees is both significant (armies marching east and west) and insignificant (the violinist – Olga Rudge in fact, as described in her daughter's account – hitching up her skirts before climbing the salita). What it tells us is something we need to know.

THE BLACK RIVER (2007)

Acknowledgments: (NZ) *Dominion Post, New Zealand Listener, Metro, New Zealand Books, Sport*; (UK) *Guardian, PN Review, Warwick Review*.

'S//CRAPBOOK': 'Seven poems each beginning with a line by Colin McCahon' – With apologies to the shade of Colin, these first lines are taken from *Rita: Seven Poems by Colin McCahon*, edited by Peter Simpson and published in a very expensive edition of 175 copies by the Holloway Press.

'Kentucky, 1853': More than one reader has said he/she feels as if this is familiar territory but can't quite 'place' it. I feel the same. The whole poem, including the very specific title, was a dream – and there was that notebook by my bed to dash it down before it was lost. I feel sure it must have some buried source in my childhood reading, not available to conscious memory – Harriet Beecher Stowe, Mark Twain, Brer Rabbit, the songs of Stephen Foster, or something else of that kind – or an amalgam. This causes me to reflect that the reading of my childhood, though 'Dominion' status hadn't quite got us out of the colonial frying pan, was not entirely British. I'm aware that the kind of 'Darkie-talk' used in the poem – though it must derive from attempts by those Classic American writers to reproduce the actual sounds of English as spoken by Black slaves – is unacceptable these days. But the whole process by which the poem arrived, its peculiarity and particularity, I find interesting – and especially the fact that there is a whole possible (and terrible) fiction potential in it; the sense of a knife-edge being walked by the Black man.

'History': The speakers in each section are as follows. They are not indicated in the poem itself because there is in all of them an element of fiction to broaden and generalise the picture.
1 Alberto Moravia
2 Winston Churchill
3 Alberto Moravia
4 Gunner Jim Henderson
5 An official in the Mussolini household
6 Mussolini
7 Olga Rudge, mistress of Ezra Pound
8 The official who speaks in 5
9 Pvte Reg Minter, 24 Btn
10 'Captain Valerio' (the name adopted to conceal the identity of the Resistance assassin)
11 *I morti in mezzo ai fiore* – the dead among flowers
12 The poet Eugenio Montale to Bernard Wall
13 C.K.S.

'Part Two, May–June 2005', was accompanied by the following note:

By way of explanation: In May 2005 I had a 'migraine' which proved to be an ischaemic stroke, an event significant only to myself and those close to me, and not for very long (apart from leaving me feeling unsafe), since all the effects were gone within a few weeks. But for a brief time I experienced complete dyslexia; and as the ability to read came back, my anxiety was to find whether I could still write. I kept a small notebook which had on its cover a symbol of a swan in pale paua, and into this I 'wrote' – scribbled – (it was like writing in the dark) what I thought were poems, composed in my head. I hope the selection which follows is of more than merely diagnostic interest. They were all written in May–June of that year. Everything in Part One of this collection was written subsequently (July 2005–September 2006).

EARLY UNCOLLECTED POEMS, 1951–61

Most of these had been published in periodicals (as indicated) but were rejected or mislaid when I put together my first collection, *Whether the Will is Free*; a few others had got no further than typescript.

Index of First Lines

Index of Poems

Part-poem titles are in *italic*.